BARRON'S

S0-BNY-479

Pass Key to the GRE®

NINTH EDITION

Sharon Weiner Green, M.A.
Ira K. Wolf, Ph.D.

© Copyright 2017, 2015, 2013, 2011, 2009, 2003, 2000, 1997, 1993
by Barron's Educational Series, Inc.

Material in this book was adapted from **New GRE, 22nd Edition**,
by Sharon Weiner Green and Ira K. Wolf.
© Copyright 2017 by Barron's Educational Series, Inc.

All inquiries should be addressed to:
Barron's Educational Series, Inc.
250 Wireless Boulevard
Hauppauge, New York 11788
www.barronseduc.com

Library of Congress Control No.: 2017939530

ISBN: 978-1-4380-0912-4

PRINTED IN CANADA
9 8 7 6 5 4 3 2 1

Contents

Preface

Welcome to the brand-new ninth edition of Barron's **Pass Key to the GRE**, the compact version of Barron's **GRE**. Designed to give you access to up-to-the-minute information about the Graduate Record Examination, **Pass Key to the GRE** provides you with a short course in GRE preparation to meet your immediate needs.

It gives you an overview of the GRE General Test, answers key questions commonly asked by undergraduates, and explains everything you need to know about the computer-delivered GRE.

It takes you step by step through dozens of verbal and mathematical questions that simulate actual GRE questions, showing you how to solve them and how to avoid going wrong.

It familiarizes you with the analytical writing task, showing you how to approach the two kinds of essays.

It provides you with dozens of proven, highlighted testing tactics that will help you attack the different types of questions on the GRE.

It offers you the compact 320-word High-Frequency Word List—words from **abate** to **zealot** that have been shown by computer analysis to occur and recur on actual published GREs.

It offers you a list of the most important Math Facts and Formulas you need to know; this is particularly valuable for students primarily involved in nonscientific disciplines.

Best of all, it offers you the opportunity to take two complete practice GREs so you can test yourself, answering questions that correspond to actual GRE questions in content, format, and level of difficulty.

Do not vacillate. As you prepare to vie for a place in a leading graduate school program, show your resolution to succeed by applying yourself sedulously to the contents of this book. Let Barron's **Pass Key to the GRE** open the door to graduate education for you.

Acknowledgments

The authors gratefully acknowledge the permission to reprint passages.

Page 58: From "So Many Female Rivals" by Christine Froula, *The New York Times Book Review*, February 7, 1988.

Pages 199–200: From *Black Leaders of the Twentieth Century*. Copyright © 1982 by the Board of Trustees of the University of Illinois. Used with permission of the University of Illinois Press.

Pages 260–261: From Vol. 15 of *Americas*. Copyright © 1963 by the Organization of American States.

Page 279: "Chapter 3, Overview: Fighting Back" by Darlene Clark Hine, from THE EYES ON THE PRIZE CIVIL RIGHTS READER by Clayborne Carson et al., copyright © 1987, 1991 by Blackside, Inc. Used by permission of Viking Penguin, a division of Penguin Group (USA) Inc.

TIMETABLE FOR A TYPICAL COMPUTER-DELIVERED GRADUATE RECORD EXAMINATION

Total Time: 4 hours

Section	Time Allowed	Description
1*	60 minutes	*Analytical Writing* Essay 1: Giving one's perspective on an issue Essay 2: Analyzing an argument (30 minutes each)
	1-minute break	
2	30 minutes	*Verbal Ability* 6 text completion questions 5 sentence equivalence questions 9 reading comprehension questions
	1-minute break	
3	35 minutes	*Quantitative Ability* 8 quantitative comparison questions 9 discrete quantitative questions 3 data interpretation questions
	10-minute break	
4	30 minutes	*Verbal Ability* 6 text completion questions 5 sentence equivalence questions 9 reading comprehension questions
	1-minute break	
5	35 minutes	*Quantitative Ability* 7 quantitative comparison questions 10 discrete quantitative questions 3 data interpretation questions
	1-minute break	
6	30 or 35 minutes	*Experimental Section* a third verbal or quantitative section

*The paper-delivered GRE splits the Analytical Writing Test into two sections, as shown below:

1	30 minutes	*Analytical Writing* Issue Essay: Giving one's perspective on an issue
2	30 minutes	*Analytical Writing* Argument Essay: Analyzing an argument

NOTE: Sections 2 through 6 can come in any order—for example, Section 2 could be a Quantitative Ability section and the Experimental Section could be any section except Section 1. Although the Experimental Section will not count in your score, it will look identical to one of the other sections—you won't know which section it is, so you must do your best on every section of the test.

What You Need to Know About the GRE

AN OVERVIEW OF THE COMPUTER-DELIVERED GRE GENERAL TEST

The GRE General Test is an examination designed by the Educational Testing Service (ETS) to measure the verbal, quantitative, and analytical writing skills you have developed in the course of your academic career. High GRE scores strongly correlate with the probability of success in graduate school: the higher you score, the more likely you are to complete your graduate degree. For this reason, many graduate and professional schools require applicants to take the GRE General Test, a test now given only on computer. (They may also require you to take a GRE Subject Test in your particular field. Subject Tests currently are available in 14 fields.)

The computer-delivered GRE General Test you take will have five or six sections. There will always be

- one Analytical Writing section composed of two 30-minute tasks (60 minutes)*
- two 20-question Verbal Ability sections (30 minutes each)
- two 20-question Quantitative Ability sections (35 minutes each)

In addition, there *may* be

- an unidentified Experimental Section, which would be a third verbal or quantitative section

Occasionally, there *may* be

- an identified optional research section (but *not* if there is an Experimental Section)

*Unlike the computer-delivered GRE, the paper-delivered GRE will include not one but two Analytical Writing sections. There will be a 30-minute section for the Issue task and a separate 30-minute section for the Argument task.

The verbal section measures your ability to use words as tools in reasoning; you are tested not only on the extent of your vocabulary but on your ability to discern the relationships that exist both within written passages and among individual groups of words. The quantitative section measures your ability to use and reason with numbers and mathematical concepts; you are tested not on advanced mathematical theory but on general concepts expected to be part of everyone's academic background. The mathematics covered should be familiar to most students who took at least two years of math in a high school in the United States. The writing section measures your ability to make rational assessments about unfamiliar, fictitious relationships and to logically present your perspective on an issue.

COMMONLY ASKED QUESTIONS ABOUT THE COMPUTER-DELIVERED GRE

How Does the GRE Differ from Other Tests?

Most tests college students take are straightforward achievement tests. They attempt to find out how much you have learned, usually in a specific subject, and how well you can apply that information. Without emphasizing memorized data, the GRE General Test attempts to measure verbal, quantitative, and analytical writing skills that you have acquired over the years both in and out of school.

Although the ETS claims that the GRE General Test measures skills that you have developed over a long period, even a brief period of intensive study can make a great difference in your eventual GRE scores. By thoroughly familiarizing yourself with the process of computer-delivered testing, the GRE test format, and the various question types, you can enhance your chances of doing well on the test and of being accepted by the graduate school of your choice.

What Is It Like to Take a Computer-Delivered GRE?

When you actually take the GRE, you sit in a carrel in a computer lab or testing center, facing a computer screen. You may be alone in the room, or other test-takers may be taking tests in nearby carrels. With your mouse, you click on an icon to start your test. The first section of the test is the Analytical Writing section, and you will have 60 minutes in which to complete the two writing tasks. When you have finished the writing section, you will have a one-minute break to take a few deep breaths and get ready for the next four or five sections, each of which will consist of 20 multiple-choice verbal or quantitative questions. When the break is over, the first question in Section 2 appears on the screen. You answer it, clicking on the oval next to your answer choice, and then, ready to move on, you click on the box marked NEXT. A new question appears on screen, and you go through the process again. Be sure to answer every question. Because there is no penalty for an incorrect answer on the GRE General Test, when you don't know an answer, try to make an educated guess by eliminating clearly incorrect choices; if you can't eliminate any choices, make a wild guess, and move on.

At the end of the second section, you are given another one-minute break. After finishing the third section, you have a ten-minute break. There will be two more one-minute breaks—after the fourth and fifth sections.

Why Do Some People Call the Computer-Delivered General Test a CAT?

CAT stands for Computer-Adaptive Test. What does this mean? It means that the test adapts to your skill level: it is customized.

What happens is that after you complete the first quantitative or verbal section, the computer program assesses your performance and adjusts the difficulty level of the questions you will have to answer in the second quantitative or verbal section. The more questions you answer correctly in the first section, the harder will be the questions that you will be given in the second section. However, the harder the questions are, the more they are worth. So your raw score depends on both the number of questions you answer correctly and the difficulty level of those questions.

Actually, the GRE is much less computer-adaptive than it used to be. It used to adapt the level of questions you received continuously; after every question the program would assess your performance and determine the level of difficulty of the next question. Now, it doesn't make that determination until you have completed an entire section.

Can I Tell How Well I'm Doing on the Test from the Questions the Computer Assigns Me?

Don't even try; it never pays to try to second-guess the computer. There's no point in wasting time and energy wondering whether it's feeding you harder questions or easier ones. Let the computer keep track of how well you're doing—you concentrate on answering correctly as many questions as you can and on pacing yourself.

Should I Guess?

Yes, you must! You are not going to know the correct answer to every question on the GRE. That's a given. But you should *never* skip a question. Remember, there is no penalty for an incorrect answer. So if a question has you stumped, eliminate any obviously incorrect answer choices, and then guess and don't worry whether you've guessed right or wrong. Your job is to get to the next question you *can* answer. Just remember to use the process of elimination to improve your guessing odds.

How Can I Determine the Unidentified Experimental Section?

You can't. Do not waste even one second in the exam room trying to identify the Experimental Section. Simply do your best on every section. Some people claim that most often the last section is the Experimental Section. Others claim that the section with unusual questions is the one that does not count. Ignore the claims: you have no sure way to tell. If you encounter a series of questions that seem strange to you, do your best. Either these are experimental and will not count, in which case you have no reason to worry about them, or they will count, in which case they probably will seem just as strange and troublesome to your fellow examinees.

How Are GRE Scores Calculated and When Are They Reported?

On both the verbal and quantitative sections of the GRE, your *raw score* is the number of questions you answered correctly, adjusted for the difficulty level of those questions. Each raw score is then adjusted to a *scaled score*, which lies between 130 and 170. The written score report that you will receive in the mail will include both your scaled scores and your percentile rank indicating the percent of examinees scoring below your scaled scores on the General Test.

> **Helpful Hint**
> After you take one of the Model Tests in the back of this book, you cannot calculate your exact scores, because there is no way to factor in the difficulty level of the questions. To give yourself a rough idea of how you did, on both the verbal and quantitative sections, assume that your raw score is equal to the number of correct answers, and that your scaled score is equal to 130 plus your raw score. For example, if you answered correctly 30 of the 40 quantitative questions, assume that your raw score would be 30 and that your scaled score would be 160.

Your analytical writing score will be the average of the scores assigned to your essays by two trained readers. These scores are rounded up to the nearest half-point. Your combined analytical writing score can vary from 0 to 6, with 6 the highest score possible.

As soon as you have finished taking the test, the computer will calculate your *unofficial* scaled scores for the verbal and quantitative sections and display them to you on the screen. Because your essays are sent to trained readers for holistic scoring, you will not receive a score for the analytical writing section on the day of the test. You should receive in the mail an *official* report containing all three scores approximately three weeks after the test date.

GRE TEST FORMAT

> ### Note
>
> For all of the multiple-choice questions in the verbal and quantitative sections of the tests and practice exercises in this book, the answer choices are labeled A, B, C, D, and E, and these letters are used in the Answer Keys and the answer explanations. On an actual GRE exam, these letters never appear on the screen. Rather, each choice is preceded by a blank oval or square, and you will answer a question by clicking with the mouse on the oval or square in front of your choice.

Verbal Reasoning

The two verbal sections consist of a total of 40 questions. These questions fall into two basic types: discrete, short-answer questions and critical reading questions.

Here is how a 20-question verbal section generally breaks down:

- 10 discrete, short-answer questions
- 10 critical reading questions (including logical reasoning questions)

Although the amount of time spent on each type of question varies from person to person, in general, discrete, short-answer questions take less time to answer than critical reading questions.

Discrete, Short-Answer Questions

In these fill-in-the blank questions, you are asked to choose the best way to complete a sentence or short passage from which one, two, or three words have been omitted. These questions test a combination of reading comprehension and vocabulary skills. You must be able to recognize the logic, style, and tone of the sentence so that you will be able to choose the answer that makes sense in context. You must also be able to recognize differences in usage. The sentences cover a wide variety of topics from a number of academic fields. They do not, however, test specific academic knowledge. You may feel more comfortable if you are familiar with the topic the sentence is discussing, but you should be able to handle any of the sentences using your knowledge of the English language.

Here is a typical fill-in-the-blank question, using one of the new question formats. In this question, you are asked to find **not one but two** correct answers; both answers must produce completed sentences that are like each other in meaning. This is what the test-makers call a **sentence equivalence** question.

| | Quit Test | Exit Section | Review | Mark | Help | Back | Next |

Select the two answer choices that, when used to complete the sentence,
fit the meaning of the sentence as a whole and produce completed sentences that are alike in meaning.

Although the two mismatched roommates are the proverbial odd couple—Felix is pedantic where Oscar is imprecise, _____ where Oscar is slovenly, cultivated where Oscar is uncouth—they nevertheless manage to share a small apartment without driving each other crazy.

☐ taciturn
☐ fastidious
☐ ebullient
☐ nice
☐ stoical
☐ egregious

Click on your choices.

Unlike Oscar, Felix is *not* slovenly (messy and untidy); instead, he is a compulsive neatnik. Felix is *fastidious* or *nice* in his habits, excessively sensitive in matters of taste. (Note the use of *nice* in a secondary sense.) See page 34 for sentence equivalence tactics and sample questions that will help you handle this new fill-in-the-blank question type.

Look at the same question, restructured into what the test-makers call a **text completion** question. In this type of question, you are asked to find only one correct answer per blank. However, you must have a correct answer for each and every blank.

Quit Test	Exit Section	Review	Mark	Help	Back	Next

For each blank select one entry from the corresponding column of choices. Fill all blanks in the way that best completes the text.

Although the two (i)_____ roommates are the proverbial odd couple—Felix is pedantic where Oscar is imprecise, (ii) _____ where Oscar is slovenly, cultivated where Oscar is (iii)_____—they nevertheless manage to share a small apartment without driving each other crazy.

Blank (i)	Blank (ii)	Blank (iii)
compatible	curious	refined
peripheral	unkempt	taciturn
mismatched	fastidious	uncouth

Click on your choices.

See page 40 for text completion question tactics and sample questions that will help you handle this new fill-in-the-blank question type.

Critical Reading Questions

Critical reading questions test your ability to understand and interpret what you read. This is probably the most important ability that you will need in graduate school and afterward.

Although the passages may encompass any subject matter, you do not need to know anything about the subject discussed in the passage in order to answer the questions on that passage. The purpose of the question is to test your reading ability, not your knowledge of history, science, literature, or art.

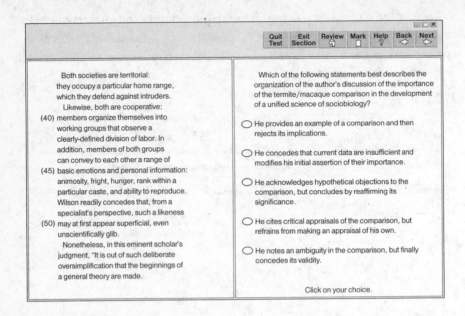

The key lines here are the passage's final sentences. Does the author *acknowledge hypothetical objections* to the comparison? Definitely. Does the author conclude by *reaffirming the significance* of the termite/macaque comparison? Clearly he does: he concludes by quoting Wilson (whom he calls an eminent scholar), in doing so giving implicit support to Wilson's assertion that such oversimplified comparisons can provide the basis for an important general theory. The correct answer is the third choice.

Quantitative Ability

The quantitative part of the GRE consists of two math sections, each with 20 questions. Of the 40 questions, there are

- 15 quantitative comparison questions—7 or 8 per section;
- 19 discrete quantitative questions, consisting of about 11 multiple-choice questions, 4 multiple-answer questions, and 4 numeric entry questions, approximately evenly split between the two sections;
- 6 data interpretation questions—3 per section—all of which are discrete quantitative questions, mostly multiple-choice.

In order to answer these questions, you need to know arithmetic, some very elementary algebra, and a little geometry. Much of this material you learned in elementary and middle school; the rest you learned during the first two years of high school. You do not need to know *any* advanced mathematics. The questions are intended to determine if you have a basic knowledge of elementary mathematics, and if you have the ability to reason clearly.

If you haven't done any mathematics in a while, go through the math review in this book before attempting the Model Tests, and certainly before registering to take the GRE. If you feel that your math skills are still pretty good, you can try the Diagnostic Test first, and then read only those sections of the math review relating to those topics that gave you trouble.

Quantitative Comparison Questions

Of the 40 mathematics questions on the GRE, 15 are what is known as quantitative comparisons. Unless you prepared for the SAT before 2005, it is very possible that you have never even seen such a question. Even if you have had some contact with this type of question, you need to review the basic idea and learn the essential tactics for answering them. Therefore, read these instructions *very* carefully.

In these questions there are two quantities—Quantity A and Quantity B— and it is your job to compare them. For these problems there are *only four possible answers*:

> Quantity A is greater.
> Quantity B is greater.
> The two quantities are equal.
> It is impossible to determine which quantity is greater.

In this book, these four answer choices will be referred to as A, B, C, and D, respectively. In some of the questions, information about the quantities being compared is centered above them. This information *must* be taken into consideration when comparing the two quantities.

In Chapter 6 you will learn several important strategies for handling quantitative comparisons. For now, let's look at three examples to make sure that you understand the concepts involved.

EXAMPLE

Quantity A	Quantity B
$(3 + 4)^2$	$3^2 + 4^2$

- Evaluate each quantity: $(3 + 4)^2 = 7^2 = $ **49**, whereas $3^2 + 4^2 = 9 + 16 = $ **25**.
- Since $49 > 25$, Quantity A is greater. The answer is **A**.

EXAMPLE

$$a + b = 16$$

Quantity A	Quantity B
The average (arithmetic mean) of a and b	8

Quantity A is the average of a and b: $\frac{a+b}{2}$. Since we are told that $a + b = 16$,

Quantity A is $\frac{a+b}{2} = \frac{16}{2} = $ **8**.

So, Quantity A and Quantity B are equal. The answer is **C**.

> **Note**
>
> We cannot determine the value of either a or b; all we know is that their sum is 16. Perhaps $a = 10$ and $b = 6$, or $a = 0$ and $b = 16$, or $a = -4$ and $b = 20$. *It doesn't matter*. The average of 10 and 6 is 8; the average of 0 and 16 is 8; and the average of –4 and 20 is 8. Since $a + b$ is 16, the average of a and b is 8, *all the time, no matter what*. The answer, therefore, is C.

EXAMPLE

Quantity A	Quantity B
a^3	a^2

- If $a = 1$, $a^3 = 1$, and $a^2 = 1$. *In this case*, the quantities in the two columns are equal.
- This means that the answer to this problem *cannot* be A or B. Why?
- The answer can be A (or B) only if Quantity A (or B) is greater *all the time*. But it isn't—not when $a = 1$.

- So, is the answer C? *Maybe*. But for the answer to be C, the quantities would have to be equal *all the time*. Are they?
- No. If $a = 2$, $a^3 = 8$, and $a^2 = 4$, and *in this case* the two quantities are *not equal.*
- The answer, therefore, is **D**.

Discrete Quantitative Questions

Of the 40 mathematics questions on the GRE, 19 are what ETS calls discrete quantitative questions. More than half of those questions are standard **multiple-choice questions**, for which there are five answer choices, exactly one of which is correct. The way to answer such a question is to do the necessary work, get the solution, and then look at the five choices to find your answer. In Chapter 6 we will discuss other techniques for answering these questions, but for now let's look at one example.

EXAMPLE

Edison High School has 840 students, and the ratio of the number of students taking Spanish to the number not taking Spanish is 4:3. How many of the students take Spanish?

Ⓐ 280   Ⓑ 360   Ⓒ 480   Ⓓ 560   Ⓔ 630

To solve this problem requires only that you understand what a ratio is. Ignore the fact that this is a multiple-choice question. *Don't even look at the choices.*

- Let $4x$ and $3x$ be the number of students taking and not taking Spanish, respectively.
- Then $4x + 3x = 840 \Rightarrow 7x = 840 \Rightarrow x = 120$.
- The number of students taking Spanish is $4 \times 120 = 480$.
- Having found the answer to be 480, *now look at the five choices*. The answer is C.

A second type of discrete quantitative question that appears on the GRE is what ETS calls a "multiple-choice question—more than one answer possible," and what for simplicity we call a **multiple-answer question**. In this type of question there could be as many as 12 choices, although usually there are no more than 7 or 8. Any number of the answer choices, from just one to all of them, could be correct. To get credit for such a question, you must select *all* of the correct answer choices and *none* of the incorrect ones. Here is a typical example.

EXAMPLE

If x is negative, which of the following statements *must* be true?
Indicate *all* such statements.

A. $x^2 < x^4$

B. $x^3 < x^2$

C. $x + \dfrac{1}{x} < 0$

D. $x = \sqrt{x^2}$

To solve this problem, examine each statement independently, and think of it as a true-false question.

A. For many negative values of x, x^2 is less than x^4, but if $x = -1$, then x^2 and x^4 are each 1, so it is not *true* that x^2 *must* be less than x^4. Statement A is false.

B. If x is negative, x^3 is negative, and so *must* be less than x^2, which is positive. Statement B is true.

C. If x is negative, so is $\dfrac{1}{x}$, and the sum of two negative numbers is negative. Statement C is true.

D. The square root of a number is *never* negative, and so could *not possibly* equal x. Statement D is false.

You must choose B and C and neither A nor D.

The third type of discrete quantitative question is called a ***numeric entry question***. The numeric entry questions are the only questions on the GRE for which no answer choices are given. For these questions, you have to determine the correct numerical answer and then use the number keys on the keyboard to enter the answer. If the answer is negative, type a hyphen for the negative sign. There are two possibilities: if the answer is an integer or a number that contains a decimal point, there will be a single box for your answer; if the answer is to be entered as a fraction, there will be two boxes—one for the numerator and one for the denominator.

Here is a typical numeric entry question.

EXAMPLE

Directions: The answer to the following question is a fraction. Enter the numerator in the upper box and the denominator in the lower box.

On Monday, $\frac{1}{5}$ of the students at Central High went on a field trip to a museum. On Tuesday, $\frac{5}{8}$ of the students who hadn't gone to the museum on Monday had the opportunity to go. What fraction of the students in the school did not go to the museum either day?

$$\boxed{}$$
$$\boxed{}$$

Of course, this problem can be solved algebraically, but on the GRE the best approach is just to assume that the school has 40 students, 40 being the least common multiple of 5 and 8, the two denominators in the problem. Then, 8 students ($\frac{1}{5}$ of 40) went to the museum on Monday, and of the remaining 32 students, 20 of them ($\frac{5}{8}$ of 32) went on Tuesday. So, 28 students went to the museum and 12 did not. So the fraction of the students in the school who did not go to the museum either day is $\frac{12}{40}$.

Enter 12 in the upper box for the numerator and 40 in the lower box for the denominator. Note that $\frac{12}{40}$ can be reduced to $\frac{6}{20}$ and $\frac{3}{10}$ and you would get full credit for either of those answers, but on the GRE it is *not* necessary to reduce fractions.

Data Interpretation Questions

In each of the two quantitative sections there are three consecutive questions that are based on the same set of data. Most data interpretation questions are multiple-choice questions, but you may have a multiple-answer and/or a numeric entry question. No data interpretation questions are quantitative comparisons. As you might guess from their name, all of these questions are based on information provided in graphs, tables, or charts. The questions test your ability to interpret the data that have been provided. You will either have to do a calculation or make an inference from the given data. The various types of questions that could arise will be explored in Chapter 6. Here is a typical data interpretation question.

EXAMPLE

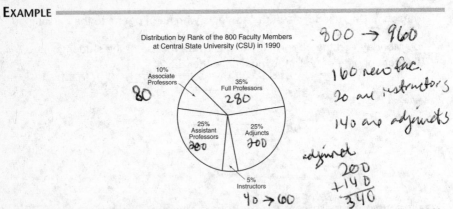

Distribution by Rank of the 800 Faculty Members at Central State University (CSU) in 1990

[handwritten notes: 800 → 960; 160 new fac.; 20 are instructors; 140 are adjuncts; adjunct 200 +140 = 340; 80; 280; 200; 40 → 60]

From 1990 to 2000, the number of faculty members at CSU increased by 20%. If the total number of assistant, associate, and full professors remained the same, and the number of instructors increased by 50%, how many adjunct faculty were there in 2000?

This question is not difficult, but it requires several calculations.

- Since the number of faculty members increased by 20%, in 2000 there were 960 people on the faculty (20% of 800 = 160, and 800 + 160 = 960).
- In 1990, 70% (35% + 10% + 25%) of the faculty were professors, and 70% of 800 = 560.

So in 1990 and also in 2000, there were 560 professors.

- In 1990, there were 40 instructors (5% of 800 = 40); since that number increased by 50%, and 50% of 40 is 20, there were 60 instructors in 2000.
- Of the 960 faculty members in 2000, 560 were professors and 60 were instructors. The remaining **340** were adjuncts (960 – 560 – 60 = 340).

Enter 340 in the box.

Analytical Writing

The analytical writing portion of the GRE consists of two tasks:

- Writing an essay presenting your point of view on an issue of general intellectual concern.
- Writing an essay analyzing the line of reasoning in an argument.

You are allotted 30 minutes to complete the issue task, and 30 minutes to complete the argument analysis task. You must finish one task before you begin the other. You will find suggestions for tackling both writing tasks in Chapter 5.

The Issue Task

In this task, you are asked to respond to a particular issue, clearly presenting your viewpoint on that issue and supporting your position with reasons and examples. This task is intended to test your ability to write logically, persuasively, and effectively.

At the test center, before you begin the timed portion of your issue writing assignment, you will first be shown a set of directions on screen. The directions for the issue task are straightforward. In essence, they say the following:

Develop an argument supporting your viewpoint on an issue.
30 Minutes

Each topic is presented as a one- to two-sentence quotation commenting on an issue of general concern. Your essay may support, refute, or qualify the views expressed in the quotation. Whatever you write, however, must be relevant to the issue under discussion, and you must support your viewpoint with reasons and examples derived from your studies and/or experience. What is more, you must carefully analyze the issue, following the specific instructions given. Your task is not to be creative but to be analytic.

Faculty members from various institutions will evaluate your essay, judging it on the basis of your skill in the following areas:

- ✔ Coverage of each of the elements in the topic instructions
- ✔ Analysis of the question's implications
- ✔ Organization and articulation of your ideas
- ✔ Use of relevant examples and arguments to support your case
- ✔ Handling of the mechanics of standard written English

To begin the timed portion of this task, click on the box labeled CONTINUE. Once you click on CONTINUE, a second screen will appear. This screen contains some general words of advice about how to write an issue essay:

- Think before you write. Plan what you are going to say.
- Work out your ideas in detail.
- Be coherent.
- Leave yourself enough time to revise.

None of this is rocket science. You already know what you are supposed to do. Don't waste your time reading pro forma advice, just click on the CONTINUE BOX and get to work.

Here are two issue topics modeled after issue tasks from the GRE. Please note that these are not official GRE issue topics, although they do resemble official topics closely in subject matter and form.

SAMPLE ISSUE TASK 1

Claim: If we are serious about solving the problem of income inequality, our primary focus should be on improving funding for public colleges and universities.

Reason: Higher education is the key to career advancement.

Compose an essay that identifies how greatly you concur (or differ) with the claim provided and its rationale.

SAMPLE ISSUE TASK 2

The key to success is found not in following your passion, but rather in bringing passion to the work you do.

Compose an essay that identifies how greatly you concur (or differ) with the statement provided, describing in detail the rationale for your argument. As you build and provide evidence for your argument, include examples that demonstrate circumstances in which the statement could (or could not) be valid. Be sure to explain the impact these examples have on your argument.

Argument Task

In this task, you are asked to critique the line of reasoning of an argument given in a brief passage, clearly pointing out that argument's strengths and weaknesses and supporting your position with reasons and examples. This task is intended to test both your ability to evaluate the soundness of a position and your ability to get your point across to an academic audience.

Again, before you begin the timed portion of your argument analysis task, you will first be shown a set of directions on screen. The directions for the argument task are straightforward. In essence, they say the following:

Evaluate an argument.
30 Minutes

In 30 minutes, prepare a critical analysis of the argument expressed in a short paragraph. You may not offer an analysis of any other argument.

As you critique the argument, think about the author's underlying assumptions. Ask yourself whether any of them are questionable. Also, evaluate any evidence that the author brings up. Ask yourself whether it actually supports the author's conclusions.

In your analysis, you may suggest additional kinds of evidence to reinforce the author's argument. You may also suggest methods to refute the argument or additional data that might be useful to you as you assess the soundness of the argument. You may not, however, present your personal views on the topic. Your job is to analyze the elements of an argument, not to support or contradict that argument.

Faculty members from various institutions will judge your essay, assessing it on the basis of your skills in the following areas:

✔ Coverage of each of the elements in the topic instructions
✔ Identification and assessment of the argument's main elements
✔ Organization and articulation of your thoughts
✔ Use of relevant examples and arguments to support your case
✔ Handling of the mechanics of standard written English

Here is an argument analysis topic modeled after argument analysis tasks from the GRE. Please note that this is not an official GRE argument analysis topic, although it does resemble the official topics closely in subject matter and form.

SAMPLE ARGUMENT TASK

The following appeared in an editorial in the *Springfield Morning Leader*.

"The time is now for Springfield to step up to the plate and demonstrate that it is a city on the move. By building a new stadium that meets the standards of Major League Baseball, we can strengthen the local economy and inspire civic pride. Building the stadium will create construction jobs for local workers. Additionally, the new stadium will help woo a Major League team to the area, which will create jobs and make Springfield more attractive to businesses that are considering relocating. Building a new stadium is an investment of public funds that will pay off for Springfield today and for generations to come."

Compose an essay that identifies and considers the evidence required to assess the validity of the argument provided. In writing your essay be sure to clarify whether this evidence would bolster or undermine the argument.

Evidence - ① other cities of comparable size did it work for them?

② discussions with Major League owners + managers to determine the likelihood they'd be willing to relocate. The likelihood would need to be extremely high in order to justify such an investment

③ consequences of building a std. if no major league team is interested in relocating. business would suffer + then the city would also be dealing with the debt from the construction

Test-Taking Tactics for the Computer-Delivered GRE

2

In this chapter, we will take you step-by-step through a discussion of all the screens you will see as you take the computer-delivered GRE. But first let's look at a few sample questions to show you what the screens actually look like, to familiarize you with the various icons, and to demonstrate how to use the mouse to navigate through the exam.

Here is a simple **_multiple-choice_** math question as it would appear on a computer screen. Right now the arrow is off to one side.

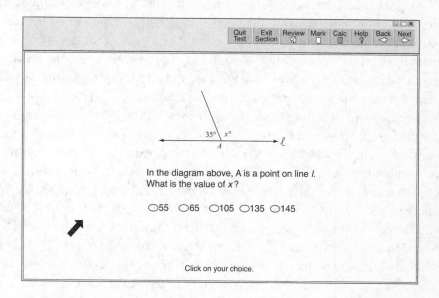

In the diagram above, A is a point on line _l_.
What is the value of _x_?

○55　○65　○105　○135　○145

Click on your choice.

Suppose that in looking at the diagram, you see that the angle is a little greater than 90° and so decide that the answer must be 105. Move the mouse until the arrow is on the circle next to 105 and click. Note that the circle on which you clicked is now black.

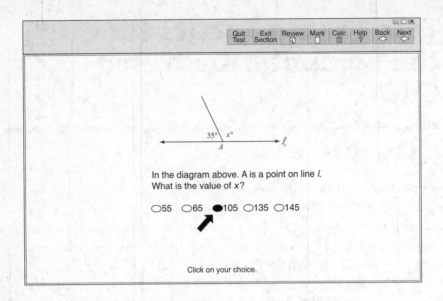

Suppose that just as you are about to click on NEXT to go to the next question, you remember that diagrams on the GRE are not drawn to scale, and so the answer may not be 105. Hopefully, you realize that the sum of the measures of the two angles in the diagram is 180°, and so to get the answer, you have to subtract 35 from 180. You can do the subtraction mentally, you can do it on your scratch paper, or you can click on the CALCULATOR icon and do it on a calculator. As soon as you click on the icon, a four-function calculator will appear on the screen. If the calculator opens up on top of the question or the answer choices, click on the top of it and drag it to wherever is convenient for you. You can either enter the numbers from your keyboard or click the numbers on the calculator. Since $180 - 35 = 145$, you want to change your answer. Simply click on the circle next to 145. That circle is now black, and the one next to 105 is white again. If you think that you might want to return to this question later, click on MARK and then click on NEXT. If you know that there is no reason to ever look at this question again, just click on NEXT. At any time, you can click on REVIEW to see which questions you have marked, and by clicking on one of the marked questions, you will immediately return to it.

Suppose the question we just discussed had been a **numeric entry** question.

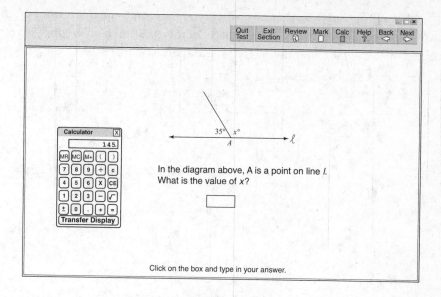

In the diagram above, A is a point on line *l*.
What is the value of *x*?

Click on the box and type in your answer.

If you subtracted 35 from 180 in your head, and you knew that the answer was 145, you could click in the box and type 145. If you used your calculator to subtract, you could still type 145 in the box, but if you prefer, instead of typing 145, you could click on the bar labeled TRANSFER DISPLAY at the bottom of the calculator, and the 145 that is in the calculator's digital readout will automatically appear in the box. Note that the only time you can click on the TRANSFER DISPLAY bar is when the question on the screen is a numeric entry question; at all other times that bar is grayed out.

Finally, let's look at a ***multiple-answer*** question. Notice that on multiple-answer questions there are squares, instead of circles, in front of each answer choice.

On multiple-answer questions, when you click on a square in front of an answer choice, an X appears in the square. In the question below, suppose you clicked on 17, 37, and 57; the screen would then look like this.

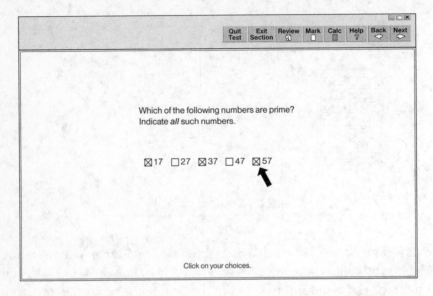

If you then realize that 47 is also a prime, just click on it; an X will appear in its square.

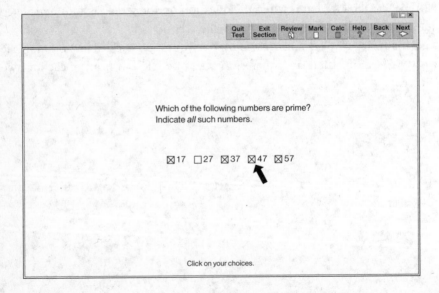

Finally, if you realize that you made another mistake, by including 57 (57 = 3 × 19), just click on the square in front of 57 and the X will go away.

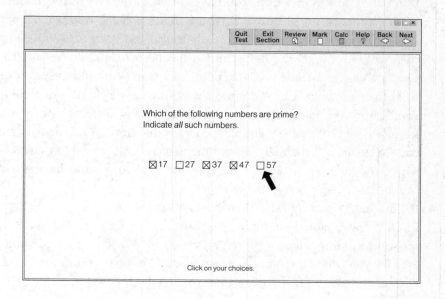

> **Note**
>
> If you use the calculator to answer a question and then click on NEXT to go to the next question, the calculator will remain on the screen (with whatever your previous answer was still in the digital readout). You may leave it there, but it is better to close it, by clicking on the X in the upper-right-hand corner, and then just clicking on the calculator icon the next time you need it.

HELPFUL HINTS

1. You should *never* click on the EXIT SECTION icon. This is tantamount to saying, "I give up. I can't deal with this section anymore." At the very least go through each question, taking a wild guess if necessary, get to the end of the section, and click CONTINUE to go to the next section.

2. You should *never* click on the HELP icon. All this will do is bring up a page of directions. Learn the directions for every type of question now and review them, if necessary, when they appear before each section begins.

Once you begin a section, the clock starts and clicking on HELP to reread the directions is just a waste of time.

3. Don't click on REVIEW until you have gotten to the end of the section. When you click on REVIEW, all you will see is a list numbered from 1–20, indicating for each question whether it has been ANSWERED or UNANSWERED and whether or not it has been MARKED. *No question should be unanswered.* If you are completely stumped and have no idea what the right answer is, just guess something before clicking on NEXT. Remember, your raw score is simply the number of correct answers you have. It would be terrible if you skipped a few questions, planning to come back to them, and then ran out of time. Instead of having a few guesses, which might result in a correct answer or two, you would have a few blanks, which earn no points whatsoever.

4. If time hasn't run out after you have answered Question 20, click on REVIEW to see which questions you marked. Click on one of them. That question will immediately appear, and you can give it a little more time. Perhaps you will figure it out; perhaps you will be able to eliminate some choices and make a better guess than you did originally.

A GUIDED TOUR OF THE COMPUTER-DELIVERED GRE

The following outline tells you exactly what you will see, screen by screen, when you take the computerized GRE. To some extent you can alter the flow of screens. For example, after answering the fourteenth math question, we assume that you would click on NEXT to bring up the screen for Question 15. However, at that point, if you chose to, you could click on MARK to put a check mark next to Question 14 in the list of questions you have looked at; you could click on BACK to return to Question 13 or click on BACK repeatedly to return to any previous question in the section; you could click on REVIEW to see exactly which questions you had already answered, which ones you had skipped, and which ones you had marked; or you could click on HELP to reread the directions for the math questions. As you will see shortly, most of those would be poor choices, but you could do any of them.

Screen 1

When you are ready to begin the test, the first screen you will see is a page of TEST CENTER REGULATIONS. You may take as much time as you like to read over this list of rules—no eating, no drinking, no smoking, no creating disturbances, no tampering with the computer—but you shouldn't need to because you should have already read it when you looked at *POWERPREP II* on the GRE website. When you are through looking at this screen, click on CONTINUE.

The second screen is a CONFIDENTIALITY AGREEMENT. This is where you promise not to cheat or to take any test materials or scrap paper out of the room. The way you say "I agree" is to click on CONTINUE.

The third screen contains GENERAL TEST INFORMATION. Much of this information—when you can take breaks; how long the breaks are; when you can leave the room—is included in this book, but feel free to take as much time as you like to read it over. When you are ready to proceed, click on CONTINUE.

This screen gives you the DIRECTIONS FOR THE ANALYTICAL WRITING section of the GRE. Again, once you read this book, you should know all of these directions. When you are ready to move on, click on CONTINUE.

This screen has the DIRECTIONS FOR TASK 1 (ANALYZE AN ISSUE). The most important point to remember is that although you have 60 minutes for Section 1, you have a maximum of 30 minutes for each of the two tasks. If, for example, you finish Task 1 in 23 minutes, you may move on to Task 2, but once you do, you can never return to Task 1 to write for 7 more minutes. Nor can you tack those 7 minutes on to the time you have for Task 2. Once you leave Task 1, you will have exactly 30 minutes for Task 2. Once you are ready to leave this screen, TAKE A DEEP BREATH: as soon as you click on CONTINUE, the test officially begins.

This screen has Task 1. On the left of the screen will be the issue you are to analyze; on the right of the screen will be a blank page on which you are to type your analysis. In the upper-right-hand corner of the screen, below the row of icons, you will see a digital readout of the amount of time remaining. If you find that distracting, you may click on HIDE TIME to make it go away, but it will reappear when there are only five minutes left. During every section, the countdown clock will be visible unless you choose to hide it. Even if you do, in every section, the clock will reappear during the last five minutes. If you finish your essay in less than 30 minutes, read it over and make any changes you like. If you still have time left, and don't want to look at the essay any more, you *can* hit NEXT, but you don't have to. You can relax. When the 30 minutes are up, the computer will automatically close that screen and take you to the next one. If you do click on NEXT, the computer will give you one last chance to change your mind.

If your full 30 minutes for Task 1 has not expired, this screen will remind you that you still have time left and give you the option of returning to Task 1 (RETURN) or moving on (CONTINUE).

Once you have left Task 1, the next screen has the DIRECTIONS FOR TASK 2 (ANALYZE AN ARGUMENT). Note: the clock is *not* running while you read these directions. So if you want an extra minute or so before starting your second essay, wait before clicking on CONTINUE.

This screen has Task 2. The argument you are to analyze will be on the left, and just as in Task 1, on the right there will be a blank page on which you are to type your analysis. And as in Task 1, the moment this screen appears, the clock will start counting down from 30:00. When you have finished your essay, you may look it over, rest a while, or click on NEXT.

If your full 30 minutes for Task 2 has not expired, this screen will remind you that you still have time left and give you the option of returning to Task 2 (RETURN) or moving on (CONTINUE).

Once you have left Task 2, the next screen will tell you that you have finished Section 1 and are about to begin Section 2. When you are ready, click on CONTINUE.

This screen will tell you that the next section will begin in 60 seconds. This is your first official break. You *should* take this short break to relax before beginning Section 2, but you don't have to. At any time before your 60 seconds are up, you can click on CONTINUE to move on.

Note

Section 2 will either be a 30-minute verbal section or a 35-minute quantitative section. In the practice tests in this book, Sections 2 and 4 are verbal and Sections 3 and 5 are quantitative. On an actual GRE, however, the sections can come in any order, and it is very likely that there will be an Experimental Section—either a third verbal section or a third quantitative section—which can come at any point in the test. The Experimental Section will not affect your score, but there is no way to know which section it is, so you must do your very best on each section.

This screen gives you the DIRECTIONS FOR THE VERBAL ABILITY sections of the GRE. Reading this screen, slowly, if you like, gives you a little longer break before resuming the test. When you are ready to begin Section 2, click on CONTINUE.

Screens 14–33 will be the 20 verbal questions in Section 2, one question per screen. Go through the section, answering *every* question, guessing whenever necessary. If, when you click on CONTINUE after Question 20, your 30 minutes for Section 2 aren't up, the next screen you see will give you the option of returning to Section 2, by clicking on RETURN, or going on to Section 3, by again clicking on CONTINUE.

This screen will tell you that the next section will begin in 60 seconds. This is your second official break. You *should* take this short break to relax before beginning Section 3, but you don't have to. At any time before your 60 seconds are up, you may click on CONTINUE to move on.

This screen gives you the DIRECTIONS FOR THE QUANTITA-TIVE ABILITY sections of the GRE. Reading this screen, slowly, if you like, gives you a little longer break before resuming the test. When you are ready to start Section 3, click on CONTINUE.

Screens 36–55 will be the 20 quantitative questions in Section 3, one question per screen. Go through the section, answering *every* question, guessing whenever necessary. If there is a question that has you stumped, you can MARK it, but still answer it (even if your answer is a wild guess) before clicking on NEXT. Just as in Section 2, after answering Question 20, you may click on CONTINUE, but if you still have time left, a screen will appear that will give you the chance to change your mind: you can click on RETURN to go back to the questions in Section 3 or you can really end the section by once again clicking on CONTINUE.

This screen will tell you that the next section will begin in 10 minutes. This is your third official break, and the only one that lasts more than 60 seconds. TAKE THIS BREAK! Whether you need to or not, go to the restroom now. If you have to go later during the test, the clock will be running. Outside the room, you can have a drink and/or a snack. And, of course, you can use this break to take some deep breaths and to relax before beginning the rest of the test. Having said this, you should know that you don't have to take the full 10-minute break. At any time before the 10 minutes are up, you may click on CONTINUE to move on.

At this point, the screens essentially repeat. There will be at least two more sections (one verbal and one quantitative), and probably three (the third section being yet another verbal or another quantitative one). Remember that if there are six sections, any section other than the writing section can be the experimental one, even Section 2 or 3. Each verbal section will have 20 questions and be 30 minutes long, just like Section 2, and each quantitative section will have 20 questions and be 35 minutes long, just like Section 3.

Final
Screens

After you have answered Question 20 in Section 6 and clicked on CONTINUE, the test is over. At this point you will see the following screen.

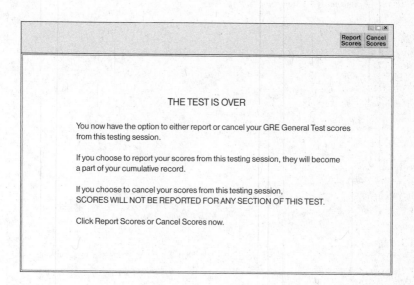

Report Scores   Cancel Scores

THE TEST IS OVER

You now have the option to either report or cancel your GRE General Test scores from this testing session.

If you choose to report your scores from this testing session, they will become a part of your cumulative record.

If you choose to cancel your scores from this testing session,
SCORES WILL NOT BE REPORTED FOR ANY SECTION OF THIS TEST.

Click Report Scores or Cancel Scores now.

Note

If you click on CANCEL, the next screen will give you a chance to avoid a disaster, in case you clicked CANCEL accidentally. Once again, you will be asked to REPORT or CANCEL, your scores, and this time your decision is irreversible.

If you choose to REPORT your scores, the next screen will give you your unofficial scores for the verbal and quantitative sections. Your official scores will arrive in the mail about three weeks after you take the test and, of course, will include your writing score, as well.

Verbal Ability: Tactics and Practice

3

In this chapter you'll learn how best to handle each type of verbal question, using strategies and tips that have helped thousands of GRE-takers before you. You'll feel confident taking the exam because you'll be familiar with the types of questions on it; your mind will switch easily into GRE gear.

> ## Long-Range Strategy
>
> The best way to have prepared for the verbal sections of the GRE is to have analyzed a great deal of good writing over the past five or ten years. As a lower division college student, you were exposed to a variety of fields, in the process increasing your vocabulary and growing accustomed to the way words are used in context. As an upper division student, however, you probably had to concentrate on your individual major. *Don't* limit your reading to your own field. Continue to expand your horizons, and, as you do, make a conscious effort to pay attention to the new words you encounter.

The key strategy for expanding your vocabulary is (once again) READ. However, it is possible to fine-tune your vocabulary by exploring unabridged dictionaries, in which usage notes make clear the fine distinctions between related words, and by studying high-level vocabulary lists such as our High-Frequency Word List, more than 300 words that have occurred and reoccurred on GREs published in the past 20 years.

Use the High-Frequency Word List as a guide in making flash cards. Scan the list looking for words you recognize but cannot use in a sentence or define. You have a feel for these words—you are on the brink of knowing them. Effort you put into mastering such "borderline" words will pay off soon.

Pay particular attention to words you thought you knew—but didn't. See whether any of them are defined in an unexpected way. If they are, make a special note of them. The GRE often stumps students with questions based on unfamiliar meanings of familiar-looking words.

To improve the effectiveness of your flash-card sessions, try following these suggestions:

Writing the Flash Card

Be brief—but include all the information you need. On one side write the word. On the other side write a *concise* definition—two or three words at most—for each major meaning of the word you want to learn. Include an antonym, too: the synonym-antonym associations can help you remember both words. To fix the word in your mind, use it in a short phrase. Then write that phrase down.

Memorizing the Flash Card

Carry a few of your flash cards with you every day. Look them over whenever you have a spare moment or two. Work in short bursts. Try going through five flash cards at a time, shuffling through them rapidly so that you can build up your rapid sight recognition of the words for the test.

Test your memory: don't look at the back of the card unless you must. Go through your five cards several times a day. Then, when you have mastered two or three of the cards and have them down pat, set those cards aside and add a couple of new ones to your working pile. That way you will always be working with a limited group, but you won't be wasting time reviewing words you already recognize on sight.

Never try to master a whole stack of flash cards in one long cram session. It won't work.

DISCRETE, SHORT-ANSWER VERBAL QUESTIONS

Discrete, short-answer verbal questions are those old favorites, fill-in-the-blank questions. They come in two formats, **sentence equivalence questions** and **text completion questions**.

Sentence equivalence questions look like this:

> The medical researchers replied to the charge that their proposed new treatment was _____ by demonstrating that it in fact observed standard medical practices.
>
> | A | deleterious |
> | B | untested |
> | C | unorthodox |
> | D | expensive |
> | E | intricate |
> | F | unconventional |

To get credit for answering a sentence equivalence question correctly, you must come up with not one correct answer choice, but **two** correct answer choices that work equally well. The answer choices to sentence equivalence questions are marked with **square boxes**, not with circles or ovals. **Square boxes** are your clue that you must select **two** answer choices to get the question right.

Correct answers: C, F

Text completion questions look like this:

> Her novel published to universal (i) _____, her literary gifts acknowledged by the chief figures of the Harlem Renaissance, her reputation as yet (ii) _____ by envious slights, Hurston clearly was at the (iii) _____ of her career.

Blank (i)	Blank (ii)	Blank (iii)
indifference	belittled	zenith
derision	resented	extremity
acclaim	untarnished	ebb

In a text completion question, you are presented with a sentence or group of sentences containing one to three blanks. Instead of seeing a single list of answer choices, you see one, two, or three independent columns of choices; for each blank in the sentence, you must select one correct answer choice from the appropriate column, mixing and matching your choices until you come up with a combination that makes sense. There is *no* partial credit: to get any credit for answering a text completion question, you must come up with a correct answer choice *for each blank.*

Correct Answers: acclaim, untarnished, zenith

Long-Range Strategy

When you encounter a new word, don't just memorize its meaning in rote fashion. Study the way it is used, and then use it correctly in three or more sentences. Try to work the word into conversations and discussions, even if it startles your friends. The way to make a word your own is to use it.

SENTENCE EQUIVALENCE QUESTIONS

TIPS TO HELP YOU COPE

1. **Before you look at the sentence, look over the answer choices to locate any obvious synonyms.** If you can spot a pair of synonyms, substitute these two words in the sentence. If both make the same sort of sense in the context, you may well have found your answer pair.

Note

Be very careful when you apply this tactic. The test-makers are very aware that some examinees simply scan the answer choices looking for synonyms. Therefore, often they will deliberately plant obvious synonym pairs among the answer choices. These eye-catchers or distractors are there to trick the unwary. Because you will recognize these words as synonyms, you may want to select them without reading the sentence closely. However, the test-makers are not testing your knowledge of vocabulary per se. They are testing your reading comprehension. The words you choose do not have to be synonyms. However, they must both make sense in the sentence in an equivalent way.

---

2. **Look at all the possible answers before you finally choose your answer pair.** You are looking for *two* words that fit the meaning of the

sentence as a whole and that can work interchangeably. In order to be sure you have not been hasty in making your decision, substitute *all* the answer choices for the missing word.

3. **If you fail to detect a pair of synonyms right away, read the sentence and think of a word that makes sense.** The word you think of may not be the exact word that appears in the answer choices, but it probably will be similar in meaning to the right answer.

4. **Consider secondary meanings of the answer choices as well as their primary meanings.** Frequently, the test-makers attempt to mislead you by using familiar words in an unfamiliar way. Suppose you have found one answer choice that perfectly fits the meaning of the sentence as a whole but cannot find a second answer choice that seems exactly right. Reread the sentence, substituting that perfect answer choice for the blank. Then take a fresh look at the other answer choices. Remember that these words or phrases may have multiple meanings. Think of contexts in which you have heard these words or phrases used. That may help you come up with additional meanings for them.

5. **Look for signal words or phrases indicating that one thing causes another or logically determines another.** (Words like *because, since, consequently,* and *hence.*)

6. **Look for words or phrases indicating that the omitted part of the sentence supports or continues a thought developed elsewhere in the sentence.** (Words like *furthermore, moreover, likewise,* and *as well.*) In such cases, a synonym or near-synonym for another word in the sentence may provide the correct answer.

7. **Look for words or phrases explicitly or implicitly indicating a contrast between one idea and another.** (Function words like *although, however, nonetheless,* and *notwithstanding,* which set up a reversal of a thought, or words like *anomaly, incongruity,* and *paradox,* whose meaning inherently indicates a contrast.) In such cases, an antonym or near-antonym for another word in the sentence may provide the correct answer.

8. **Use your knowledge of word parts and parts of speech to get at the meanings of unfamiliar words.** If a word used by the author is unfamiliar, or if an answer choice is unknown to you, break down the word into its component parts—prefixes, suffixes, roots—to see whether they provide any clues to its meaning. Change the unfamiliar word from one part of speech to another to see whether it is more recognizable in an alternate form. You may not recognize the noun *inebriety*; you probably are familiar with the adjective *inebriated.*

Examples to Get You Started

EXAMPLE 1

Try spotting the synonyms among the following six answer choices.

> A   extravagant
> B   tawdry
> C   parsimonious
> D   optimistic
> E   profligate
> F   pedestrian

Extravagant and *profligate* are synonyms; both mean spendthrift, or wasteful.

Now here is the sentence. Do the synonyms that you spotted work in this context?

> Although the young duke's trustees had tried to teach him
> fiscal prudence, they feared he would never learn to curb
> his _____ ways.

Clearly, they do. If the young duke has not learned to be careful about his finances, it is understandable that his trustees might worry about his inability to curb or restrain his *profligate* and *extravagant* ways.

EXAMPLE 2

Be sure to consider all the answer choices before you select your answer pair.

> The evil of class and race hatred must be eliminated while it is still in
> _____ state; otherwise it may grow to dangerous proportions.

> A   an amorphous
> B   an overt
> C   a rudimentary
> D   a threatening
> E   an independent
> F   an embryonic

On the basis of a loose sense of this sentence's meaning, you might be tempted to select the first choice, *amorphous*. After all, this sentence basically tells you that you should wipe out hatred before it gets too dangerous. Clearly, if hatred is vague or *amorphous*, it is less formidable than if it is well-defined. However, this reading of the sentence is inadequate: it fails to take into account the sentence's key phrase.

The key phrase here is "may grow to dangerous proportions." The writer fears that class and race hatred may grow large enough to endanger society. He wants us to wipe out this hatred before it is fully grown. Examine each answer choice, eliminating those answers that carry no suggestion that something lacks its full growth or development. Does *overt* suggest that something isn't fully grown? No, it suggests that something is obvious or evident. Does *rudimentary* suggest that something isn't fully grown? Yes, it suggests that something is unfinished or immature. This may well be one of your two correct answer choices.

Look for a second word that suggests a lack of full growth. Does *independent* suggest that something isn't fully grown? No, it suggests that something is free and unconstrained. Does *threatening* suggest that something isn't fully grown? No, it suggests that something is a source of danger or cause for alarm. Only one word is left: *embryonic* (at an early, incomplete stage of development). If you substitute *embryonic* for *rudimentary* in the sentence, you will not change the sentence's essential meaning. The correct answer choices are *rudimentary* and *embryonic*.

EXAMPLE 3

Try coming up with your own word to complete the following sentence.

> Because experience had convinced her that Hector was both self-seeking and avaricious, she rejected the possibility that the motivation behind his donation had been wholly _____.

This sentence presents a simple case of cause and effect. The key phrase here is *self-seeking* and *avaricious*. The woman has found the man to be selfish and greedy. *Therefore*, she refuses to believe his motivation for donating money can be _____. She expects selfishness (*self-seeking*) and greed (*avaricious*), not their opposite.

You are looking for words that are antonyms for selfish. What words immediately come to mind? *Selfless, generous, charitable*?

Now look at the answer choices.

> A redundant
>
> B frivolous
>
> C egotistical
>
> D ephemeral
>
> E altruistic
>
> F benevolent

The missing words are, of course, *altruistic* and *benevolent*. They are the correct answer pair.

EXAMPLE 4

In tackling the following sentence equivalence question, be on the lookout for words with multiple meanings.

> Snakes are the most stationary of all vertebrates; as long as a locality
> _____ them a sufficiency of food and some shelter to which they can
> readily retreat, they have no inducement to change it.
>
> A provides
>
> B constitutes
>
> C affords
>
> D denies
>
> E disallows
>
> F withholds

Snakes tend to be stationary creatures. Why? They stay put because a particular locality meets their needs: it *provides* or offers them food and shelter.

Look at the other answer choices. Can you rule out any of them? *Denies, disallows,* and *withholds* are all negative terms; none of them seem appropriate in this context. After all, if a locality *denied* or *disallowed* the snakes food and shelter or *withheld* food and shelter from them, that would not be an inducement or incentive for the snakes to stay put. Likewise, *constitutes* (composes; establishes) does not seem appropriate in the context. It feels awkward, even ungrammatical (the verb does not normally take an indirect object).

Only *affords* is left. Here it clearly is *not* used with its primary meaning, "to be able to meet the expense of," as in affording to buy a new car.

Try to think of other contexts for *afford*. "It affords me great pleasure to be here." "Gustavo's Facebook entries afford us a glimpse into the daily life of a musician on tour." These sentences use *afford* with a secondary meaning: to give, offer, or provide. The correct answers to this sentence equivalence question are *affords* and *provides*.

EXAMPLE 5

Note the function of a contrast signal word in the following question.

Paradoxically, the more _____ the details this artist chooses, the better able she is to depict her fantastic, other-worldly landscapes.

- A ethereal
- B realistic
- C fanciful
- D mundane
- E extravagant
- F sublime

The artist creates imaginary landscapes that do not seem to belong to this world. We normally would expect the details comprising these landscapes to be as fantastic and other-worldly as the landscapes themselves. The truth of the matter, however, is *paradoxical*: it contradicts what we expect. The details she chooses may be *realistic* (true to life) or *mundane* (ordinary, everyday), yet the more lifelike and unremarkable they are, the more fantastic the paintings seem. The correct answers are *realistic* and *mundane*.

EXAMPLE 6

Note how the knowledge of prefixes, suffixes, and roots and of parts of speech can help you with the following sentence equivalence question.

This island is a colony; however, in most matters it is _____ and receives no orders from the mother country.

- A synoptic
- B independent
- C methodical
- D autonomous
- E heretical
- F disinterested

First, locate any answer choices that are obviously correct. If a colony receives no orders from its mother country, it is *independent* to act according to its own wishes: it is essentially self-governing.

Then eliminate any answer choices that are most likely incorrect. It is not necessarily *methodical* (systematic), nor is it by definition *heretical* (unorthodox) or *disinterested* (impartial). Thus, you may rule out Choices C, E, and F.

The two answer choices remaining may be unfamiliar to you. Analyze them, using what you know of related words. *Synoptic* is related to the noun *synopsis*, a summary or abridgement. Does this term have anything to do with how a colony might govern itself? Definitely not. *Autonomous*, however, comes from the prefix *auto-* (self) and the root *nom-* (law). An autonomous nation is independent; it rules itself. Thus, the correct answers are *independent* and *autonomous*.

TEXT COMPLETION QUESTIONS

🗝 TIPS TO HELP YOU COPE

1. In double- and triple-blank texts, go through one column at a time, eliminating the answer choices that do not fit. First read through the entire text to get a sense of it as a whole. Pay special attention to the parts of the text (subordinate clauses, participial phrases, etc.) *without* any blanks. See whether you can predict what the first missing word may be. Then go through the first column, inserting each word in the sentence's first blank. Ask yourself whether a given word would make sense in this blank. If it makes no sense, eliminate it. If it makes possible sense, keep it in mind as you work on filling in the next blank.

2. Break down complex passages into simpler components. Rephrase dependent clauses and long participial phrases, turning them into simple sentences.

3. If a sentence contains a metaphor, check to see whether that metaphor controls the writer's choice of words (and your answer choice).

4. Once you have filled in all the blanks to your satisfaction, reread the completed passage to be sure it makes sense. No matter how confident you are that you have filled in an individual blank correctly, you cannot be sure you have successfully completed the passage until you have confirmed your word choice(s) by rereading the entire text. Remember: you are aiming for closure. Do not omit this stage in the procedure.

Examples to Get You Started

EXAMPLE 1

Here is an example of how to work through a text one blank at a time.

> Critics of the movie version of *The Color Purple* (i) _____ its saccharine, overoptimistic tone as out of keeping with the novel's more (ii) _____ quality.

Blank (i)
Ⓐ acclaimed
Ⓑ decried
Ⓒ echoed

Blank (ii)
Ⓓ acerbic
Ⓔ cloying
Ⓕ sanguine

For a quick, general sense of the opening clause, break it down. What does it say? *Critics _____ the movie's sugary sweet tone.*

How would critics react to something sugary sweet and overly hopeful? Most likely they would *not* acclaim or praise it. You are probably safe to cross out the word *acclaimed*. However, they might well *decry* or disparage it. They might even *echo* or copy it, although that answer choice seems unlikely.

You have two possibilities for the first blank, *decried* and *echoed,* the former more likely than the latter. Now consider the second blank. The movie's sugary, overly hopeful tone is out of keeping with the novel's quality: the two tones disagree. Therefore, the novel's tone is not *sanguine* (hopeful) or *cloying* (sickly sweet). It is instead on the bitter or sour side; in a word, *acerbic*.

Now that you are sure of your second answer choice, go back to the first blank. Reread the sentence:

Critics of the movie version of The Color Purple _____ *its saccharine, overoptimistic tone as out of keeping with the novel's more acerbic quality.* Clearly, the critics would not echo the movie's tone. Instead, they decried or disparaged it. By rereading the text you have confirmed your answer choices.

Helpful Hint

Do *not* assume that you have to work your way through the blanks sequentially. Depending on the text, it may be easier to fill in the second or third blank first!

EXAMPLE 2

Here is an example of how to break down a complex passage into simpler components.

> Museum director Hoving (i) _____ refers to the smuggled Greek urn as the "hot pot," not because there are doubts about its authenticity or even great reservations as to its price, but because the (ii) _____ of its acquisition is open to question.

Blank (i)
(A) characteristically
(B) colloquially
(C) repeatedly

Blank (ii)
(D) timeliness
(E) manner
(F) expense

What do we know?

✔ The urn has been smuggled.
✔ Hoving calls it a "hot pot."
✔ It is genuine. (There are no doubts about its authenticity.)
✔ It did not cost too much. (There are no great reservations as to its price.)

In calling the smuggled urn a "hot pot," Hoving is not necessarily speaking *characteristically:* we have no information about his typical mode of speech. Similarly, we have no evidence that Hoving has *repeatedly* called it a hot pot: we know only that he called it a hot pot at least once. Hoving is speaking *colloquially*, that is, informally. (*Hot* here is a slang term meaning stolen or illegally obtained.) You have your first correct answer choice, *colloquially*.

Now consider the second blank. The urn's *expense* is not being questioned, nor is the *timeliness* (well-timed occurrence) of its acquisition. However, because the urn has been smuggled into the country, there clearly are unresolved questions about how it got here, in other words, about its mode or *manner* of acquisition. The second correct answer choice is *manner*.

EXAMPLE 3

Note how the extended metaphor in the following sentence governs the writer's choice of words.

> The mind of a bigot is like the pupil of the eye: the more light you pour upon it, the more it will _____.

Ⓐ	blink
Ⓑ	veer
Ⓒ	stare
Ⓓ	reflect
Ⓔ	contract

The image of light unifies this sentence. In choosing an answer, you must complete the sentence in such a way as to develop that metaphor fully and accurately. Exactly what takes place when you shine a light into someone's eye? The person may stare back or blink; you may see the light reflected in the person's eye. But what happens to the pupil of the eye? It neither blinks nor reflects. Instead it shrinks in size: it *contracts*. Likewise, exposed to the light of tolerance, the bigot's mind resists illumination, shrinking from light. *Contract* completes the metaphor; it is the correct answer choice.

READING COMPREHENSION QUESTIONS

The reading comprehension portions of the GRE contain some surprises for test-takers. Some reading comprehension questions require you to click on a sentence within the passage that fits a particular description; others require you to select one or more answer choices to get a question right. In addition, logical reasoning questions appear in the reading comprehension portions of the test. These logical reasoning questions resemble questions found on the Logical Reasoning sections of the LSAT, the Verbal sections of the GMAT, etc. These questions ask you to determine the logical conclusion of an argument, to analyze the function and relationship of individual statements within an argument, to isolate the assumptions underlying an argument, and to distinguish what strengthens an argument from what weakens it.

The reading comprehension questions take more time than any other questions on the test because you have to read an entire passage before you can answer them. They test your ability to understand what you read—both content and technique.

> ### Long-Range Strategy
> **Read, Read, Read! Just do it.**
> There is no substitute for extensive reading as a preparation for the GRE and for graduate school. The only way to obtain proficiency in reading is by reading books of all kinds. The GRE tends to take its reading passages from *Scientific American*, from prestigious university presses (Harvard, Princeton, Oxford), and from scholarly journals. If you want to turn yourself into the kind of reader graduate schools are looking for, you must develop the habit of reading complex material—every day.

⌐━━ TIPS TO HELP YOU COPE

1. **First read the question; then read the passage.** In responding to reading comprehension questions on the GRE, you often will have to consider more material than can fit conveniently on a single screen. On your monitor, you will confront a split screen. On one-half of the screen you will see the question you must answer; on the other you will see a segment of the passage under consideration. You will have to scroll through the passage in order to read the text in its entirety. Under these conditions, clearly only one tactic works: first read the question, then read the passage.

> ### Note
> It is particularly important to follow this tactic when you are dealing with the logical reasoning questions on the GRE. Rather than jumping in blindly and analyzing each and every aspect of the argument—assumptions, evidence, further application, logical flaws—do no more work than necessary. Look at the question stem. Then examine the argument. Know what aspect of the argument you are to concentrate on, and focus on it. You will save time and effort.

2. **Read the question carefully, so that you are sure you understand what it is asking.** Decide whether it is asking about a specific, readily identifiable detail within the passage, or whether it is asking

about the passage as a whole. Note any key words in the question that may help you spot where the answer may be found.

3. **Next, turn to the passage.** Read as rapidly as you can with understanding, but do not force yourself. Do not worry about the time element. If you worry about not finishing the test, you will begin to take shortcuts and miss the correct answer in your haste.

4. **As you read the opening sentences, try to anticipate what the passage will be about.** Ask yourself who or what the author is talking about.

5. **As you continue reading, try to identify what *kind* of writing this is, what *techniques* are being used, who its intended *audience* may be, and what *feeling* (if any) the author has toward his subject.** Try to retain names, dates, and places for quick reference later. In particular, try to remember where in the passage the author makes *major points*. Then, when you start looking for the phrase or sentence that will justify your choice of answer, you will be able to save time by going back to that section of the passage immediately without having to reread the entire selection.

6. **When you tackle the questions, *go back to the passage* to verify your choice of answer.** Do not rely on your memory alone.

7. **Watch out for words or phrases in the question that can alert you to the kind of question being asked.**

Questions asking about the main idea of the passage:
The main point of the passage is to . . .
The passage is primarily concerned with . . .
The author's primary purpose in this passage is to . . .
The chief theme of the passage can best be described as . . .

Questions asking for information stated in the passage:
According to the author . . .
The author states all of the following EXCEPT . . .
According to the passage, which of the following is true of the . . .
Which of the following is NOT cited in the passage as evidence of . . .

Questions asking you to draw a conclusion:
It can be inferred from the passage that . . .
The author implies that . . .

The passage suggests that . . .

Which of the following statements about . . . can be inferred from the passage?

It can be argued that . . .

The author would most likely . . .

The author probably considers . . .

Questions asking how the author's ideas apply to other situations:

With which of the following aphorisms would the author be in strongest agreement?

The author's argument would be most weakened by the discovery of which of the following?

The author's contention would be most clearly strengthened if which of the following were found to be true?

Which of the following examples could best be substituted for the author's example of . . .

Questions asking about the author's emotional state:

The author's attitude toward . . . is . . .

The author regards the idea that . . . with . . .

The author's tone in the passage . . .

Questions asking about the passage's method of organization:

Which of the following best describes the development of this passage?

In presenting the argument, the author does all of the following EXCEPT . . .

The relationship between the second paragraph and the first paragraph can best be described as . . .

In the passage, the author makes the central point primarily by . . .

Questions asking about contextual meaning:

As used in the passage, the term . . . can best be described as . . .

The phrase . . . is used in the passage to mean that . . .

As used by the author, the term . . . refers to . . .

The author uses the phrase . . . to describe . . .

8. **When asked to find the main idea, be sure to check the opening and summary sentences of each paragraph.** Authors typically provide readers with a sentence that expresses a paragraph's main idea succinctly. Although such *topic sentences* may appear anywhere in the paragraph, readers customarily look for them in the opening or closing sentences.

   Note that in GRE reading passages, topic sentences are sometimes implied rather than stated directly. If you cannot find a topic sentence, ask yourself these questions:

   Who or what is this passage about?
   What aspect of this subject is the author talking about?
   What is the author trying to get across about this aspect of the subject?

9. **When asked about specific details in the passage, spot key words in the question and scan the passage to find them (or their synonyms).** To answer questions about supporting details, you *must* find a word or group of words in the passage supporting your choice of answer. Do not be misled into choosing an answer (even one that makes good sense) if you cannot find it supported by the text.

10. **When asked to make inferences, take as your answer what the passage logically suggests, not what it states directly.** Look for clues in the passage; then choose as your answer a statement that is a logical development of the information the author has provided.

11. **When asked to determine questions of attitude, mood, or tone, look for words that convey emotion, express values, or paint pictures.** These images and descriptive phrases get the author's feelings across.

12. **When asked to give the meaning of an unfamiliar word, look for nearby context clues.** Often authors will use an unfamiliar word and then immediately define it within the same sentence. The two words or groups of words are juxtaposed—set beside one another—to make their relationship clear. Often an unfamiliar word in one clause of a sentence will be defined or clarified in the sentence's other clause.

13. **In tackling logical reasoning questions, pay particular attention to signal words in the question (and in the argument as well).** These signal words can clarify the situation. Words like *accordingly*, *consequently*, and *therefore* often signal the conclusion of an argument. Words like *although*, *however*, and *nonetheless* often suggest a reversal of thought within an argument or question stem.

14. **In questions about weakening or strengthening an argument, examine the argument for any unstated assumptions it makes.** Pinpoint what the argument assumes. Then compare that assumption with the answer choices. If the question asks you to choose an answer that most strengthens the argument, look for the answer choice that is most in keeping with the argument's basic assumption. If the question asks you to choose an answer that most weakens the argument, look for the answer choice that casts the most doubt on that assumption.

Examples to Get You Started

Read the following passage, which examines the nature of visual recognition.

What is involved in the process of visual recognition? First, like computer data, visual memories of an object must be stored; then, a mechanism must exist for them to be retrieved. But how does this process
Line work? The eye triggers the nerves into action. This neural activity con-
(5) structs a picture in the brain's memory system, an internal image of the object observed. When the eye once again confronts that object, the object is compared with its internal image; if the two images match, recognition takes place.

Among psychologists, the question as to whether visual recognition is
(10) a parallel, single-step operation or a sequential, step-by-step one is the subject of much debate. Gestalt psychologists contend that objects are perceived as wholes in a parallel operation: the internal image is matched with the retinal impression in one single step. Psychologists of other schools, however, suggest the opposite, maintaining that the individual
(15) features of an object are matched serially with the features of its internal image. Some experiments have demonstrated that the more well-known an object is, the more holistic its internal image becomes, and the more parallel the process of recognition tends to be. Nonetheless, the bulk of the evidence appears to uphold the serial hypothesis, at least for simple
(20) objects that are relatively unfamiliar to the viewer.

EXAMPLE 1

Now look at the following question on a specific detail in the passage.

According to the passage, psychologists of the Gestalt school assume which of the following about the process of visual recognition?

Select *all* that apply.

A The image an object makes on the retina is exactly the same as its internal image.

B The mind recognizes a given object as a whole; it has no need to analyze the object's constituent parts individually.

C The process of matching an object with its internal image takes place in a single step.

You can arrive at the correct answer to this question by elimination.

First, quickly scan the passage looking for the key word *Gestalt*. The sentence mentioning Gestalt psychologists states they maintain that objects are recognized as wholes in a parallel procedure. The sentence immediately preceding defines a parallel procedure as one that takes only one step.

Now examine the statements. Do Gestalt psychologists maintain that an object's retinal image is exactly the same as its internal image? Statement A is unsupported by the passage.

Statement B is supported by the passage: lines 11–13 indicate that Gestalt psychologists believe objects are recognized as wholes.

Statement C is supported by the passage: lines 13–15 indicate that Gestalt psychologists believe matching is a parallel process that occurs in one step.

Choices B and C are both correct.

Note how necessary it is to point to specific lines in the passage when you answer questions on specific details.

EXAMPLE 2

Try this relatively easy inference question, based on the previous passage about visual recognition.

> One can infer from the passage that, in visual recognition, the process of matching
>
> (A) requires neural inactivity.
> (B) cannot take place if an attribute of a familiar object has been altered in some way.
> (C) cannot occur when the observer looks at an object for the very first time.
> (D) has now been proven to necessitate both serial and parallel processes.
> (E) can only occur when the brain receives a retinal image as a single unit.

Go through the answer choices, eliminating any choices that obviously contradict what the passage states or implies. Remember that in answering inference questions you must go beyond the obvious, beyond what the authors explicitly state, to look for logical implications of what they say.

Choice A is incorrect. Nothing in the passage suggests that the matching process requires or demands neural inactivity. Rather, the entire process of visual recognition, including the matching of images, requires neural *activity*.

Choice D is incorrect. It is clear from the passage that the matching process is not fully understood; nothing yet has been absolutely *proven*. The weight of the evidence seems to support the serial hypothesis, but controversy still surrounds the entire question.

Choice E is incorrect. It can be eliminated because it directly contradicts information in the passage stating that recognition most likely is a serial or step-by-step process rather than a parallel one receiving an image as a single unit.

Choices B and C are left. Which is a possible inference? Choice C seems a possible inference. Although the author never says so, it seems logical that you could not match an object if you had never seen it before. After all, if you had never seen the object before, you would have no prior internal image of it and would have nothing with which to match it. What of Choice B? Nothing in the passage mentions altering any attributes or features of a familiar object. Therefore, *on the basis of the passage* you have no way to deduce whether matching would or would not be possible if such a change took place. There is not enough information in the passage to justify Choice B as an inference. The correct answer is Choice C.

EXAMPLE 3

Refer once more to the passage on visual recognition on page 48 to answer the following question.

Which of the following phrases could best replace "the more holistic its internal image becomes" (line 17) without significantly changing the sentence's meaning?

Ⓐ the more its internal image increases in detail
Ⓑ the more integrated its internal image grows
Ⓒ the more its internal image decreases in size
Ⓓ the more it reflects its internal image
Ⓔ the more indistinct its internal image appears

What words or phrases in the vicinity of "the more holistic its internal image becomes" give you a clue to the phrase's meaning? The phrase immediately following, "becomes more parallel." If the recognition process becomes more parallel as an object becomes more familiar, then matching takes place in one step in which all the object's features are simultaneously transformed into a single internal representation. Thus, to say that an object's internal image becomes more holistic is to say that it becomes more integrated or whole. The correct answer is Choice B.

Look at the words in the immediate vicinity of the word or phrase you are defining. They will give you a sense of the meaning of the unfamiliar word.

PRACTICE QUESTIONS

The purpose of this section is to familiarize you with the kinds of questions that appear on the GRE by presenting practice questions closely modeled on published samples of the new question types and on actual questions from recent GREs. Knowing what to expect when you take the examination is an important step in preparing for the test and succeeding on it.

Sentence Equivalence Questions

> _Directions:_ For the following questions, select the **two** answer choices that, when used to complete the sentence, fit the meaning of the sentence as a whole **and** produce completed sentences that are alike in meaning.

1. Truculent in defending their individual rights of sovereignty under the Articles of Confederation, the newly formed states _____ constantly.

   - [A] digressed
   - [B] conferred
   - [C] bickered
   - [D] dismembered
   - [E] rebuffed
   - [F] squabbled

2. In Anglo Saxon times, the monastic scribes made _____ distinction between Latin texts and texts in the vernacular by assigning the former an Anglo-Caroline script and reserving the pointed insular script for texts in Old English.

   - [A] a nice
   - [B] a subtle
   - [C] a pointless
   - [D] an obvious
   - [E] an unconventional
   - [F] a judgmental

3. Written in an amiable style, the book provides a comprehensive overview of European wines that should prove _____ to both the virtual novice and the experienced connoisseur.

   A inviting

   B tedious

   C engaging

   D inspirational

   E perplexing

   F opaque

4. Shy and hypochondriacal, Madison was uncomfortable at public gatherings; his character made him a most _____ orator and practicing politician.

   A conscientious

   B unlikely

   C fervent

   D gregarious

   E improbable

   F effective

5. Alec Guinness has few equals among English-speaking actors, and in his autobiography he reveals himself to possess an uncommonly _____ prose style as well.

   A ambivalent

   B infamous

   C felicitous

   D happy

   E redundant

   F ephemeral

Text Completion Questions

Directions: For the following questions, select one entry for each blank from the corresponding column of choices. Fill all blanks in the way that best completes the text.

6. Chaotic in conception but not in _____, Kelly's canvases are as neat as the proverbial pin.

Ⓐ	conceit
Ⓑ	execution
Ⓒ	intent
Ⓓ	origin
Ⓔ	theory

7. During the middle of the eighteenth century, the (i) _____ style in furniture and architecture, marked by elaborate scrollwork and (ii) _____ decoration, flourished.

Blank (i)		Blank (ii)	
Ⓐ abstract		Ⓓ austere	
Ⓑ medieval		Ⓔ excessive	
Ⓒ rococo		Ⓕ functional	

8. Tocqueville decided to swear the oath of loyalty to the new Orleanist king in part (i) _____ (he wanted to keep his position as magistrate), and in part (ii) _____ (he was convinced that the democratization of politics represented by the new regime was inevitable).

Blank (i)		Blank (ii)	
Ⓐ opportunistically		Ⓓ altruistically	
Ⓑ selflessly		Ⓔ irresolutely	
Ⓒ theoretically		Ⓕ pragmatically	

9. In seeking to rediscover Zora Neale Hurston, it is intriguing to look at the figure she cut in the minds of her contemporaries, the high regard she (i) _____ before shifting aesthetic values (ii) _____ her to curio status.

Blank (i)	Blank (ii)
(A) deplored	(D) elevated
(B) enjoyed	(E) relegated
(C) offered	(F) suspended

10. The tapeworm is an example of (i) _____ organism, one that lives within or on another creature, (ii) _____ some or all of its nutrients from its host.

Blank (i)	Blank (ii)
(A) an autonomous	(D) converting
(B) a hospitable	(E) deriving
(C) a parasitic	(F) sublimating

Reading Comprehension Questions

Directions: The passage is followed by questions based on its content. After reading the passage, choose the best answer to each question. Answer all questions following the passage on the basis of what is *stated* or *implied* in the passage.

One phase of the business cycle is the expansion phase. This phase is a twofold one, including recovery and prosperity. During the recovery period there is ever-growing expansion of existing facilities, and new
Line facilities for production are created. More businesses are created and
(5) older ones expanded. Improvements of various kinds are made. **There is an ever-increasing optimism about the future of economic growth.** Much capital is invested in machinery or "heavy" industry. More labor is employed. More materials are required. As one part of the economy develops, other parts are affected. For example, a great expansion in
(10) automobiles results in an expansion of the steel, glass, and rubber industries. Roads are required; thus the cement and machinery industries are stimulated. Demand for labor and materials results in greater prosperity for workers and suppliers of raw materials, including farmers. This increases purchasing power and the volume of goods bought and sold.
(15) Thus, prosperity is diffused among the various segments of the population. This prosperity period may continue to rise and rise without an apparent end. However, a time comes when this phase reaches a peak and stops spiraling upwards. This is the end of the expansion phase.

11. Which of the following statements best exemplifies the optimism mentioned in the **boldfaced** sentence of the passage as being part of the expansion phase?

Ⓐ Public funds are designated for the construction of new highways designed to stimulate tourism.

Ⓑ Industrial firms allocate monies for the purchase of machine tools.

Ⓒ The prices of agricultural commodities are increased at the producer level.

Ⓓ Full employment is achieved at all levels of the economy.

Ⓔ As technology advances, innovative businesses replace antiquated firms.

12. It can be inferred from the passage that the author believes that

    (A) when consumers lose their confidence in the market, a recession follows.
    (B) cyclical ends to business expansion are normal.
    (C) luxury goods such as jewelry are unaffected by industrial expansion.
    (D) with sound economic policies, prosperity can become a fixed pattern.
    (E) the creation of new products is essential for prosperity.

13. Which of the following statements would be most likely to begin the paragraph immediately following the passage?

    (A) Union demands may also have an effect on business cycles.
    (B) Some industries are, by their very nature, cyclical, having regular phases of expansion and recession.
    (C) Information is a factor that must be taken into consideration in any discussion of the expansion phase.
    (D) The farmer's role during the expansion phase is of vital importance.
    (E) The other phase of the business cycle is called the recession phase.

Both plants and animals of many sorts show remarkable changes in form, structure, growth habits, and even mode of reproduction in becoming adapted to different climatic environments, types of food supply, or
Line modes of living. This divergence in response to evolution is commonly
(5) expressed by altering the form and function of some part or parts of the organism, the original identity of which is clearly discernible. For example, the creeping foot of the snail is seen in related Marine pteropods to be modified into a flapping organ useful for swimming, and is changed into prehensile arms that bear suctorial disks in the squids and other
(10) cephalopods. The limbs of various mammals are modified according to several different modes of life—for swift running (cursorial) as in the horse and antelope; for swinging in trees (arboreal) as in the monkeys; for digging (fossorial) as in the moles and gophers; for flying (volant) as in the bats; for swimming (aquatic) as in the seals, whales, and dolphins;
(15) and for other adaptations. The structures or organs that show main change in connection with this adaptive divergence are commonly identified readily as **homologous**, in spite of great alterations. Thus, the finger and wrist bones of a bat and whale, for instance, have virtually nothing in common except that they are definitely equivalent elements of the
(20) mammalian limb.

14. The author provides information that would answer which of the following questions?

Select *all* that apply.

A What factors can cause change in organisms?

B What is the theory of evolution?

C How are horses' legs related to seals' flippers?

15. Which of the following words could best be substituted for the boldfaced word **homologous** without substantially changing the author's meaning?

Select *all* that apply.

A altered

B mammalian

C corresponding

D divergent

E tactile

"The emancipation of women," James Joyce told one of his friends, "has caused the greatest revolution in our time in the most important relationship there is—that between men and women." Other modernists
Line agreed: Virginia Woolf, claiming that in about 1910 "human character
(5) changed"; and, illustrating the new balance between the sexes, urged, "Read the 'Agamemnon,' and see whether...your sympathies are not almost entirely with Clytemnestra." D.H. Lawrence wrote, "perhaps the deepest fight for 2000 years and more, has been the fight for women's independence."
(10)   But if modernist writers considered women's revolt against men's domination one of their "greatest" and "deepest" themes, only recently— in perhaps the past 15 years—has literary criticism begun to catch up with it. Not that the images of sexual antagonism that abound in modern literature have gone unremarked; far from it. But what we are able to see
(15) in literary works depends on the perspectives we bring to them, and now that women—enough to make a difference—are reforming canons and interpreting literature, the landscapes of literary history and the features of individual books have begun to change.

16. According to the passage, women are changing literary criticism by

   (A) noting instances of hostility between men and women.
   (B) seeing literature from fresh points of view.
   (C) studying the works of early twentieth-century writers.
   (D) reviewing books written by feminists.
   (E) resisting masculine influence.

17. The author quotes James Joyce, Virginia Woolf, and D.H. Lawrence primarily in order to show that

   (A) these were feminist writers.
   (B) although well-meaning, they were ineffectual.
   (C) before the twentieth century, there was little interest in women's literature.
   (D) modern literature is dependent on the women's movement.
   (E) the interest in feminist issues is not new.

18. The author's attitude toward women's reformation of literary canons can best be described as one of

   (A) ambivalence.
   (B) antagonism.
   (C) indifference.
   (D) endorsement.
   (E) skepticism.

19. Which of the following titles best describes the content of the passage?

   (A) Modernist Writers and the Search for Equality
   (B) The Meaning of Literary Works
   (C) Toward a New Criticism
   (D) Women in Literature, from 1910 On
   (E) Transforming Literature: What Women See

Although there are no physical differences between the visual organs of the two groups, the inhabitants of the Bilge Islands, when shown a card displaying a spectrum of colors, perceived fewer colors than do most persons in the United States.

20. Which of the following conclusions can most reliably be drawn from the information above?

Ⓐ Human color perception is at least partly determined by factors other than the physical structure of the visual organs.

Ⓑ The Bilge Islanders in all probability are taught in childhood to recognize fewer colors than are persons in the United States.

Ⓒ Differences in social structure most likely affect color perception.

Ⓓ Color perception in humans is influenced by differences in physical environment.

Ⓔ Bilge Islanders may have fewer terms denoting colors in their language than do English-speaking persons.

Answer Key

1. **C, F**	5. **C, D**	9. **B, E**	13. **E**	17. **E**
2. **A, B**	6. **B**	10. **C, E**	14. **A, C**	18. **D**
3. **A, C**	7. **C, E**	11. **B**	15. **C**	19. **E**
4. **B, E**	8. **A, F**	12. **B**	16. **B**	20. **A**

Answer Explanations

1. **(C)(F)** The key word here is *truculent*, quick to argue or fight. The states are quick to take action to defend their rights from outside interference. Thus, they *bicker* and *squabble* (quarrel, often about trivial things).

2. **(A)(B)** Watch out for words that have uncommon secondary meanings. At first glance none of the answer choices appear to be alike in meaning. However, *nice*, which commonly means *enjoyable* or *good*, as in having a nice time, has the secondary meaning of *very slight* or *subtle*. In using one script for Latin texts and a different script for Old English texts, the scribes subtly distinguished the texts from one another.

3. **(A)(C)** The book is described in positive terms: it is "(w)ritten in an amiable (agreeable; pleasing) style;" it "provides a comprehensive (broad, wide-ranging) overview." Therefore, it should be *engaging* or *inviting* to anyone with an interest in wine. However, it would not necessarily be *inspirational* (soul-stirring; emotionally moving) to such a person.

4. **(B)(E)** Would you expect someone shy and uncomfortable at public gatherings to be a natural politician? No, he would be an *unlikely, improbable* politician.

5. **(C)(D)** As an actor, Guinness is described in highly positive terms: he "has few equals among . . . actors." His writing is described in similarly positive terms: it is "uncommonly *felicitous* (well expressed) or *happy* (apt, as in "a happy turn of phrase"). Again, check words for possible secondary meanings. *Happy*, commonly means *joyful* or *merry*, as in "Have a happy birthday!," which has the secondary meaning of *fitting* or *apt*.

6. **(B)** The key word here is "conception," which here means the forming or devising of an idea. Kelly is a painter. The ideas behind his paintings may be chaotic (messy, disorganized), but the paintings themselves are neat as a pin. So, the paintings are messy in conception, but neat in *execution* (the way a plan or course of action is carried out). Note that the writer is using a secondary meaning of the noun *execution* here.

7. **(C)(E)** By definition, the *rococo* style in furniture was characterized by elaborate scrollwork and *excessive* ornamentation. It was over the top.

8. **(A)(F)** The missing words are explained by the parentheses following each blank.

Go through the answer choices, testing each one to see whether it makes sense. Eliminate any choices that you can. If you don't know the meaning of an answer choice, go on to the next one to see whether you can eliminate that. If you can eliminate two answer choices, the third choice must be the correct answer. If you swear an oath of loyalty in order to keep your job, are you being *opportunistic*? The word is unfamiliar; go on to the next answer choice.

If you swear an oath of loyalty in order to keep your job, are you being *selfless* (unselfish, altruistic)? No, you are thinking of yourself. You can eliminate Choice B. If you swear an oath of loyalty in order to keep your job, are you being *theoretical* (conceptual, not practical)? No, you are being practical. You can eliminate Choice C. The correct answer must be Choice A, *opportunistically*. To be opportunistic is to be ready to exploit immediate opportunities, regardless of principle. Toqueville decided to swear an oath that he was loyal because that was his chance to keep his job.

Now, go through the answer choices for the second blank. If you swear an oath of loyalty because you believe that the new government's policies inevitably will win, are you being *altruistic* (unselfish)? No, you are simply accepting the inevitable. You can eliminate Choice D. Are you being *irresolute* (indecisive or uncertain)? No, you are certain that the democratization of politics will inevitably occur. You can eliminate Choice E. Are you being *pragmatic* (practical)? Yes, it was practical for Toqueville to go along with the regime whose success he believed was inevitable. Choice F is correct.

9. **(B)(E)** The key words here are "rediscover" and "curio status." Someone who needs to be rediscovered is someone who has been forgotten. Once, Hurston was respected as a writer: she *enjoyed* or possessed the "high regard" of literary society. Then, aesthetic values shifted. Her writing was no longer valued. The change in aesthetic values *relegated* (downgraded or consigned) her to curio status, the status of a no longer fashionable literary curiosity.

10. **(C)(E)** Use the process of elimination to fill in the first blank. A tapeworm is an organism that lives within or on another creature. By definition it is

not *autonomous* (independent, self-sufficient). You can eliminate Choice A. A tapeworm is an organism that depends on a host (an animal or plant that provides nutrition for an organism living within or on it). It is not *hospitable* in any sense of the word. You can eliminate Choice B. A tapeworm, however, by definition is *parasitic, deriving* (obtaining) some or all of its nutrients from its host.

11. **(B)** Take a close look at the sentences that immediately precede and follow the boldfaced sentence. What do they discuss? They talk about changes in business, in the facilities for production, in investments in "machinery or 'heavy' industry." These changes reflect business owners' optimism about the future of economic growth. If the owners of industrial firms were not optimistic that their businesses were going to grow, they would be unwilling to invest money in purchasing new equipment. The correct answer is Choice B.

12. **(B)** To the author, it is no big deal that an end comes to the business cycle's expansion phase. He describes the end of the prosperity cycle in a matter-of-fact manner: "a time comes when this phase reaches a peak and stops spiraling upwards." To him, *cyclical ends to business expansion are normal.*

    Use the process of elimination to make sure you have come up with the correct answer. Does the author believe that *when consumers lose their confidence in the market, a recession follows*? There is no evidence to support this statement: the passage never even mentions recessions or consumer loss of confidence. You can eliminate Choice A. Does the author believe that *luxury goods such as jewelry are unaffected by industrial expansion*? While the author discusses industrial expansion, he never mentions luxury goods. You can eliminate Choice C. Does the author believe that *with sound economic policies, prosperity can become a fixed pattern*? Definitely not. He states that a time comes when the prosperity period stops spiraling upwards; rather than becoming a fixed pattern, prosperity comes to an end. You can eliminate Choice D. Does the author believe that *the creation of new products is essential for prosperity*? Most likely not. He doesn't talk about new products; he certainly never asserts that their creation is essential for prosperity. You can eliminate Choice E. Only Choice B is left. It is the correct answer.

13. **(E)** What is the topic of this passage? It is the business cycle's expansion phase. From the passage's opening sentence ("One phase of the business cycle is the expansion phase") to its concluding sentence ("This is

the end of the expansion phase"), the author has been describing this one phase. By definition, a phase is one stage in a process of change or development. The business cycle therefore must consist of more than one phase. Thus, it is likely that the paragraph immediately following a description of the business cycle's expansion phase would describe a different phase of the business cycle. Choice E, *The other phase of the business cycle is called the recession phase*, is a likely introductory sentence for such a paragraph.

14. **(A)(C)** The passage's opening sentence lists factors that may cause plants and animals to change or adapt. These factors include changes in the climate or in the sort of food supply available. Thus, the author provides information to answer the question "What factors can cause change in organisms?" Choice A is correct.

Although the passage mentions the word *evolution*, it fails to provide information that would serve to answer the question "What is the theory of evolution?" Choice B is incorrect.

The passage also answers the question of how horses' legs are related to seals' flippers. Although adaptive divergence has caused them to look very different and to serve very different functions, they are definitely related as "equivalent elements of the mammalian limb." Choice C also is correct.

Pay particular attention to the instruction "Select *all* that apply." One, two, or three answers may be correct.

15. **(C)** The term *homologous*, as used in biology, means similar in position, structure, and evolutionary origin but not necessarily in function. In spite of great alterations, the structures or organs are equivalent elements; they *correspond* to one another.

16. **(B)** Scan the passage looking for the key phrase "literary criticism." You will find the phrase, and the answer to this question in lines 18–20, and the sentences immediately following. Women are interpreting literature from their own perspective; thus, they are changing literary criticism by *seeing literature from* their own *fresh points of view*.

17. **(E)** The passage's opening paragraph uses quotes from Joyce, Woolf, and Lawrence to establish the point that *the interest in feminist issues is not new*. Indeed, the passage states that Woolf claimed the shift took place early in the 20th century.

18. **(D)** The author describes literary critics as only beginning to "catch up" with the modernist writers (Joyce, Woolf, Lawrence) in recognizing the importance of women's revolt against male domination as one of the great themes of our times. Clearly, the author agrees with the modernists as to the positive impact that women are making on the interpretation of literature. Thus, her attitude toward women's reformation of literary canons can best be described as one of *endorsement* or support.

19. **(E)** Use the process of elimination to answer this question. Does the title *Modernist Writers and the Search for Equality* adequately describe the content of this passage? No. Although the passage cites several modernist writers, its emphasis is on the impact women are having on the interpretation of literature. Does the title *The Meaning of Literary Works* adequately describe the content of this passage? No. It is far too broad. Does the title *Toward a New Criticism* adequately describe the content of this passage? No. New Criticism was a 20th century literary movement that stressed the close reading of poetry. The term has nothing to do with the passage. Does the title *Women in Literature, from 1910 on* adequately describe the content of this passage? No. The passage discusses how women's perspective is causing readers to reinterpret literature; it does not discuss women in literature. The title that best describes the contents of the passage is Choice D: *Transforming Literature: What Women See.*

20. **(A)** The brief passage clearly states that there are no physical differences between the visual organs of Bilge Islanders and the visual organs of most persons in the United States. It also states that the Bilge Islanders perceived fewer colors than most persons in the United States do. Both the Bilge Islanders and the U.S. residents perceive colors; however, they perceive colors differently. Therefore, we can reliably conclude that *(h)uman color perception is at least partly determined by factors other than the physical structure of the visual organs.* Note that we have *no* information as to what these factors might be. Therefore, we can rule out Choices B, C, D, and E, all of which suggest possible factors that might affect color perception in humans.

Building Your Vocabulary

4

Now that you have mastered the appropriate strategies for dealing with the types of questions on the Graduate Record Examination that test your verbal ability, you have the opportunity to spend some time refining your vocabulary and acquainting yourself with the fine shades of meaning that words possess. Studies show that whereas the average high school graduate recognizes about 50,000 words, the average college graduate recognizes around 70,000. That indicates that during your four years of college you have rapidly acquired about 20,000 new words (many of them technical terms from a variety of disciplines), some of which may have connotations and nuances that still escape you.

Graduate school will tax your vocabulary building skills even further. To succeed in your graduate program, you must be able to absorb new words and concepts rapidly. The time you devote now to learning vocabulary-building techniques for the GRE will pay off later, and not just on the GRE. In this chapter you'll find a fundamental tool that will help you enlarge your vocabulary: Barron's GRE High-Frequency Word List.

No matter how little time you have before you take the GRE, you can familiarize yourself with the level of vocabulary you will confront on the test. Look over the words on our GRE High-Frequency Word List. Study them well: these words, ranging from everyday words such as *ambiguous* and *partisan* to less commonly known ones such as *aberrant* and *plethora*, have occurred and reoccurred (as answer choices or as question words) in GREs published in the past 20 years.

Long-Range Strategy

There is only one effective long-range strategy for vocabulary building: READ. Read widely and well. Sample different subjects—astrophysics, sociobiology, Arthurian romances, art history—and different styles. Extensive reading is the one sure way to make your vocabulary grow.

As you read, however, take some time to acquaint yourself specifically with the sorts of words you must know to do well on the GRE. To get an idea of the level of vocabulary you must master, look over the High-Frequency Word List on the following pages.

TIPS TO HELP YOU COPE

For those of you who wish to work your way through the word list and feel the need for a plan, we recommend that you follow the procedure described below in order to use the list most profitably:

1. Divide the list into groups of 30 words.
2. Allot a definite time each day for the study of a group.
3. Devote at least one hour to each group.
4. First go through the group looking at the short, simple-looking words (6 letters at most). Mark those you don't know. In studying, pay particular attention to them.
5. Go through the group again looking at the longer words. Pay particular attention to words with more than one meaning and familiar-looking words that have unusual definitions that come as a surprise to you. Study these secondary definitions.
6. List unusual words on index cards that you can shuffle and review from time to time. (Study no more than 5 cards at a time.)
7. Use the illustrative sentences as models and make up new sentences of your own.
8. In making up new sentences, use familiar examples and be concrete: the junior high school band tuning up sounds *discordant;* Ebenezer Scrooge, before he reforms, is *parsimonious.*

For each word, the following is provided:

1. The word (printed in heavy type).
2. Its part of speech (abbreviated).
3. A brief definition.
4. A sentence illustrating the word's use.
5. Whenever appropriate, related words are provided, together with their parts of speech.

The word list is arranged in strict alphabetical order.

THE GRE HIGH-FREQUENCY WORD LIST

abate v. subside or moderate. Rather than leaving immediately, they waited for the storm to *abate*.

aberrant ADJ. abnormal or deviant. Given the *aberrant* nature of the data, we came to doubt the validity of the entire experiment.

abeyance N. suspended action. Hostilities between the two rival ethnic groups have been in *abeyance* since the arrival of the United Nations peacekeeping force last month.

abscond v. depart secretly and hide. The teller who *absconded* with the bonds went uncaptured until someone recognized him from his photograph on *America's Most Wanted*.

abstemious ADJ. sparing in eating and drinking; temperate. Concerned whether her vegetarian son's *abstemious* diet provided him with sufficient protein, the worried mother pressed food on him.

admonish v. warn; reprove. He *admonished* his listeners to change their wicked ways. admonition, N.

adulterate v. make impure by adding inferior or tainted substances. It is a crime to *adulterate* foods without informing the buyer; when consumers learned that Beechnut had *adulterated* its apple juice by mixing the juice with water, they protested vigorously. adulteration, N.

aesthetic ADJ. artstic; dealing with or capable of appreciating the beautiful. The beauty of Tiffany's stained glass appealed to Alice's *aesthetic* sense. aesthete, N.

aggregate v. gather; accumulate. Before the Wall Street scandals, dealers in so-called junk bonds managed to *aggregate* great wealth in short periods of time. also ADJ. aggregation, N.

alacrity N. cheerful promptness; eagerness. Phil and Dave were raring to get off to the mountains; they packed up their ski gear and climbed into the van with *alacrity*.

alleviate v. relieve. This should *alleviate* the pain; if it does not, we shall have to use stronger drugs.

amalgamate v. combine; unite in one body. The unions will attempt to *amalgamate* their groups into one national body.

ambiguous ADJ. unclear or doubtful in meaning. His *ambiguous* instruction misled us; we did not know which road to take. ambiguity, N.

ambivalence N. the state of having contradictory or conflicting emotional attitudes. Torn between loving her parents one minute and hating them the next, she was confused by the *ambivalence* of her feelings. ambivalent, ADJ.

ameliorate v. improve. Many social workers have attempted to *ameliorate* the conditions of people living in the slums.

anachronism N. something or someone misplaced in time. Shakespeare's reference to clocks in *Julius Caesar* is an *anachronism*; no clocks existed in Caesar's time. anachronistic, ADJ.

analogous ADJ. comparable. Actors exploring a classic text often improvise, working through an *analogous* situation closer to their own experience: for example, to explore the balcony scene in *Romeo and Juliet*, they may improvise a doorstep "goodnight" scene between newly met boy and girl.

anarchy N. absence of governing body; state of disorder. The assassination of the leaders led to a period of *anarchy*.

anomalous ADJ. abnormal; irregular. She was placed in the *anomalous* position of seeming to approve procedures that she despised.

antipathy N. aversion; dislike. Tom's extreme *antipathy* for disputes keeps him from getting into arguments with his temperamental wife. Noise in any form is *antipathetic* to him. Among his other *antipathies* are honking cars, boom boxes, and heavy metal rock.

apathy N. lack of caring; indifference. A firm believer in democratic government, she could not understand the *apathy* of people who never bothered to vote. apathetic, ADJ.

appease v. pacify or soothe; relieve. Tom and Jody tried to *appease* the crying baby by offering him one toy after another. However, he would not calm down until they *appeased* his hunger by giving him a bottle. appeasement, N.

apprise v. inform. When she was *apprised* of the dangerous weather conditions, she decided to postpone her trip.

approbation N. approval. Wanting her parents' regard, she looked for some sign of their *approbation*.

appropriate v. acquire; take possession of for one's own use. The ranch owners *appropriated* the lands that had originally been set aside for the Indian's use.

arduous ADJ. hard; strenuous. Her *arduous* efforts had sapped her energy.

artless ADJ. without guile; open and honest. Red Riding Hood's *artless* comment, "Grandma, what big eyes you have!" indicates the child's innocent surprise at her "grandmother's" changed appearance.

ascetic ADJ. practicing self-denial; austere. The wealthy, self-indulgent young man felt oddly drawn to the strict, *ascetic* life led by members of some monastic orders. also N. asceticism, N.

assiduous ADJ. diligent. It took Rembrandt weeks of *assiduous* labor before he was satisfied with his portrait of his son.

assuage V. ease or lessen (pain); satisfy (hunger); soothe (anger). Jilted by Jane, Dick tried to *assuage* his heartache by indulging in ice cream. One gallon later, he had *assuaged* his appetite but not his grief. assuagement, N.

attenuate V. make thin; weaken. By withdrawing their forces, the generals hoped to *attenuate* the enemy lines.

audacious ADJ. daring; bold. Audiences cheered as Luke Skywalker and Princess Leia made their *audacious,* death-defying leap to freedom and escaped Darth Vader's troops. audacity, N.

austere ADJ. forbiddingly stern; severely simple and unornamented. The headmaster's *austere* demeanor tended to scare off the more timid students, who never visited his study willingly. The room reflected the man, *austere* and bare, like a monk's cell, with no touches of luxury to moderate its *austerity.*

autonomous ADJ. self-governing. Although the University of California at Berkeley is just one part of the state university system, in many ways Cal Berkeley is *autonomous,* for it runs several programs that are not subject to outside control. autonomy, N.

aver V. state confidently. I wish to *aver* that I am certain of success.

banal ADJ. hackneyed; commonplace; trite; lacking originality. The hack writer's worn-out clichés made his comic sketch seem *banal.* He even resorted to the *banality* of having someone slip on a banana peel!

belie V. contradict; give a false impression. His coarse, hard-bitten exterior *belied* his innate sensitivity.

beneficent ADJ. kindly; doing good. The overgenerous philanthropist had to curb his *beneficent* impulses before he gave away all his money and left himself with nothing.

bolster V. support; reinforce. The debaters amassed file boxes full of evidence to *bolster* their arguments.

bombastic ADJ. pompous; using inflated language. Puffed up with conceit, the orator spoke in such a *bombastic* manner that we longed to deflate him. bombast, N.

boorish ADJ. rude; insensitive. Though Mr. Potts constantly interrupted his wife, she ignored his *boorish* behavior, for she had lost hope of teaching him courtesy.

burgeoning ADJ. flourishing; growing quickly; putting out buds. Phil and Adam could scarcely keep up with the *burgeoning* demand for the services of their production company.

burnish V. make shiny by rubbing; polish. The maid *burnished* the brass fixtures until they reflected the lamplight.

buttress V. support; prop up. Just as architects *buttress* the walls of cathedrals with flying *buttresses,* debaters *buttress* their arguments with facts. also N.

cacophonous ADJ. discordant; inharmonious. Do the students in the orchestra enjoy the *cacaphonous* sounds they make when they're tuning up? I don't know how they can stand the racket. cacophony, N.

capricious ADJ. unpredictable; fickle. The storm was *capricious;* it changed course constantly. Jill was *capricious,* too; she changed boyfriends almost as often as she changed clothes.

castigation N. punishment; severe criticism. Sensitive even to mild criticism, Virginia Woolf could not bear the *castigation* that she found in certain reviews. castigate, V.

catalyst N. agent that brings about a chemical change while it remains unaffected and unchanged. Many chemical reactions cannot take place without the presence of a *catalyst.*

caustic ADJ. burning; sarcastically biting. The critic's *caustic* remarks angered the hapless actors who were the subjects of his sarcasm.

chicanery N. trickery; deception. Those sneaky lawyers misrepresented what occurred, made up all sorts of implausible alternative scenarios to confuse the jurors, and in general depended on *chicanery* to win the case.

cogent ADJ. convincing. It was inevitable that David chose to go to Harvard; he had several *cogent* reasons for doing so, including a full-tuition scholarship. Katya argued her case with such *cogency* that the jury had to decide in favor of her client.

commensurate ADJ. equal in extent. Your reward will be *commensurate* with your effort; what you earn will depend on how hard you work.

compendium N. brief, comprehensive summary. This text can serve as a *compendium* of the tremendous amount of new material being developed in this field.

complaisant ADJ. trying to please; obliging. Accustomed to VIP treatment, the star expected the hotel manager to be *complaisant*, if not totally obsequious. Imagine her shock when she was greeted curtly and then ignored.

compliant ADJ. yielding; conforming to requirements. Because Joel usually gave in and went along with whatever his friends desired, his mother worried that he might be too *compliant*.

conciliatory ADJ. reconciling; soothing. She was still angry despite his *conciliatory* words. conciliate, V.

condone V. overlook; forgive; give tacit approval; excuse. Unlike Widow Douglas, who *condoned* Huck's minor offenses, Miss Watson did nothing but scold.

confound V. confuse; puzzle. No mystery could *confound* Sherlock Holmes for long.

connoisseur N. person competent to act as a judge of art, etc.; a lover of an art. She had developed into a *connoisseur* of fine china.

contention N. claim; thesis. It is our *contention* that, if you follow our tactics, you will boost your score on the GRE. contend, V.

contentious ADJ. quarrelsome. Disagreeing violently with the referees' ruling, the coach became so *contentious* that the referees threw him out of the game.

contrite ADJ. penitent. Her *contrite* tears did not influence the judge when he imposed sentence. contrition, N.

conundrum N. riddle; difficult problem. During the long car ride, she invented *conundrums* to entertain the children.

converge V. approach; tend to meet; come together. African-American men from all over the United States *converged* on Washington to take part in the historic Million Man March. convergence, N.

convoluted ADJ. coiled around; involved; intricate. His argument was so *convoluted* that few of us could follow it intelligently.

craven ADJ. cowardly. Lillian's *craven* refusal to join the protest was criticized by her comrades, who had expected her to be brave enough to stand up for her beliefs.

daunt V. intimidate; frighten. "Boast all you like of your prowess. Mere words cannot *daunt* me," the hero answered the villain.

decorum N. propriety; orderliness and good taste in manners. Even the best-mannered students have trouble behaving with *decorum* on the last day of school. decorous, ADJ.

default N. failure to act. When the visiting team failed to show up for the big game, they lost the game by *default*. When Jack failed to make the payments on his Jaguar, the dealership took back the car because he had *defaulted* on his debt.

deference N. courteous regard for another's wish. In *deference* to the minister's request, please do not take photographs during the wedding service.

delineate V. portray; depict; sketch. Using only a few descriptive phrases, Austen *delineates* the character of Mr. Collins so well that we can predict his every move. delineation, N.

denigrate V. belittle or defame; blacken. All attempts to *denigrate* the character of our late President have failed; the people still love him and cherish his memory.

deride V. ridicule; make fun of. The critics *derided* his pretentious dialogue and refused to consider his play seriously. derision, N.

derivative ADJ. unoriginal; obtained from another source. Although her early poetry was clearly *derivative* in nature, the critics thought she had promise and eventually would find her own voice.

desiccate V. dry up. A tour of this smokehouse will give you an idea of how the pioneers used to *desiccate* food in order to preserve it.

desultory ADJ. aimless; haphazard; digressing at random. In prison Malcolm X set himself the task of reading straight through the dictionary; to him, reading was purposeful, not *desultory*.

deterrent N. something that discourages; hindrance. Does the threat of capital punishment serve as a *deterrent* to potential killers? also ADJ.

diatribe N. bitter scolding; invective. During the lengthy *diatribe* delivered by his opponent he remained calm and self-controlled.

dichotomy N. split; branching into two parts (especially contradictory ones). Willie didn't know how to resolve the *dichotomy* between his ambition to go to college and his childhood longing to run away and join the circus. Then he heard about Ringling Brothers Circus College, and he knew he'd found his school.

diffidence N. shyness. You must overcome your *diffidence* if you intend to become a salesperson.

diffuse ADJ. wordy; rambling; spread out (like a gas). If you pay authors by the word, you tempt them to produce *diffuse* manuscripts rather than brief ones. also V. diffusion, N.

digression N. wandering away from the subject. Nobody minded when Professor Renoir's lectures wandered away from their official theme; his *digressions* were always more fascinating than the topic of the day. digress, V.

disabuse V. correct a false impression; undeceive. Once Sharon started teaching junior high on the Lower East Side, she was quickly *disabused* of any romantic notions she had about her role.

discerning ADJ. mentally quick and observant; having insight. Though no genius, the star was sufficiently *discerning* to tell her true friends from the countless phonies who flattered her.

discordant ADJ. not harmonious; conflicting. Nothing is quite so *discordant* as the sound of a junior high school orchestra tuning up.

discredit V. defame; destroy confidence in; disbelieve. The campaign was highly negative in tone; each candidate tried to *discredit* the other.

discrepancy N. lack of consistency; difference. The police noticed some *discrepancies* in his description of the crime and did not believe him.

discrete ADJ. separate; unconnected. The universe is composed of *discrete* bodies.

disingenuous ADJ. lacking genuine candor; insincere. Now that we know the mayor and his wife are engaged in a bitter divorce fight, we find their earlier remarks regretting their lack of time together remarkably *disingenuous*.

disinterested ADJ. unprejudiced. Given the judge's political ambitions and the lawyers' financial interest in the case, the only *disinterested* person in the courtroom may have been the court reporter.

disjointed ADJ. disconnected. His remarks were so *disjointed* that we could not follow his reasoning.

dismiss V. eliminate from consideration; reject. Believing in John's love for her, she *dismissed* the notion that he might be unfaithful. (secondary meaning)

disparage V. belittle. A doting mother, Emma was more likely to praise her son's crude attempts at art than to *disparage* them.

disparate ADJ. basically different; unrelated. Unfortunately, Tony and Tina have *disparate* notions of marriage: Tony sees it as a carefree extended love affair, while Tina sees it as a solemn commitment to build a family and a home.

dissemble V. disguise; pretend. Even though John tried to *dissemble* his motive for taking modern dance, we all knew he was there not to dance but to meet girls.

disseminate V. distribute; spread; scatter (like seeds). By their use of the Internet, propagandists have been able to *disseminate* their pet doctrines to new audiences around the globe.

dissolution N. breaking of a union; decay; termination. Which caused King Lear more suffering: the *dissolution* of his kingdom into warring factions, or the *dissolution* of his aged, failing body? dissolve, V.

dissonance N. discord; opposite of harmony. Composer Charles Ives often used *dissonance*—clashing or unresolved chords—for special effects in his musical works. dissonant, ADJ.

distend V. expand; swell out. I can tell when he is under stress by the way the veins on his forehead *distend*.

distill V. purify; refine; concentrate. A moonshiner *distills* mash into whiskey; an epigrammatist *distills* thoughts into quips.

diverge V. vary; go in different directions from the same point. The spokes of the wheel *diverge* from the hub.

divest V. strip; deprive. Before Eisenhower appointed Charlie Wilson the Secretary of Defense, he required Wilson to *divest* himself of his holdings in General Motors (Wilson sold his stock at a considerable financial loss.)

document V. provide written evidence. She kept all the receipts from her business trip in order to *document* her expenses for the firm. also N.

dogmatic ADJ. opinionated; arbitrary; doctrinal. We tried to discourage Doug from being so *dogmatic,* but never could convince him that his opinions might be wrong.

dormant ADJ. sleeping; lethargic; latent. At fifty her long-*dormant* ambition to write flared up once more; within a year she had completed the first of her great historical novels. dormancy, N.

dupe N. someone easily fooled. While the gullible Watson often was made a *dupe* by unscrupulous parties, Sherlock Holmes was far more difficult to fool.

ebullient ADJ. showing excitement; overflowing with enthusiasm. Amy's *ebullient* nature could not be repressed; she was always bubbling over with excitement. ebullience, N.

eclectic ADJ. selective; composed of elements drawn from disparate sources. His style of interior decoration was *eclectic:* bits and pieces of furnishings from widely divergent periods, strikingly juxtaposed to create a unique decor. eclecticism, N.

efficacy N. power to produce desired effect. The *efficacy* of this drug depends on the regularity of the dosage. efficacious, ADJ.

effrontery N. insolent boldness; temerity. The classic example of unmitigated *effrontery* or "chutzpah" is the man who killed his parents and then asked the judge for mercy because he was an orphan.

elegy N. poem or song expressing lamentation. On the death of Edward King, Milton composed the *elegy* "Lycidas." elegiacal, ADJ.

elicit V. draw out by discussion. The detectives tried to *elicit* where he had hidden his loot.

embellish V. adorn; ornament; enhance, as a story. The costume designer *embellished* the leading lady's ball gown with yards and yards of ribbon and lace.

empirical ADJ. based on experience. He distrusted hunches and intuitive flashes; he placed his reliance entirely on *empirical* data.

emulate V. imitate; rival. In a brief essay, describe a person you admire, someone whose virtues you would like to *emulate*.

endemic ADJ. prevailing among a specific group of people or in a specific area or country. This disease is *endemic* in this part of the world; more than 80 percent of the population are at one time or another affected by it.

enervate V. weaken. She was slow to recover from her illness; even a short walk to the window *enervated* her. enervation, N.

engender V. cause; produce. To receive praise for real accomplishments *engenders* self-confidence in a child.

enhance V. increase; improve. You can *enhance* your chances of being admitted to the college of your choice by learning to write well; an excellent essay can *enhance* any application.

ephemeral ADJ. short-lived; fleeting. The mayfly is an *ephemeral* creature: its adult life lasts little more than a day.

equanimity N. calmness of temperament; composure. Even the inevitable strains of caring for an ailing mother did not disturb Bea's *equanimity*.

equivocate V. intentionally mislead; attempt to conceal the truth. Rejecting the candidate's attempts to *equivocate* about his views on abortion, the reporters pressed him to state clearly where he stood on the issue. equivocal, ADJ.

erudite ADJ. learned; scholarly. Though his fellow students thought him *erudite*, Paul knew he would have to spend many years in serious study before he could consider himself a scholar. erudition, N.

esoteric ADJ. hard to understand; known only to the chosen few. *New Yorker* short stories often include *esoteric* allusions to obscure people and events; the implication is, if you are in the in-crowd, you'll get the reference; if you come from Cleveland, you won't. esoterica, N.

eulogy N. expression of praise, often on the occasion of someone's death. Instead of delivering a spoken *eulogy* at Genny's memorial service, Jeff sang a song he had written in her honor. eulogize, V.

euphemism N. mild expression in place of an unpleasant one. The expression "he passed away" is a *euphemism* for "he died."

exacerbate V. worsen; embitter. The latest bombing *exacerbated* England's already existing bitterness against the IRA, causing the Prime Minister to break off the peace talks abruptly. exacerbation, N.

exculpate V. clear from blame. Fearful of being implicated as a conspirator in the plot to kill Hitler, General Fromm equivocated, prevaricated, and lied outright in an attempt to *exculpate* himself.

exigency N. urgent state; demand or requirement. Given the *exigency* of the current near-riot conditions, the mayor felt it necessary to call for federal help. Packing enough food and fuel to last the week, the hiker felt well prepared to face the *exigencies* of wilderness life. exigent. ADJ.

extrapolation N. projection; conjecture. Based on their *extrapolation* from the results of the primaries on Super Tuesday, the networks predicted that George Bush would be the Republican candidate for the presidency. extrapolate, V.

facetious ADJ. joking (often inappropriately); humorous. I'm serious about this project; I don't need any *facetious,* smart-alecky cracks about do-good little rich girls.

facilitate V. help bring about; make less difficult. Rest and proper nourishment should *facilitate* the patient's recovery.

fallacious ADJ. false; misleading. Paradoxically, *fallacious* reasoning does not always yield erroneous results; even though your logic may be faulty, the answer you get may be correct. fallacy, N.

fatuous ADJ. foolish; inane. She is far too intelligent to utter such *fatuous* remarks.

fawning ADJ. courting favor by cringing and flattering. She was constantly surrounded by a group of *fawning* admirers who hoped to win her favor. fawn, V.

felicitous ADJ. apt; suitably expressed; well chosen. Famous for his *felicitous* remarks, he was called upon to serve as master-of-ceremonies at many a banquet.

fervor N. glowing ardor; intensity of feeling. At the protest rally, the students cheered the strikers and booed the dean with equal *fervor*.

flag V. droop; grow feeble. When the opposing hockey team scored its third goal only minutes into the first period, the home team's spirits *flagged*. flagging, ADJ.

fledgling ADJ. inexperienced. While it is necessary to provide these *fledgling* poets with an opportunity to present their work, it is not essential that we admire everything they write. also N.

flout V. reject; mock. The headstrong youth *flouted* all authority; he refused to be curbed.

foment V. stir up; instigate. Cher's archenemy Heather spread some nasty rumors that *fomented* trouble in the club. Do you think Cher's foe meant to *foment* such discord?

forestall V. prevent by taking action in advance. By setting up a prenuptial agreement, the prospective bride and groom hoped to *forestall* any potential arguments about money in the event of a divorce.

frugality N. thrift; economy. In these economically difficult days businesses must practice *frugality* or risk bankruptcy. frugal, ADJ.

futile ADJ. useless; hopeless; ineffectual. It is *futile* for me to try to get any work done around here while the telephone is ringing every 30 seconds. futility, N.

gainsay V. deny. She was too honest to *gainsay* the truth of the report.

garrulous ADJ. loquacious; wordy; talkative. My Uncle Henry can out-talk any other three people I know. He is the most *garrulous* person in Cayuga County. garrulity, N.

goad V. urge on; prod; incite. Laurie was furious with herself for having lost her temper, and even more furious with Jo for having *goaded* her into losing it.

grandiloquent ADJ. pompous; bombastic; using high-sounding language. The politician could never speak simply; she was always *grandiloquent*.

gregarious ADJ. sociable. Typically, party-throwers are *gregarious;* hermits are not.

guileless ADJ. without deceit. He is naive, simple, and *guileless;* he cannot be guilty of fraud.

gullible ADJ. easily deceived. *Gullible* people have only themselves to blame if they fall for con artists repeatedly. As the saying goes, "Fool me once, shame on you. Fool me twice, shame on me."

harangue N. long, passionate, and vehement speech. In her lengthy *harangue,* the principal berated the offenders. also V.

homogeneous ADJ. of the same kind. Because the student body at Elite Prep was so *homogeneous,* Sara and James decided to send their daughter to a school that offered greater cultural diversity. homogeneity, N.

hyperbole N. exaggeration; overstatement. As far as I'm concerned, Apple's claims about the new computer are pure *hyperbole*; no machine is that good! hyperbolic, ADJ.

iconoclastic ADJ. attacking cherished traditions. Deeply *iconoclastic,* Jean Genet deliberately set out to shock conventional theatergoers with his radical plays. iconoclasm, N.

idolatry N. worship of idols; excessive admiration. "(P)ublic display of the ruler's countenance, whether on the coinage, the postage stamp, or the wall, is very recent, and in the more conservative countries is still regarded as a blasphemy verging on *idolatry*." (Bernard Lewis)

immutable ADJ. unchangeable. All things change over time; nothing is *immutable*.

impair V. injure; hurt. Drinking alcohol can *impair* your ability to drive safely; if you're going to drink, don't drive.

impassive ADJ. without feeling; imperturbable; stoical. Refusing to let the enemy see how deeply shaken he was by his capture, the prisoner kept his face *impassive*.

impede V. hinder; block. The special prosecutor determined that the Attorney General, though inept, had not intentionally set out to *impede* the progress of the investigation.

impermeable ADJ. impervious; not permitting passage through its substance. This new material is *impermeable* to liquids; it will be an excellent fabric for raincoats.

imperturbable ADJ. calm; placid. Wellington remained *imperturbable* and in full command of the situation in spite of the hysteria and panic all around him. imperturbability, N.

impervious ADJ. impenetrable; incapable of being damaged or distressed. The carpet salesman told Simone that his most expensive brand of floor covering was warranted to be *impervious* to ordinary wear and tear. Having read so many negative reviews of his acting, the movie star had learned to ignore them, and was now *impervious* to criticism.

implacable ADJ. incapable of being pacified. Madame Defarge was the *implacable* enemy of the Evremonde family.

implicit ADJ. understood but not stated. Jack never told Jill he adored her; he believed his love was *implicit* in his deeds.

implode V. burst inward. If you break a vacuum tube, the glass tube *implodes*. implosion, N.

inadvertently ADV. unintentionally; by oversight; carelessly. Judy's great fear was that she might *inadvertently* omit a question on the exam and mismark her whole answer sheet.

inchoate ADJ. recently begun; rudimentary; elementary. Before the Creation, the world was an *inchoate* mass.

incongruity N. lack of harmony; absurdity. The *incongruity* of his wearing sneakers with formal attire amused the observers. incongruous, ADJ.

inconsequential ADJ. insignificant; unimportant. Brushing off Ali's apologies for having broken the wine glass, Tamara said, "Don't worry about it; it's *inconsequential*."

incorporate V. introduce something into a larger whole; combine; unite. Breaking with precedent, President Truman ordered the military to *incorporate* blacks into every branch of the armed services. also ADJ.

indeterminate ADJ. uncertain; not clearly fixed; indefinite. That interest rates shall rise appears certain; when they will do so, however, remains *indeterminate*.

indigence N. poverty. Neither the economists nor the political scientists have found a way to wipe out the inequities of wealth and eliminate *indigence* from our society.

indolent ADJ. lazy. Couch potatoes lead an *indolent* life lying back in their Lazyboy recliners watching TV. indolence, N.

inert ADJ. inactive; lacking power to move. "Get up, you lazybones," Tina cried to Tony, who lay in bed *inert*. inertia, N.

ingenuous ADJ. naive and trusting; young; unsophisticated. The woodsman did not realize how *ingenuous* Little Red Riding Hood was until he heard that she had gone off for a walk in the woods with the Big Bad Wolf. ingenue, N.

inherent ADJ. firmly established by nature or habit. Katya's *inherent* love of justice caused her to champion anyone she considered to be treated unfairly by society.

innocuous ADJ. harmless. An occasional glass of wine with dinner is relatively *innocuous* and should have no ill effect on most people.

insensible ADJ. unconscious; unresponsive. Sherry and I are very different; at times when I would be covered with embarrassment, she seems *insensible* to shame.

insinuate V. hint; imply; creep in. When you said I looked robust, did you mean to *insinuate* that I'm getting fat?

insipid ADJ. lacking in flavor; dull. Flat prose and flat ginger ale are equally *insipid;* both lack sparkle.

insularity N. narrow-mindedness; isolation. The *insularity* of the islanders manifested itself in their suspicion of anything foreign. insular, ADJ.

intractable ADJ. unruly; stubborn; unyielding. Charlie Brown's friend Pigpen was *intractable;* he absolutely refused to take a bath.

intransigence N. refusal of any compromise; stubbornness. The negotiating team had not expected such *intransigence* from the striking workers, who rejected any hint of a compromise. intransigent, ADJ.

inundate V. overwhelm; flood; submerge. This semester I am *inundated* with work; you should see the piles of paperwork flooding my desk. Until the great dam was built, the waters of the Nile used to *inundate* the river valley every year.

inured ADJ. accustomed; hardened. Although she became *inured* to the Alaskan cold, she could not grow accustomed to the lack of sunlight.

irascible ADJ. irritable; easily angered. Miss Minchin's *irascible* temper intimidated the younger schoolgirls, who feared she'd burst into a rage at any moment.

irresolute ADJ. uncertain how to act; weak. Once you have made your decision, don't waver; a leader should never appear *irresolute.*

itinerary N. plan of a trip. Disliking sudden changes in plans when she traveled abroad, Ethel refused to make any alterations in her *itinerary.*

laconic ADJ. brief and to the point. Many of the characters portrayed by Clint Eastwood are *laconic* types: strong men of few words.

lassitude N. languor; weariness. After a massage and a long soak in the hot tub, I surrendered to my growing *lassitude* and lay down for a nap.

latent ADJ. potential but undeveloped; dormant; hidden. Polaroid pictures were popular at parties because you could see the *latent* photographic image gradually appear before your eyes. latency, N.

laud V. praise. The NFL *lauded* Boomer Esiason's efforts to raise money to combat cystic fibrosis. also N. laudable, laudatory, ADJ.

lethargic ADJ. drowsy; dull. The stuffy room made her *lethargic:* she felt as if she was about to nod off. lethargy, N.

levity N. lack of seriousness or steadiness; frivolity. Stop giggling and wriggling around in the pew; such *levity* is improper in church.

log N. record of a voyage or flight; record of day-to-day activities. "Flogged two seamen today for insubordination," wrote Captain Bligh in the *Bounty's log.* To see how much work I've accomplished recently, just take a look at the number of new files listed on my computer *log.* also V.

loquacious ADJ. talkative. Though our daughter barely says a word to us these days, put a phone in her hand and see how *loquacious* she can be; our phone bills are out of sight! loquacity, N.

lucid ADJ. easily understood; clear; intelligible. Lexy makes an excellent teacher; her explanations of technical points are *lucid* enough for a child to grasp. lucidity, N.

luminous ADJ. shining; issuing light. The sun is a *luminous* body.

magnanimity N. generosity. Noted for his *magnanimity,* philanthropist Eugene Lang donated millions to charity. magnanimous, ADJ.

malingerer N. one who feigns illness to escape duty. The captain ordered the sergeant to punish all *malingerers* and force them to work. malinger, V.

malleable ADJ. capable of being shaped by pounding; impressionable. Gold is a *malleable* metal, easily shaped into bracelets and rings. Fagin hoped Oliver was a *malleable* lad, easily shaped into a thief.

maverick N. rebel; nonconformist. To the masculine literary establishment, George Sand with her insistence on wearing trousers and smoking cigars was clearly a *maverick* who fought her proper womanly role.

mendacious ADJ. lying; habitually dishonest. Distrusting Huck from the start, Miss Watson assumed he was *mendacious* and refused to believe a word he said. mendacity, N.

metamorphosis N. change of form. The *metamorphosis* of caterpillar to butterfly is typical of many such changes in animal life. metamorphose, V.

meticulous ADJ. excessively careful; painstaking; scrupulous. Martha Stewart was a *meticulous* housekeeper, fussing about each and every detail that went into making up her perfect home.

misanthrope N. one who hates mankind. In *Gulliver's Travels*, Swift portrays human beings as vile, degraded beasts; for this reason, various critics consider him a *misanthrope*. misanthropic, ADJ.

mitigate V. appease; moderate. Nothing Jason did could *mitigate* Medea's anger; she refused to forgive him for betraying her.

mollify V. soothe. The airline customer service representative tried to *mollify* the angry passenger by offering her a seat in first class.

morose ADJ. ill-humored; sullen; melancholy. Forced to take early retirement, Bill acted *morose* for months; then, all of a sudden, he shook off his gloom and was his usual cheerful self.

mundane ADJ. worldly as opposed to spiritual; everyday. Uninterested in philosophical or spiritual discussions, Tom talked only of *mundane* matters such as the daily weather forecast or the latest basketball results.

negate V. cancel out; nullify; deny. A sudden surge of adrenalin can *negate* the effects of fatigue; there's nothing like a good shock to wake you up. negation, N.

neophyte N. recent convert; beginner. This mountain slope contains slides that will challenge experts as well as *neophytes*.

obdurate ADJ. stubborn. In this retelling of Barrie's *Peter Pan*, Fiona Button as Wendy is heartbreaking in her stoical disappointment at Peter's *obdurate* refusal to grow up.

obsequious ADJ. slavishly attentive; servile; sycophantic. Helen valued people who behaved as if they respected themselves; nothing irrtated her more than an excessively *obsequious* waiter or a fawning salesclerk.

obviate V. make unnecessary; prevent problems. If you can house-sit for me for the next two weeks, that will *obviate* my need to find someone to feed the cats while I am gone.

officious ADJ. meddlesome; excessively pushy in offering one's services. After her long flight, Jill just wanted to nap, but the *officious* bellboy was intent on showing her all the special features of the deluxe suite.

onerous ADJ. burdensome. She asked for an assistant because her work load was too *onerous*.

opprobrium N. infamy; vilification. He refused to defend himself against the slander and *opprobrium* hurled against him by the newspapers; he preferred to rely on his record.

oscillate V. vibrate pendulumlike; waver. It is interesting to note how public opinion *oscillates* between the extremes of optimism and pessimism.

ostentatious ADJ. showy; pretentious; trying to attract attention. Trump's latest casino in Atlantic City is the most *ostentatious* gambling palace in the East; it easily out-glitters its competitors. ostentation, N.

paragon N. model of perfection. Her fellow students disliked Lavinia because Miss Minchin always pointed her out as a *paragon* of virtue.

partisan ADJ. one-sided; prejudiced; committed to a party. Rather than joining forces to solve our nation's problems, the Democrats and Republicans spend their time on *partisan* struggles. also N.

pathological ADJ. related to the study of disease; diseased or markedly abnormal. Jerome's *pathological* fear of germs led him to wash his hands a hundred times a day. pathology, N.

paucity N. scarcity. They closed the restaurant because the *paucity* of customers made it uneconomical to operate.

pedantic ADJ. showing off learning; bookish. Leavening her decisions with humorous, down-to-earth anecdotes, Judge Judy was not at all the *pedantic* legal scholar. pedantry, N.

penchant N. strong inclination; liking. Dave has a *penchant* for taking risks; one semester he went steady with three girls, two of whom were stars on the school karate team.

penury N. severe poverty; stinginess. When his pension fund failed, George feared he would end his days in *penury*. He became such a penny-pincher that he turned into a closefisted, *penurious* miser.

perennial N. something long-lasting. These plants are hardy *perennials* and will bloom for many years. also ADJ.

perfidious ADJ. treacherous; disloyal. When Caesar realized that Brutus had betrayed him, he reproached his *perfidious* friend. perfidy, N.

perfunctory ADJ. superficial; not thorough; lacking interest, care, or enthusiasm. The auditor's *perfunctory* inspection of the books overlooked many errors.

permeable ADJ. penetrable; porous; allowing liquids or gas to pass through. If your jogging clothes weren't made out of *permeable* fabric, you'd drown in your own sweat (figuratively speaking). permeate, V.

pervasive ADJ. spread throughout. Despite airing them for several hours, she could not rid her clothes of the *pervasive* odor of mothballs that clung to them. pervade, V.

phlegmatic ADJ. calm; not easily disturbed. The nurse was a cheerful but *phlegmatic* person, unexcited in the face of sudden emergencies.

piety N. devoutness; reverence for God. Living her life in prayer and good works, Mother Teresa exemplified the true spirit of *piety*. pious, ADJ.

placate V. pacify; conciliate. The store manager tried to *placate* the angry customer, offering to replace the damaged merchandise or to give back her money.

plasticity N. ability to be molded. When clay dries out, it loses its *plasticity* and becomes less malleable.

platitude N. trite remark; commonplace statement. In giving advice to his son, old Polonius expressed himself only in *platitudes;* every word out of his mouth was a truism.

plethora N. excess; overabundance. She offered a *plethora* of excuses for her shortcomings.

porous ADJ. full of pores; like a sieve. Dancers like to wear *porous* clothing because it allows the ready passage of water and air.

pragmatic ADJ. practical (as opposed to idealistic); concerned with the practical worth or impact of something. This coming trip to France should provide me with a *pragmatic* test of the value of my conversational French class.

precarious ADJ. uncertain; risky. Saying the stock was currently overpriced and would be a *precarious* investment, the broker advised her client against purchasing it.

precipitate ADJ. rash; premature; hasty; sudden. Though I was angry enough to resign on the spot, I had enough sense to keep myself from quitting a job in such a *precipitate* fashion.

precursor N. forerunner. Though Gray and Burns share many traits with the Romantic poets who followed them, most critics consider them *precursors* of the Romantic Movement, not true Romantics.

presumptuous ADJ. overconfident; impertinently bold; taking liberties. Matilda thought it *presumptuous* of the young man to address her without first being introduced. Perhaps manners were freer here in the New World. presumption, N.

prevaricate V. lie. Some people believe that to *prevaricate* in a good cause is justifiable and regard such misleading *prevarications* as "white lies."

pristine ADJ. characteristic of earlier times; primitive, unspoiled. This area has been preserved in all its *pristine* wildness.

probity N. uprightness; incorruptibility. Everyone took his *probity* for granted; his indictment for embezzlement, therefore, shocked us all.

problematic ADJ. doubtful; unsettled; questionable; perplexing. Given the way building costs have exceeded estimates for the job, whether the arena will ever be completed is *problematic*.

prodigal ADJ. wasteful; reckless with money. Don't be so *prodigal* spending my money; when you've earned some money, you can waste as much of it as you want! also N.

profound ADJ. deep; not superficial; complete. Freud's remarkable insights into human behavior caused his fellow scientists to honor him as a *profound* thinker. profundity, N.

prohibitive ADJ. tending to prevent the purchase or use of something; inclined to prevent or forbid. Susie wanted to buy a new Volvo but had to settle for a used Dodge because the new car's price was *prohibitive*. prohibition, N.

proliferate V. grow rapidly; spread; multiply. Times of economic hardship inevitably encourage countless get-rich-quick schemes to *proliferate*. proliferation, N.

propensity N. natural inclination. Convinced of his own talent, Sol has an unfortunate *propensity* to belittle the talents of others.

propitiate V. appease. The natives offered sacrifices to *propitiate* the angry gods.

propriety N. fitness; correct conduct. Miss Manners counsels her readers so that they may behave with *propriety* in any social situation and not embarrass themselves.

proscribe V. ostracize; banish; outlaw. Antony, Octavius, and Lepidus *proscribed* all those who had conspired against Julius Caesar.

qualified ADJ. limited; restricted. Unable to give the candidate full support, the mayor gave him only a *qualified* endorsement. (secondary meaning)

quibble N. minor objection or complaint. Aside from a few hundred teensy-weensy *quibbles* about the set, the script, the actors, the director, the costumes, the lighting, and the props, the hypercritical critic loved the play. also V.

quiescent ADJ. at rest; dormant; temporarily inactive. After the devastating eruption, fear of Mount Etna was great; people did not return to cultivate its rich hillside lands until the volcano had been *quiescent* for a full two years. quiescence, N.

rarefied ADJ. made less dense [of a gas]. The mountain climbers had difficulty breathing in the *rarefied* atmosphere. rarefy, V. rarefaction, N.

recalcitrant ADJ. obstinately stubborn; determined to resist authority; unruly. Which animal do you think is more *recalcitrant*, a pig or a mule?

recant V. disclaim or disavow; retract a previous statement; openly confess error. Hoping to make Joan of Arc *recant* her sworn testimony, her English captors tried to convince her that her visions had been sent to her by the Devil.

recondite ADJ. difficult to understand; profound; secret. While Holmes happily explored arcane subjects such as paleography and ancient Near Eastern languages, Watson claimed they were far too *recondite* for a simple chap like him.

refractory ADJ. stubborn; unmanageable. The *refractory* horse was eliminated from the race when he refused to obey the jockey.

refute V. disprove. The defense called several respectable witnesses who were able to *refute* the false testimony of the prosecution's only witness. refutation, N.

relegate V. banish to an inferior position; delegate; assign. After Ralph dropped his second tray of drinks that week, the manager swiftly *relegated* him to a minor post cleaning up behind the bar.

reproach V. express disapproval or disappointment. He never could do anything wrong without imagining how the look on his mother's face would *reproach* him afterwards. also N. reproachful, ADJ.

reprobate N. person hardened by sin, devoid of a sense of decency. "After all, as a conservative of fairly recent vintage, I've seen how easy it is for liberals, assisted by a compliant press, to cast ideological foes as moral *reprobates* and thus avoid engaging their ideas." (Harry Stein)

repudiate V. disown; disavow. On separating from Tony, Tina announced that she would *repudiate* all debts incurred by her soon-to-be ex-husband.

rescind V. cancel. Because of the public outcry against the new taxes, the senator proposed a bill to *rescind* the unpopular financial measure.

resolution N. determination. Nothing could shake his *resolution* to succeed despite all difficulties. resolute, ADJ.

resolve N. determination; firmness of purpose. How dare you question my *resolve* to take up sky-diving! Of course I haven't changed my mind! also V.

reticent ADJ. reserved; uncommunicative; inclined to silence. Fearing his competitors might get advance word about his plans from talkative staff members, Hughes preferred *reticent* employees to loquacious ones. reticence, N.

reverent ADJ. respectful; worshipful. Though I bow my head in church and recite the prayers, sometimes I don't feel properly *reverent*. revere, V. reverence, N.

sage N. person celebrated for wisdom. Hearing tales of a mysterious Master of All Knowledge who lived in the hills of Tibet, Sandy was possessed with a burning desire to consult the legendary *sage*. also ADJ.

salubrious ADJ. healthful. Many people with hay fever move to more *salubrious* sections of the country during the months of August and September.

sanction V. approve; ratify. Nothing will convince me to *sanction* the engagement of my daughter to such a worthless young man.

satiate V. satisfy fully. Having stuffed themselves until they were *satiated*, the guests were so full they were ready for a nap.

saturate V. soak thoroughly. Thorough watering is the key to lawn care; you must *saturate* your new lawn well to encourage its growth.

savor V. enjoy; have a distinctive flavor, smell, or quality. Relishing his triumph, Costner especially *savored* the chagrin of the critics who had predicted his failure.

secrete V. hide away or cache; produce and release a substance into an organism. The pack rat *secretes* odds and ends in its nest; the pancreas *secretes* insulin in the islets of Langerhans.

shard N. fragment, generally of pottery. The archaeologist assigned several students the task of reassembling earthenware vessels from the *shards* he had brought back from the expedition.

skeptic N. doubter; person who suspends judgment until having examined the evidence supporting a point of view. I am a *skeptic* about the new health plan; I want some proof that it can work. skeptical, ADJ. skepticism, N.

solicitous ADJ. worried, concerned. The employer was very *solicitous* about the health of her employees because replacements were difficult to get. solicitude, N.

soporific ADJ. sleep-causing; marked by sleepiness. Professor Pringle's lectures were so *soporific* that even he fell asleep in class. also N.

specious ADJ. seemingly reasonable but incorrect; misleading (often intentionally). To claim that, because houses and birds both have wings, both can fly is extremely *specious* reasoning.

spectrum N. colored band produced when a beam of light passes through a prism. The visible portion of the *spectrum* includes red at one end and violet at the other.

sporadic ADJ. occurring irregularly. Although you can still hear *sporadic* outbursts of laughter and singing outside, the big Halloween parade has passed; the party's over till next year.

stigma N. token of disgrace; brand. I do not attach any *stigma* to the fact that you were accused of this crime; the fact that you were acquitted clears you completely. stigmatize, N.

stint V. be thrifty; set limits. "Spare no expense," the bride's father said, refusing to *stint* on the wedding arrangements.

✓ **stipulate** V. make express conditions, specify. Before agreeing to reduce American military forces in Europe, the president *stipulated* that NATO teams be allowed to inspect Soviet bases.

stolid ADJ. dull; impassive. The earthquake shattered Stuart's usual *stolid* demeanor; trembling, he crouched on the no longer stable ground. stolidity, N.

subpoena N. writ of summoning a witness to appear. The prosecutor's office was ready to serve a *subpoena* on the reluctant witness. also V.

subside V. settle down; descend; grow quiet. The doctor assured us that the fever would eventually *subside*.

substantiate V. establish by evidence; verify; support. These endorsements from satisfied customers *substantiate* our claim that Barron's *New GRE* is the best GRE-prep book on the market.

supersede V. cause to be set aside; replace; make obsolete. Bulk mailing postal regulation 326D *supersedes* bulk mailing postal regulation 326C. If, in bundling your bulk mailing, you follow regulation 326C, your bulk mailing will be returned. supersession, N.

supposition N. hypothesis; surmise. I based my decision to confide in him on the *supposition* that he would be discreet. suppose, V.

tacit ADJ. understood; not put into words. We have a *tacit* agreement based on only a handshake.

tangential ADJ. peripheral; only slightly connected; digressing. Despite Clark's attempts to distract her with *tangential* remarks, Lois kept on coming back to her main question: why couldn't he come out to dinner with Superman and her?

tenuous ADJ. thin; rare; slim. The allegiance of our allies is held by rather *tenuous* ties; let us hope they will remain loyal.

tirade N. extended scolding; denunciation; harangue. Every time the boss holds a meeting, he goes into a lengthy *tirade,* scolding us for everything from tardiness to padding our expenses.

torpor N. lethargy; sluggishness; dormancy. Throughout the winter, nothing aroused the bear from his *torpor*; he would not emerge from hibernation until spring. torpid, ADJ.

tortuous ADJ. winding; full of curves. Because this road is so *tortuous*, it is unwise to go faster than twenty miles an hour on it.

tractable ADJ. docile; easily managed. Although Susan seemed a *tractable* young woman, she had a stubborn streak of independence that occasionally led her to defy the powers-that-be when she felt they were in the wrong. tractability, N.

transgression N. violation of a law; sin. Forgive us our *transgressions;* we know not what we do. transgress, V.

truculence N. aggressiveness; ferocity. Tynan's reviews were noted for their caustic attacks and general tone of *truculence.* truculent, ADJ.

vacillate V. waver; fluctuate. Uncertain which suitor she ought to marry, the princess *vacillated,* saying now one, now the other. vacillation, N.

venerate V. revere. In Tibet today, the common people still *venerate* their traditional spiritual leader, the Dalai Lama.

veracious ADJ. truthful. Did you believe that Kato Kaelin was *veracious* when he testified about what he heard the night Nicole Brown Simpson was slain? Some people question his *veracity.*

verbose ADJ. wordy. We had to make some major cuts in Senator Foghorn's speech because it was far too *verbose.* verbosity, N.

viable ADJ. practical or workable; capable of maintaining life. That idea won't work. Let me see whether I can come up with a *viable* alternative. viability. N.

viscous ADJ. sticky, gluey. Melted tar is a *viscous* substance. viscosity, N.

vituperative ADJ. abusive; scolding. He became more *vituperative* as he realized that we were not going to grant him his wish.

volatile ADJ. changeable; explosive; evaporating rapidly. The political climate today is extremely *volatile;* no one can predict what the electorate will do next. Maria Callas's temper was extremely *volatile;* the only thing you could predict was that she would blow up. Acetone is an extremely *volatile* liquid; it evaporates instantly. volatility, N.

warranted ADJ. justified; authorized. Before the judge issues the injunction, you must convince her this action is *warranted.*

wary ADJ. very cautious. The spies grew *wary* as they approached the sentry.

welter N. turmoil; bewildering jumble. The existing *welter* of overlapping federal and state programs cries out for immediate reform.

whimsical N. capricious; fanciful. In *Mrs. Doubtfire,* the hero is a playful, *whimsical* man who takes a notion to dress up as a woman so that he can look after his children, who are in the custody of his ex-wife. whimsy, N.

zealot N. fanatic; person who shows excessive zeal. Though Glenn was devout, he was no *zealot;* he never tried to force his religious beliefs on his friends.

Analytical Writing: Tactics and Practice | 5

PREPARING FOR THE WRITING TEST

Tactic 1: **Take Advantage of the GRE's Free Study Aids**

When you sign up to take the GRE General Test, you will be able to download their *PowerPrep II* test preparation software for the General Test and Writing Assessment. The download is available on the GRE website at *www.ets.org/gre/revised_general/prepare/powerprep2.*

 PowerPrep II is helpful because it uses the same GRE word processing software that you will have to use to write your essays when you take your computer-based test. It is a very basic word processor that lets you perform very basic tasks. You can insert text, delete text, and move text around using a cut-and-paste function. You can also undo an action you've just performed.

 Familiarize yourself with this word processing software so that, on the test date, you'll be comfortable using it. This software simulates actual testing conditions and presents actual essay topics. Practice writing your essays while you keep one eye on the clock. You need to develop a sense of how much time to allow for thinking over your essay and how much time to set aside for the actual writing.

Tactic 2: **Practice Taking Shortcuts to Maximize Your Typing Efficiency**

Slow and steady is not the way to go, at least not when you're taking the analytical writing test on the GRE. Fast typists have a decided advantage here. Unfortunately, you cannot turn yourself into a typing whiz overnight. However, you can practice some shortcuts to help you on the day of the test.

 First, using the GRE's own word processing program, practice using the cut-and-paste function to copy phrases that you want to repeat in your essay. In an argument essay, for example, you might reuse such phrases as "the author makes the following assumption" or "another flaw in the author's argument is that. . . ." In an issues essay, if you are running out of time and still haven't written your opening and summary paragraphs (which we advise you to compose *after* you've written the body of your text), you can write just your concluding paragraph, cutting and pasting it to both the beginning and end of the essay. Then, in a few seconds, you can change the wording of that initial paragraph so that it works as an introduction, not as a conclusion. It's easy to do, using cut-and-paste.

Second, you can also practice abbreviating multiword names or titles. Instead of writing out Collegiate High School in full, refer to it as Collegiate or CHS.

Similarly, instead of typing out "for example," substitute the abbreviation "e.g."

Tactic 3: Acquaint Yourself with the Actual Essay Topics You Will Face

The GRE has posted its entire selection of potential essay topics on its website. The pool of issue topics can be found at *www.ets.org/gre/revised_general/prepare/analytical_writing/issue/pool*. The pool of argument topics can be found at *www.ets.org/gre/revised_general/prepare/analytical_writing/argument/pool*. There is no point in trying to memorize these topics or in trying to write an essay for each one. There are well over 200 items in the pool of issue topics alone. There is, however, a real point to exploring these potential topics and to noting their common themes.

Some of these themes involve contrasts:

- Tradition versus innovation and modernization.
- Competition versus cooperation.
- Present social needs versus future social needs.
- Conformity versus individualism.
- Imagination versus knowledge.
- Pragmatism versus idealism.

Many of the issue topics pose a simple question:

- What makes an effective leader?
- What are education's proper goals?
- How does technology affect our society?
- Why should we study history (or art, literature)?
- What is government's proper role (in education, art, wilderness preservation, and so on)?
- How do we define progress?

Others ask you to question conventional wisdom:

- Is loyalty *always* a virtue?
- Is "moderation in all things" *truly* good advice?
- Does conformity *always* have a negative impact?

Go over these recurrent questions and themes. If you have old notebooks from your general education courses, skim through them to refresh your memory of classroom discussions of such typical GRE issues. In the course of flipping through these old notes, you're very likely to come across examples that you might want to note for possible use in writing the issue essay.

Tactic 4: Acquaint Yourself with the Actual Essay Prompts You Will Face

Although there are 200 possible topics in the Issue Essay topic pool, and another 200 topics in the Argument Essay topic pool, there are only fourteen sets of specific task instructions for those topics (six for the Issue Essay and eight for the Argument Essay). GRE essay readers require that you not only adhere to the subject of the assigned essay topic, but that you also *meet each of the requirements found in the task instructions*. Writing a strong essay on the assigned topic is not enough to receive a high score; you must do so in the manner described in the task instructions.

You can review the task instructions for the Issue Essay at *www.ets.org/ gre/revised_general/prepare/analytical_writing/issue/*. The task instructions for the Argument Essay can be located at *www.ets.org/gre/revised_general/prepare/ analytical_writing/argument/*. As you examine the sets of task instructions, break them down into their essential components. What do the task instructions require? Take, for example, the Argument Essay task instructions below, which are modeled on actual task instructions used in the GRE.

> *Compose an essay identifying the questions that must be answered before reaching a conclusion about whether the recommendation and the argument supporting it make sense. In writing your essay, you should describe the impact that the answers to these questions would have on your assessment of the recommendation.*

These task instructions contain two requirements. First, your essay must identify the questions that must be answered in order to evaluate the recommendation. Second, your essay must explain *how* the answers to these questions would weaken or strengthen the argument and assist in evaluating the soundness of the recommendation. Failing to meet *both* of these requirements will result in a poor score.

WRITING THE ISSUE ESSAY

Tactic 5: **Break Down the Topic Statement into Separate Areas to Consider**

Here is an example of an issue topic, modeled on actual topics found in the GRE pool.

> *Compose an essay that identifies how greatly you concur (or differ) with the statement provided, describing in detail the rationale for your argument. As you build and provide evidence for your argument, include examples that demonstrate circumstances in which the statement could (or could not) be valid. Be sure to explain the impact these examples have on your argument.*
>
> *"The end does not justify the means, if the end is truly meritorious."*

Break down the statement into its component elements. Look for key words and phrases. First, consider **ends** or goals. These can be divided into personal goals—taking a trip to a foreign country, for example, or providing for one's family—and societal goals—preserving endangered species, for example, or protecting the health of the elderly.

Next, consider what **means** you might use to reach these goals. If you have to spend your savings and take a leave of absence from college to travel abroad, thereby postponing or potentially jeopardizing your eventual graduation, then perhaps your goal is insufficiently meritorious to justify the means. If, however, your goal is not simply to take a pleasure trip but to use the time abroad working in a refugee camp, the worthiness of the cause you are serving might well outweigh the expense and the risk of your not graduating.

Finally, consider the phrase **truly meritorious**. The author is begging the question, qualifying his assertion to make it appear incontrovertible. But what makes an action meritorious? Even more, what makes an action *truly* meritorious? How do you measure merit? Whose standards do you use?

Breaking down the topic statement into its components helps start you thinking analytically about the subject. It's a good way to begin composing your issue essay.

Tactic 6: **Write the Body of Your Essay Before You Write Your Opening and Summary Paragraphs**

Once you've determined your general line of reasoning, the direction you want your argument to take, you need to spend the bulk of your time writing the body of your essay. Allow 15 to 20 minutes for this. Outline the points you plan to make. Then as rapidly as you can, write two to three sentences to flesh out each reason or example in your outline. Do not worry if time pressure doesn't allow you to deal with every point you dreamed up. Start with a reason or example that you can easily put into words, preferably your best, most compelling reason or example. Given the 30-minute time limit you're working under, you want to be sure you cover your best points right away, before you run out of time. During the revision period, you can always rearrange your paragraphs, putting the strongest paragraph immediately before the conclusion, so that your essay builds to a solid climax.

Once you've written the body of your essay, work on your opening and concluding paragraphs. It may seem strange to write your introductory paragraph after you have written the body of your essay, but it is a useful technique. Many writers launch into writing the introduction, only to find, once they have finished the essay, that their conclusion is unrelated to, or even contradicts, what they had written in the introduction. By writing the introduction *after* you have composed the bulk of the essay, you will avoid having to rewrite the introduction to support the conclusion that you *actually* reached, rather than the conclusion that you *expected* to reach.

Your conclusion comes last. It should restate your thesis and summarize the arguments that you make in its support. You should mention your supporting arguments in the same order in which they appear in the body of the essay. This technique underscores the organization of your essay, giving it a predictable and orderly appearance.

Tactic 7: **Adopt a Balanced Approach**

Consider your readers. Who are they? Academics, junior members of college faculties. What are they looking for? They are looking for articulate and persuasive arguments expressed in scholarly, well-reasoned prose. In other words, they are looking for the sort of essay they might write themselves.

How do you go about writing for an academic audience? First, avoid extremes. You want to come across as a mature, evenhanded writer, someone who can take a strong stand on an issue, but who can see others' positions as well. Restrain yourself: don't get so carried away by the "rightness" of your argument that you wind up sounding fanatical or shrill. Second, be sure to acknowledge that other viewpoints exist. Cite them; you'll win points for scholarly objectivity.

Draw examples to support your position from "the great world" and from the academic realm. In writing about teaching methods, for example, you'll win more points citing current newspaper articles about magnet schools or relevant passages from John Dewey and Maria Montessori than telling anecdotes about your favorite gym teacher in junior high school. While it is certainly acceptable for you to offer an occasional example from personal experience, for the most part your object is to show the readers the *breadth* of your knowledge (without showing off by quoting the most obscure sources you can find!).

One additional point: Do not try to second-guess your readers. Yes, they want you to come up with a scholarly, convincing essay. But there is no "one true answer" that they are looking for. You can argue for the position. You can argue against the position. You can strike a middle ground, arguing both for and against the position, hedging your bet. The readers don't care what position you adopt. Don't waste your time trying to psych them out.

Tactic 8: **Make Use of Transitions or Signal Words to Point the Way**

Assume that typical GRE readers must read hundreds of issue essays in a day. You want to make the readers' job as easy as possible, so that when they come to your essay they breathe a sigh of relief, saying, "Ah! Someone who knows how to write!"

One way to make the readers' job easy is to lead them by the hand from one idea to the next, using signal words to point the way. The GRE readers like it when test-takers use signal words (transitions); in their analyses of sample essays scoring a 5 or 6, they particularly mention the writers' use of transitions as a good thing.

Here are a few helpful transitions. Practice using them precisely: you earn no points for sticking them in at random!

Support Signal Words

Use the following words or abbreviations to signal the reader that you are going to support your claim with an illustration or example:

e.g., (short for Latin *exempli gratia*, for the sake of an example)
for example
for instance
let me illustrate
such as

Use these words to signal the reader that you are about to add an additional reason or example to support your claim:

additionally	*furthermore*	*likewise*
also	*in addition*	*moreover*

Contrast Signal Words

Use the following words to signal a switch of direction in your argument.

although	*in contrast*	*on the other hand*
but	*in spite of*	*rather than*
despite	*instead of*	*still*
even though	*nevertheless*	*unlike*
except	*not*	*yet*
however	*on the contrary*	

Cause and Effect Signal Words

Use the following words to signal the next step in your line of reasoning or the conclusion of your argument.

accordingly	*in conclusion*	*therefore*
consequently	*in short*	*thus*
for this reason	*in summary*	*when . . . then*
hence	*so . . . that*	

See Tactic 12 for a discussion of how signal words can be helpful to you in the second of your two writing tasks, the argument critique.

WRITING THE ARGUMENT CRITIQUE

Tactic 9: **Learn to Spot Common Logical Fallacies**

You may remember studying a list of logical fallacies during your undergraduate education. It probably included Latin terms such as "post hoc ergo propter hoc" and "argumentum ad hominem." Fortunately, you do not need to memorize these terms to perform well on the GRE argument essay. The GRE's essay readers are not concerned with whether you know the name of a given logical fallacy; they are more concerned with whether you can recognize and explain fallacies as they occur in simulated real-world situations. Labeling a claim a "post hoc" fallacy will not win you a 6 (the top score) unless you can *explain* the flaw in the argument. And a straightforward logical explanation of the argument's flaw can get you a 6, whether or not you use the fancy Latin terminology.

This does not mean, however, that brushing up on the common logical fallacies is a waste of your time. A decent understanding of the ways in which arguments can be wrong will help you write a better essay by enabling you to identify more flaws in the assigned argument (GRE argument statements generally include more than one logical error), and by giving you a clearer understanding of the nature of those flaws. Our advice is, therefore, to review the common logical fallacies without spending too much time trying to memorize their names.

COMMON LOGICAL FALLACIES

Causal Fallacies

The classic fallacy of causation is often known by a Latin phrase, "post hoc ergo propter hoc," or its nickname, "the post hoc fallacy." The Latin phrase translates to "after this, therefore because of this." The post hoc fallacy confuses correlation with causation, assuming that when one event follows another, the second event must have been caused by the first. It is as if you were to say that because your birthday precedes your husband's by one month, your birth must have caused him to be born.

Inductive Fallacies

Fallacies of induction involve the drawing of general rules from specific examples. They are among the most common fallacies found in the GRE argument essay topics. To induce a general rule correctly from specific examples, it is crucial that the specific examples be representative of the larger group. All too often, this is not the case.

The **hasty generalization** (too small sample) is the most common inductive fallacy. A hasty generalization is a general conclusion that is based on too small a sample set. If, for example, you wanted to learn the most popular flavor of ice cream in Italy, you would need to interview a substantial number of Italians. Drawing a conclusion based on the taste of the three Italian tourists you met last week would not be justified.

Small sample size is a problem because it increases the risk of drawing a general conclusion from an **unrepresentative sample**. If, for example, you wanted to learn who was most likely to be elected president of the United States, you could not draw a reliable conclusion based on the preferences of the citizens of a single city, or even a single state.

To learn more about common logical fallacies, consult standard works on rhetoric and critical reasoning. Two currently popular texts are James Herrick's *Argumentation* and T. Edward Damer's *Attacking Faulty Reasoning*.

Tactic 10: Remember That Your Purpose Is to Analyze, *Not* to Persuade

You are not asked to agree or disagree with the argument in the prompt. Do not be distracted by your feelings on the subject of the prompt, and do not give in to the temptation to write your own argument. Be especially vigilant against this temptation if the topic is on a subject that you know very well. If, for example, the prompt argues that class size reduction is a poor idea because it did not improve test scores in one city, do not answer this argument with data you happen to know about another city in which test scores improved after class sizes were reduced. Instead, point out that one city is not a large enough sample on which to base a general conclusion. Go on to identify other factors that could have caused test scores to remain the same, despite lower class size. (Perhaps test scores in the sample city were already nearly as high as they could go, or the student population in that city was changing at the time class sizes were reduced.) Remember, the readers are not interested in how much you *know* about the subject of the prompt; they want to know how well you *think*.

Tactic 11: Examine the Argument for Unstated Assumptions and Missing Information

An argument is based upon certain assumptions made by its author. If an argument's basic premises are sound, the argument is strengthened. If the argument's basic premises are flawed, the argument is weakened.

Pinpoint what the argument assumes but never states. Then consider the validity of these unstated assumptions.

Ask yourself what additional evidence would strengthen or weaken the claim. Generally, GRE argument prompts are flawed but could be true under some circumstances. Only rarely will you find an argument that is absolutely untrue. Instead, you will find plausible arguments for which support is lacking.

Put yourself in the place of the argument's author. If you were trying to prove this argument, what evidence would you need? What missing data should you assemble to support your claim? Use your concluding paragraph to list this evidence and explain how its presence would solve the shortcomings that you identified earlier in your essay.

Tactic 12: **Pay Particular Attention to Signal Words in the Argument**

In analyzing arguments, be on the lookout for transitions or signal words that can clarify the structure of the argument. These words are like road signs, pointing out the direction the author wants you to take, showing you the connection between one logical step and the next. When you spot such a word linking elements in the author's argument, ask yourself whether this connection is logically watertight. Does A unquestionably lead to B? These signal words can indicate vulnerable areas in the argument, points you can attack.

In particular, be alert for:

Cause and Effect Signal Words

The following words often signal the conclusion of an argument.

accordingly	*in conclusion*	*therefore*
consequently	*in short*	*thus*
for this reason	*in summary*	
hence	*so*	

Contrast Signal Words

The following words often signal a reversal of thought within an argument.

although	*in contrast*	*rather than*
but	*instead*	*still*
despite	*nevertheless*	*unlike*
even though	*not*	*yet*
except	*on the contrary*	
however	*on the other hand*	

Tactic 13: **Allow Plenty of Time to Reread and Revise**

Expert writers often test their work by reading it aloud. In the exam room, you cannot read out loud. However, when you read your essay silently, take your time and listen with your inner ear to how it sounds. Read to get a sense of your essay's logic and rhythm. Does one sentence flow smoothly into the next? Would they flow more smoothly if you were to add a transition word or phrase (*therefore, however, nevertheless, in contrast, similarly*)? Do the sentences follow a logical order? Is any key idea or example missing? Does any sentence seem out of place? How would things sound if you cut out that awkward sentence or inserted that transition word?

Take a minute to act on your response to hearing your essay. If it sounded to you as if a transition word was needed, insert it. If it sounded as if a sentence should be cut, delete it. If it sounded as if a sentence was out of place, move it. Trust your inner ear, but do not attempt to do too much. Have faith in your basic outline for the essay. You have neither the need nor the time to revise everything.

Now think of yourself as an editor, not an auditor. Just as you need to have an ear for problems of logic and language, you also need to have an eye for errors that damage your text. Take a minute to look over your essay for problems in spelling and grammar. From your English classes you should know which words and grammatical constructions have given you trouble in the past. See whether you can spot any of these words or constructions in your essay. Correct any really glaring errors that you find. Do not worry if you fail to catch every mechanical error or awkward phrase. The readers understand that 30 minutes doesn't give you enough time to produce polished, gem-like prose. They won't penalize you for an occasional mechanical glitch.

PRACTICE EXERCISES

Practice for the Issue Task

1. Brainstorm for 5 minutes, jotting down any words and phrases that are triggered by one of the following questions:
   - What should the goals of higher education be?
   - Why should we study history?
   - How does technology affect our society?
   - What is the proper role of art?
   - Which poses the greater threat to society, individualism or conformity?
   - Which is more socially valuable, preserving tradition or promoting innovation?
   - Is it better to be a specialist or a generalist?
   - Can a politician be both honest and effective?

2. In a brief paragraph, define one of the following words:
   - Freedom
   - Originality
   - Honesty
   - Progress

3. Choosing an issue topic from the GRE's published pool of topics, write an essay giving your viewpoint concerning the particular issue raised. Set no time limit; take as long as you want to complete this task, then choose a second issue topic from the pool. *In only 30 minutes*, write an essay presenting your perspective on this second issue.

   Compare your two essays. Ask yourself how working under time pressure affected your second essay. Did its major problems stem from a lack of fluency? A lack of organization? A lack of familiarity with the subject matter under discussion? A lack of knowledge of the mechanics of formal written English? Depending on what problems you spot, review the appropriate sections of this chapter, as well as style manuals or writing texts.

Practice for the Argument Task

1. Choosing a sample of argument topics from the GRE's published pool of topics (*www.ets.org/gre/revised_general/prepare/analytical_writing/ argument/pool*), practice applying the list of logical fallacies to the published prompts. See how many fallacies you can find for each argument. If you have time, write practice essays for some of these arguments. If you are short of time, or would simply like to move more quickly, get together with a friend and explain the fallacies you have found in the argument essay prompts. This will be especially rewarding if you can work with a friend who is also preparing to take the GRE.

2. Write an "original" argument topic, modeling it on one of the argument prompts in the GRE's published pool. Your job is to change the details of the situation (names, figures, and so on) without changing the types of logical fallacies involved. By doing this, you will learn to spot the same old fallacies whenever they crop up in a new guise.

3. Choosing an argument prompt from the GRE's published pool of topics (*www.ets.org/gre/revised_general/prepare/analytical_writing/argument/pool*), write an essay critiquing the particular argument expressed. Set no time limit; take as long as you want to complete this task, then choose a second argument prompt from the pool. *In only 30 minutes*, write an essay critiquing this second argument.

   Compare your two critiques. Ask yourself how working under time pressure affected your second critique. Would more familiarity with the common logical fallacies have helped you? Depending on what problems you spot, review the appropriate sections of this chapter, as well as standard logic and rhetoric texts.

Quantitative Ability: Tactics and Practice

6

CALCULATORS ON THE GRE

You may *not* bring your own calculator to use when you take the GRE. However, you will have access to an onscreen calculator. While you are working on the math sections, one of the icons at the top of the screen will be a calculator icon. During the verbal and writing sections of the test, either that icon will be grayed out (meaning that you can't click on it) or it will simply not be there at all. During the math sections, however, you will be able to click on that icon at anytime; when you do, a calculator will instantly appear on the screen. Clicking the X in the upper-right-hand corner of the calculator will hide it.

Note that when the calculator appears on the screen, it may cover part of the question or the answer choices. If this occurs, just click on the top of the calculator and drag it to a convenient location. If you use the calculator to answer a question and then click NEXT to go to the next question, the calculator remains on the screen, exactly where it was, with the same numerical read-out. This is actually a distraction. So, if you do use the calculator to answer a question, as soon as you have answered that question, click on the X to remove the calculator from the screen. Later, it takes only one click to get it back.

The onscreen calculator is a simple four-function calculator, with a square root key. It is not a graphing calculator; it is not a scientific calculator. The only operations you can perform with the onscreen calcu-lator are adding, subtracting, multiplying, dividing, and taking square roots. Fortunately, these are the only operations you will ever need to answer any GRE question.

At the bottom of the onscreen calculator is a bar labeled TRANSFER DISPLAY. If you are using the calculator on a numeric entry question, and the result of your final calculation is the answer that you want to enter in the box, click on TRANSFER DISPLAY—the number currently displayed in the calculator's readout will instantly appear in the box under the question. This saves the few seconds that it would otherwise take to enter your answer; more important, it guarantees that you won't make an error typing in your answer.

Remember

Use your calculator only when you need to.

Note: You cannot use TRANSFER DISPLAY to enter either the numerator or denominator of a fraction—you must use the keyboard to enter a number in each box. Also, you must be attentive to what the question is asking. Suppose the question asks for a value rounded to the nearest hundredth, and the last calculation results in a calculator display of 0.8333333. You have two choices: either you use the keyboard to enter .83 or use TRANSFER DISPLAY, and then use the delete button to remove all of the extra 3s.

Just because you have a calculator at your disposal does not mean that you should use it very much. In fact, you shouldn't. The vast majority of questions that appear on the GRE do not require any calculations.

⌐━━ᴛ FACTS AND FORMULAS

1. **Sum:** the result of an addition: 8 is the sum of 6 and 2

2. **Difference:** the result of a subtraction: 4 is the difference of 6 and 2

3. **Product:** the result of a multiplication: 12 is the product of 6 and 2

4. **Quotient:** the result of a division: 3 is the quotient of 6 and 2

5. **Integers:** $\{\ldots, -3, -2, -1, 0, 1, 2, 3, \ldots\}$

6. **Remainder:** when 15 is divided by 6, the quotient is 2 and the remainder is 3: $15 = 6 \times 2 + 3$

7. **Factor or Divisor:** any integer that leaves no remainder (i.e., a remainder of 0) when it is divided into another integer: 1, 2, 5, 10 are the factors (or divisors) of 10

8. **Multiple:** the product of one integer by a second integer: 7, 14, 21, 28, . . . are multiples of 7 ($7 = 1 \times 7$, $14 = 2 \times 7$, and so on)

9. **Even integers:** the multiples of 2: $\{\ldots, -4, -2, 0, 2, 4, \ldots\}$

10. **Odd integers:** the non-multiples of 2: $\{\ldots, -3, -1, 1, 3, 5, \ldots\}$

11. **Consecutive integers:** two or more integers, written in sequence, each of which is 1 more than the preceding one. For example:

$$7, 8, 9 \qquad -2, -1, 0, 1, 2 \qquad n, n+1, n+2$$

12. **Prime number:** a positive integer that has exactly two divisors. The first few primes are 2, 3, 5, 7, 11, 13, 17 (*not* 1).

13. **Exponent:** a number written as a superscript: the 3 in 7^3. On the GRE, exponents are almost always positive integers:

$$2^n = 2 \times 2 \times 2 \times \cdots \times 2, \text{ where 2 appears as a factor } n \text{ times.}$$

14. **Laws of Exponents:**

For any numbers b, c, m, and n:

(i) $b^m b^n = b^{m+n}$ (ii) $\dfrac{b^m}{b^n} = b^{m-n}$ (iii) $(b^m)^n = b^{mn}$ (iv) $b^m c^m = (bc)^m$

15. **Square root of a positive number:** if a is positive, $\sqrt{a}$ is the only positive number whose square is a: $\left(\sqrt{a}\right)^2 = \sqrt{a} \times \sqrt{a} = a$.

16. **The product and the quotient of signed numbers:** The product and the quotient of two positive numbers or two negative numbers are positive; the product and the quotient of a positive number and a negative number are negative.

- The product of an *even* number of negative factors is positive.
- The product of an *odd* number of negative factors is negative.

17. For any positive numbers a and b:

$$\sqrt{ab} = \sqrt{a} \times \sqrt{b} \qquad \text{and} \qquad \sqrt{\dfrac{a}{b}} = \dfrac{\sqrt{a}}{\sqrt{b}}$$

18. The **Distributive Law:** for any real numbers a, b, and c:

- $a(b + c) = ab + ac$
- $a(b - c) = ab - ac$

and, if $a \neq 0$,

- $\dfrac{b+c}{a} = \dfrac{b}{a} + \dfrac{c}{a}$
- $\dfrac{b-c}{a} = \dfrac{b}{a} - \dfrac{c}{a}$

19. **Inequalities:** for any numbers a and b:

- $a > b$ means that $a - b$ is positive.
- $a < b$ means that $a - b$ is negative.

20. **To compare two fractions**, convert them to decimals by dividing the numerator by the denominator.

21. **To multiply two fractions**, multiply their numerators and multiply their denominators:

$$\frac{3}{5} \times \frac{4}{7} = \frac{3 \times 4}{5 \times 7} = \frac{12}{35}$$

22. **To divide any number by a fraction**, multiply that number by the reciprocal of the fraction.

$$\frac{3}{5} \div \frac{2}{3} = \frac{3}{5} \times \frac{3}{2} = \frac{9}{10}$$

23. **To add or subtract fractions with the same denominator**, add or subtract the numerators and keep the denominator:

$$\frac{4}{9} + \frac{1}{9} = \frac{5}{9} \quad \text{and} \quad \frac{4}{9} - \frac{1}{9} = \frac{3}{9} = \frac{1}{3}$$

24. **To add or subtract fractions with different denominators**, first rewrite the fractions as equivalent fractions with the same denominator:

$$\frac{1}{6} + \frac{3}{4} = \frac{2}{12} + \frac{9}{12} = \frac{11}{12}$$

25. **Percent:** a fraction whose denominator is 100:

$$15\% = \frac{15}{100} = 0.15$$

26. The **percent increase** of a quantity is

$$\frac{\text{actual increase}}{\text{original amount}} \times 100\%$$

The **percent decrease** of a quantity is

$$\frac{\text{actual decrease}}{\text{original amount}} \times 100\%$$

27. **Ratio:** a fraction that compares two quantities that are measured in the same units. The ratio 2 to 3 can be written $\frac{2}{3}$ or 2:3.

28. In any ratio problem, write the letter x after each number and use some given information to solve for x.

29. **Proportion:** an equation that states that two ratios (fractions) are equal. Solve proportions by cross-multiplying: if $\dfrac{a}{b} = \dfrac{c}{d}$, then $ad = bc$.

30. **Average (arithmetic mean) of a set of n numbers:** the sum of those numbers divided by n:

$$\text{average} = \frac{\text{sum of the numbers}}{n} \quad \text{or simply} \quad A = \frac{\text{sum}}{n}$$

31. **Tactic for average problems:** If you know the average, A, of a set of n numbers, multiply A by n to get their sum: sum $= nA$.

32. **To multiply two binomials, use the FOIL method:** multiply each term in the first parentheses by each term in the second parentheses and simplify by combining terms, if possible.

$$(2x - 7)(3x + 2) = (2x)(3x) + (2x)(2) + (-7)(3x) + (-7)(2) =$$

First terms   Outer terms   Inner terms   Last terms

$$6x^2 + 4x - 21x - 14 = 6x^2 - 17x - 14$$

33. The three most **important binomial products** on the GRE are these:

- $(x - y)(x + y) = x^2 - y^2$
- $(x - y)^2 = (x - y)(x - y) = x^2 - 2xy + y^2$
- $(x + y)^2 = (x + y)(x + y) = x^2 + 2xy + y^2$

34. All **distance problems** involve one of three variations of the same formula:

$$\text{distance} = \text{rate} \times \text{time} \qquad \text{rate} = \frac{\text{distance}}{\text{time}}$$

$$\text{time} = \frac{\text{distance}}{\text{rate}}$$

35.

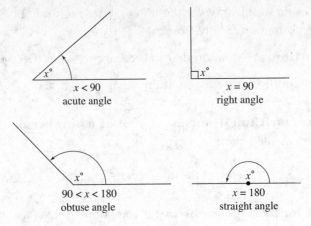

$x < 90$	$x = 90$
acute angle	right angle

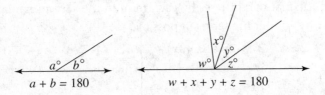

$90 < x < 180$	$x = 180$
obtuse angle	straight angle

36. If two or more angles form a **straight angle**, the sum of their measures is 180°.

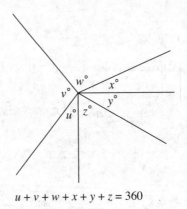

$$a + b = 180 \qquad w + x + y + z = 180$$

37. The sum of all the measures of all the angles around a point is 360°.

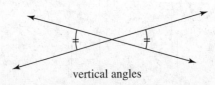

$$u + v + w + x + y + z = 360$$

38. Vertical angles are the opposite angles formed by the intersecting lines.

vertical angles

Vertical angles have equal measures.

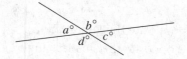

$$a = c \text{ and } b = d.$$

39. If a pair of **parallel lines** is cut by a **transversal** that is *not* perpendicular to the parallel lines:

- Four of the angles are acute, and four are obtuse.
- All four acute angles are equal: $a = c = e = g$.
- All four obtuse angles are equal: $b = d = f = h$.
- The sum of any acute angle and any obtuse angle is 180°: for example, $d + e = 180$, $c + f = 180$, $b + g = 180$, ...

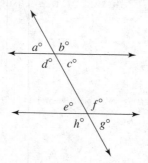

40. The sum of the measures of the three angles of a triangle is 180°:

$$x + y + z = 180.$$

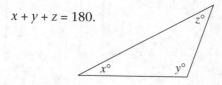

41. The measure of an exterior angle of a triangle is equal to the sum of the measures of the two opposite interior angles.

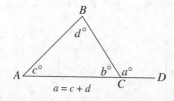

$$a = c + d$$

42. The lengths of the sides of a triangle

In any triangle:

- the longest side is opposite the largest angle;
- the shortest side is opposite the smallest angle;
- sides with the same length are opposite angles with the same measure.

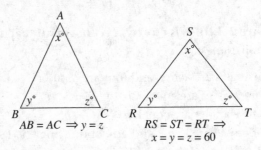

$$AB = AC \Rightarrow y = z \qquad RS = ST = RT \Rightarrow$$
$$x = y = z = 60$$

43. In any **right triangle**, the sum of the measures of the two acute angles is 90°.

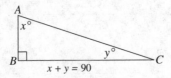

$$x + y = 90$$

44. Pythagorean theorem

In a right triangle with legs a, b, and hypotenuse c: $a^2 + b^2 = c^2$.

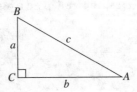

45. In a **45-45-90 right triangle**, the sides are x, x, and $x\sqrt{2}$.

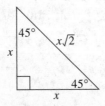

46. In a **30-60-90 right triangle**, the sides are x, $x\sqrt{3}$, and $2x$.

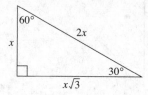

47. The triangle inequality

- The sum of the lengths of any two sides of a triangle is greater than the length of the third side.
- The difference between the lengths of any two sides of a triangle is less than the length of the third side.

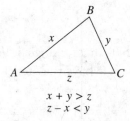

$$x + y > z$$
$$z - x < y$$

48. The **area of a triangle** is given by $A = \frac{1}{2}bh$, where b is the base and h is the height.

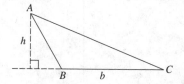 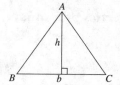

49. If A represents the **area of an equilateral triangle** with side s, then $A = \dfrac{s^2\sqrt{3}}{4}$.

50. In any **quadrilateral**, the sum of the measures of the four angles is 360°.

51. A **trapezoid** is a quadrilateral in which exactly one pair of sides is parallel. A **parallelogram** is a quadrilateral in which both pairs of opposite sides are parallel. A **rectangle** is a parallelogram in which all four angles are right angles. A **square** is a rectangle in which all four sides have the same length.

52. **Properties of a parallelogram**

In parallelogram *ABCD*:

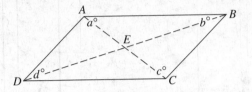

- Opposite sides are equal: $AB = CD$ and $AD = BC$.
- Opposite angles are equal: $a = c$ and $b = d$.
- Consecutive angles add up to 180°: $a + b = 180$, $b + c = 180$, and so on.
- The two diagonals bisect each other: $AE = EC$ and $BE = ED$.

53. **Properties of a rectangle**

In any rectangle:

- The measure of each angle in a rectangle is 90°.
- The diagonals of a rectangle have the same length: $AC = BD$.

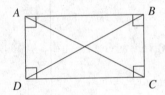

54. **Properties of a square**

In any square:

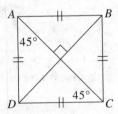

- All four sides have the same length.
- Each diagonal divides the square into two 45-45-90 right triangles.
- The diagonals are perpendicular to each other: $AC \perp BD$.

55. Formulas for perimeter and area:

- For a parallelogram: $A = bh$ and $P = 2(a + b)$.
- For a rectangle: $A = \ell w$ and $P = 2(\ell + w)$.
- For a square: $A = s^2$ or $A = \dfrac{1}{2}d^2$ and $P = 4s$.
- For a trapezoid: $A = \dfrac{1}{2}(b_1 + b_2)h$.

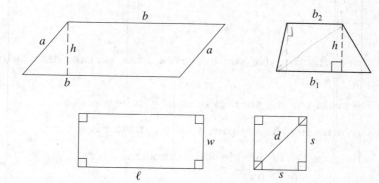

56. Circle formulas

Let r be the radius, d the diameter, C the circumference, and A the area of a circle. Then

$$d = 2r \qquad C = \pi d = 2\pi r \qquad A = \pi r^2$$

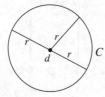

57. The formula for the volume of a rectangular solid is $V = \ell wh$.

In a cube, all the edges are equal. Therefore, if e is the edge, the formula for the volume is $V = e^3$.

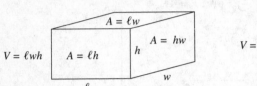 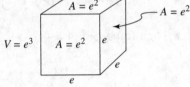

58. The formula for the surface area of a rectangular solid is $A = 2(\ell w + \ell h + wh)$.

The formula for the surface area of a cube is $A = 6e^2$.

59. The formula for the volume, V, of a cylinder is $V = \pi r^2 h$.

The surface area, A, of the side of the cylinder is $A = 2\pi rh$. The area of the top and bottom are each πr^2.

60. The distance, d, between two points, $A(x_1, y_1)$ and $B(x_2, y_2)$, can be calculated using the distance formula:

$$d = \sqrt{(x_2 - x_1)^2 + (y_2 - y_1)^2}$$

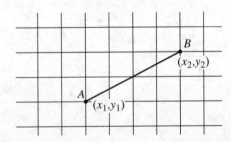

61. Slope formula

The slope of line AB is given by slope $= \dfrac{y_2 - y_1}{x_2 - x_1}$

62. Slope facts:

- The slope of any horizontal line is 0.
- The slope of any line that goes up as you move from left to right is positive.
- The slope of any line that goes down as you move from left to right is negative.

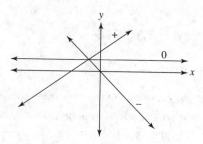

63. Formula for the equation of a line:

- For any real number a: $x = a$ is the equation of the vertical line that crosses the x-axis at $(a, 0)$.
- For any real number b: $y = b$ is the equation of the horizontal line that crosses the y-axis at $(0, b)$.
- For any real numbers b and m: $y = mx + b$ is the equation of the line that crosses the y-axis at $(0, b)$ and whose slope is m.

64. The Counting Principle:
If two jobs need to be completed and there are m ways to do the first job and n ways to do the second job, then there are $m \times n$ ways to do one job followed by the other. This principle can be extended to any number of jobs.

65.
If E is any event, the **probability** that E will occur is given by

$$P(E) = \frac{\text{number of favorable outcomes}}{\text{total number of possible outcomes}}$$

assuming that all of the possible outcomes are equally likely.

66. Probability Facts:

Let E be an event, and let $P(E)$ be the probability that it will occur.

- If E is **impossible**, then $P(E) = 0$.
- If it is **certain** that E will occur, then $P(E) = 1$.
- In all other cases, $0 < P(E) < 1$.
- The probability that event E will *not* occur is $1 - P(E)$.
- If an experiment is done 2 (or more) times, the probability that first one event will occur, and then a second event will occur, is the product of the probabilities.

GENERAL MATH TACTICS

Tactic 1: **Draw a Diagram**

On any geometry question for which a figure is not provided, draw one (as accurately as possible) on your scrap paper. If a diagram is provided, copy it onto your scrap paper, unless you *instantly* see the solution.

Let's consider some examples.

EXAMPLE 1

What is the area of a rectangle whose length is twice its width and whose perimeter is equal to that of a square whose area is 1?

Ⓐ 1 Ⓑ 6 Ⓒ $\frac{2}{3}$ Ⓓ $\frac{4}{3}$ Ⓔ $\frac{8}{9}$

SOLUTION

Don't even think of answering this question until you have drawn a square and a rectangle and labeled each of them: each side of the square is 1; and if the width of the rectangle is w, its length is $2w$.

Now, write the required equation and solve it:

$$6w = 4 \Rightarrow w = \frac{4}{6} = \frac{2}{3} \Rightarrow 2w = \frac{4}{3}$$

The area of the rectangle $= lw = \left(\frac{4}{3}\right)\left(\frac{2}{3}\right) = \frac{8}{9}$ (E).

Drawings should not be limited, however, to geometry questions; there are many other questions on which drawings will help.

EXAMPLE 2

A jar contains 10 red marbles and 30 green ones. How many red marbles must be added to the jar so that 60% of the marbles will be red?

Ⓐ 25　Ⓑ 30　Ⓒ 35　Ⓓ 40　Ⓔ 60

SOLUTION

Draw a diagram and label it.

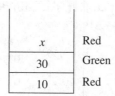

From the diagram it is clear that there are now $40 + x$ marbles in the jar, of which $10 + x$ are red. Since we want the fraction of red marbles to be

$60\% \left(= \frac{3}{5}\right)$, we have $\frac{10 + x}{40 + x} = \frac{3}{5}$.

Cross-multiplying, we get:

$$50 + 5x = 120 + 3x \Rightarrow 2x = 70 \Rightarrow x = 35 \text{ (C)}$$

Of course, you could have set up the equation and solved it without the diagram, but the drawing makes the solution easier and you are less likely to make a careless mistake.

Tactic 2: • **Trust Diagrams That Are Drawn to Scale**
    • **Redraw Diagrams That Are Not Drawn to Scale**

EXAMPLE 3

In the figure at the right, what is the sum of
the measures of all of the marked angles?

Ⓐ 360°
Ⓑ 540°
Ⓒ 720°
Ⓓ 900°
Ⓔ 1080°

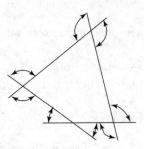

SOLUTION

Since the diagram contains no values for the lengths of segments or the measures
of angles, there is nothing that could cause the diagram to not be drawn to scale.
So, trust it. Make your best estimate of each angle, and add up the values. The
five choices are so far apart that, even if you're off by 15° or more on some of
the angles, you'll get the right answer. The sum of the estimates shown is 690°,
so the correct answer *must* be 720° (C).

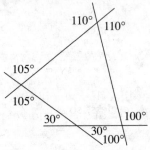

EXAMPLE 4

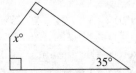

Quantity A	Quantity B
x	170

SOLUTION

Since the diagram appears to be drawn to scale (the angle labeled 35° looks to be about 35°), trust it. Look at x: it appears to be *about* 90 + 50 = 140; it is *definitely* less than 170.

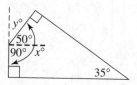

Also, y, drawn above is clearly more than 10, so x is less than 170. Choose (B).

Tactic 3: **When Necessary, Change a Diagram, and Then Trust Your Figure**

EXAMPLE 5

In △*ACB*, what is the value of x?

Ⓐ 75
Ⓑ 60
Ⓒ 45
Ⓓ 30
Ⓔ 15

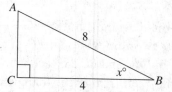

SOLUTION

The figure provided here is useless, so you can't trust it. We are told that $AB = 8$ and $BC = 4$, but in the figure AB is ever so slightly longer than BC; it is *certainly not* twice as long as BC. On your scrap paper redraw the triangle so that AB *is* twice as long as BC. Now, just look: x is about 60 (B).

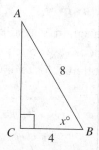

In fact, *x* is exactly 60. If the hypotenuse of a right triangle is twice the length of one of the legs, you have a 30-60-90 triangle, and the angle formed by the hypotenuse and that leg is 60°.

EXAMPLE 6

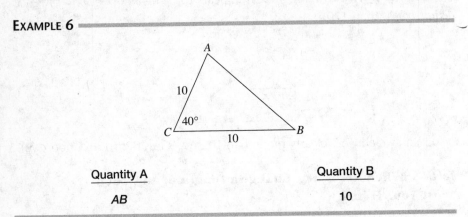

Quantity A	Quantity B
AB	10

SOLUTION

Again, the diagram is not drawn to scale and so cannot be trusted. Actually, there are two things wrong: ∠*C* is labeled 40°, but looks much more like 60° or 70°, and *AC* and *BC* are each labeled 10, but *BC* is drawn much longer. On your scrap paper redraw the triangle with a 40° angle and two sides of the same length. Since *your* diagram is drawn to scale, you may trust it, and it's clear that *AB* < 10. Choose (B).

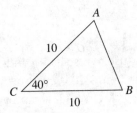

Tactic 4: **Add a Line to a Diagram**

Occasionally, after staring at a diagram, you still have no idea how to solve the problem to which it applies. It looks as though there isn't enough given information. When this happens, it often helps to draw another line in the diagram.

EXAMPLE 7

In the figure below, *Q* is a point on the circle whose center is *O* and whose radius is *r*, and *OPQR* is a rectangle. What is the length of diagonal *PR*?

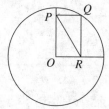

Ⓐ *r*   Ⓑ r^2 Ⓒ $\dfrac{r^2}{\pi}$ Ⓓ $\dfrac{r\sqrt{2}}{\pi}$

Ⓔ It cannot be determined from the information given.

SOLUTION

If, after staring at the diagram and thinking about rectangles, circles, and the Pythagorean theorem, you're still lost, don't give up. Ask yourself, "Can I add another line to this diagram?" As soon as you think to draw in *OQ*, the other diagonal, the problem becomes easy: the two diagonals are equal, and, since *OQ* is a radius, it is equal to *r* (A).

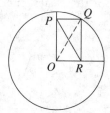

Tactic 5: Subtract to Find Shaded Regions

Whenever part of a figure is white and part is shaded, the straightforward way to find the area of the shaded portion is to find the area of the entire figure and then subtract from it the area of the white region. Of course, if you are asked for the area of the white region, you can, instead, subtract the shaded area from the total area. Occasionally, you may see an easy way to calculate the shaded area directly, but usually you should subtract.

EXAMPLE 8

In the figure below, *ABCD* is a rectangle, and *BE* and *CF* are arcs of circles centered at *A* and *D*. What is the area of the shaded region?

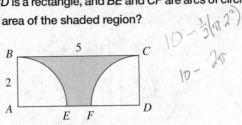

$$10 - \tfrac{1}{2}(\pi \cdot 2^2)$$

$$10 - 2\pi$$

Ⓐ $10 - \pi$ Ⓑ $2(5 - \pi)$ Ⓒ $2(5 - 2\pi)$ Ⓓ $6 + 2\pi$ Ⓔ $5(2 - \pi)$

SOLUTION

The entire region is a 2×5 rectangle whose area is 10. Since each white region is a quarter-circle of radius 2, the combined area of these regions is that of a semicircle of radius 2:

$$\frac{1}{2}\pi(2)^2 = 2\pi$$

Therefore, the area of the shaded region is $10 - 2\pi = 2(5 - \pi)$ (B).

Tactic 6: **Don't Do More Than You Have To**

Look for shortcuts. Since a problem can often be solved in more than one way, you should always look for the easiest method. Consider the following examples.

EXAMPLE 9

If $5(3x - 7) = 20$, what is $3x - 8$?

Ⓐ $\frac{11}{3}$ Ⓑ 0 Ⓒ 3 Ⓓ 14 Ⓔ 19

It's not difficult to solve for x:

$$5(3x - 7) = 20 \Rightarrow 15x - 35 = 20 \Rightarrow 15x = 55 \Rightarrow x = \frac{55}{15} = \frac{11}{3}$$

But it's too much work. Besides, once you find that $x = \frac{11}{3}$, you still have

to multiply to get $3x$: $3\frac{11}{3} = 11$, and then subtract to get $3x - 8$: $11 - 8 = 3$.

SOLUTION

The key is to recognize that you don't need x. Finding $3x - 7$ is easy (just divide the original equation by 5), and $3x - 8$ is just 1 less:

$$5(3x - 7) = 20 \Rightarrow 3x - 7 = 4 \Rightarrow 3x - 8 = 3$$

EXAMPLE 10

Zach worked from 9:47 A.M. until 12:11 P.M.

Sam worked from 9:11 A.M. until 12:47 P.M.

Quantity A	Quantity B
The number of minutes Zach worked	The number of minutes Sam worked

SOLUTION

Don't spend any time calculating how many minutes either boy worked. You need to know only which column is greater; and since Sam started earlier and finished later, he clearly worked longer. The answer is B.

Tactic 7: **Pay Attention to Units**

Often the answer to a question must be in units different from those used in the given data. As you read the question, write down and underline or circle exactly what you are being asked. Do the examiners want hours or minutes or seconds, dollars or cents, feet or inches, meters or centimeters? On multiple-choice questions an answer with the wrong units is almost always one of the choices.

EXAMPLE 11

At a speed of 48 miles per hour, how many minutes will be required to drive 32 miles?

(A) $\dfrac{2}{3}$ (B) $\dfrac{3}{2}$ (C) 40   (D) 45   (E) 2400

SOLUTION

This is a relatively easy question. Just be attentive. Since $\frac{32}{48} = \frac{2}{3}$, it will take $\frac{2}{3}$ of an *hour* to drive 32 miles. Choice A is $\frac{2}{3}$; but that is *not* the correct answer because you are asked how many *minutes* will be required. The correct answer is $\frac{2}{3}(60) = 40$ (C).

Tactic 8: Systematically Make Lists

When a question asks "how many," often the best strategy is to make a list of all the possibilities. It is important that you make the list in a *systematic* fashion so that you don't inadvertently leave something out. Often, shortly after starting the list, you can see a pattern developing and can figure out how many more entries there will be without writing them all down.

EXAMPLE 12

The product of three positive integers is 300. If one of them is 5, what is the least possible value of the sum of the other two?

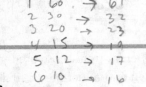

60

$$\boxed{16}$$

the one closest to the middle

SOLUTION

Since one of the integers is 5, the product of the other two is 60 ($5 \times 60 = 300$). Systematically, list all possible pairs, (a, b), of positive integers whose product is 60, and check their sums. First, let $a = 1$, then 2, and so on.

<u>a</u>	<u>b</u>	<u>a + b</u>
1	60	61
2	30	32
3	20	23
4	15	19
5	12	17
6	10	16

The answer is 16.

EXAMPLE 13

A palindrome is a number, such as 93539, that reads the same forward and backward. How many palindromes are there between 100 and 1000?

[handwritten:]
101   202   909
111   212   914
121   222... 929
131
191   242   999
10 × 9

SOLUTION

First, write down the numbers in the 100's that end in 1:

101, 111, 121, 131, 141, 151, 161, 171, 181, 191

Now write the numbers beginning and ending in 2:

202, 212, 222, 232, 242, 252, 262, 272, 282, 292

By now you should see the pattern: there are 10 numbers beginning with 1, and 10 beginning with 2, and there will be 10 beginning with 3, 4, . . . , 9 for a total of 9 × 10 = 90 palindromes.

PRACTICE QUESTIONS

1. In the figure below, if the radius of circle O is 10, what is the length of diagonal AC of rectangle $OABC$?

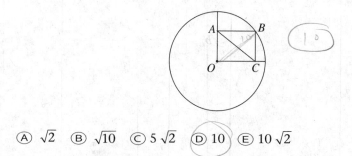

[handwritten: 10]

(A) $\sqrt{2}$ (B) $\sqrt{10}$ (C) $5\sqrt{2}$ (D) 10 (E) $10\sqrt{2}$

2. In the figure below, *ABCD* is a square and *AED* is an equilateral triangle. If *AB* = 2, what is the area of the shaded region?

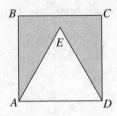

Ⓐ $\sqrt{3}$ Ⓑ 2 Ⓒ 3 Ⓓ $4 - 2\sqrt{3}$ Ⓔ $4 - \sqrt{3}$

3. If $5x + 13 = 31$, what is the value of $\sqrt{5x + 31}$?

Ⓐ $\sqrt{13}$ Ⓑ $\sqrt{\dfrac{173}{5}}$ Ⓒ 7 Ⓓ 13 Ⓔ 169

4. At Nat's Nuts a $2\frac{1}{4}$-pound bag of pistachio nuts costs $6.00. At this rate, what is the cost, in cents, of a bag weighing 9 ounces?

5. In the figure below, three circles of radius 1 are tangent to one another. What is the area of the shaded region between the circles?

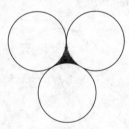

Ⓐ $\dfrac{\pi}{2} - \sqrt{3}$ Ⓑ 1.5 Ⓒ $\pi - \sqrt{3}$ Ⓓ $\sqrt{3} - \dfrac{\pi}{2}$ Ⓔ $2 - \dfrac{\pi}{2}$

6.

Quantity A	Quantity B
The number of odd positive factors of 30	The number of even positive factors of 30

7.

Quantity A	Quantity B
In writing all of the integers from 1 to 300, the number of times the digit 1 is used.	150

8.

$$a + 2b = 14$$
$$5a + 4b = 16$$

Quantity A	Quantity B
The average (arithmetic mean) of a and b.	2.5

9.

A bag contains 4 marbles, 1 of each color:
red, blue, yellow, and green.
The marbles are removed at random,
1 at a time. The first marble is red.

Quantity A	Quantity B
The probability that the yellow marble is removed before the blue marble	.5

10.

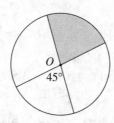

The area of circle O is 12.

Quantity A	Quantity B
The area of the shaded sector	$\dfrac{\pi}{2}$

Answer Key

1. **D**	3. **C**	5. **D**	7. **A**	9. **C**
2. **E**	4. **150**	6. **C**	8. **C**	10. **B**

Answer Explanations

1. **(D)** There is nothing wrong with the diagram, so trust it. *AC* is clearly longer than *OC*, and very close to radius *OE*.

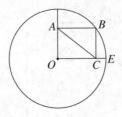

   Therefore, *AC* must be about 10. Check the choices. They are approximately as follows:

   Ⓐ $\sqrt{2} = 1.4$; Ⓑ $\sqrt{10} = 3.1$; Ⓒ $5\sqrt{2} = 7$; Ⓓ 10; Ⓔ $10\sqrt{2} = 14$.

   The answer must be 10.

   The answer *is* 10. The two diagonals are equal, and diagonal *OB* is a radius.

2. **(E)** Use Tactic 5: subtract to find the shaded area. The area of square *ABCD* is 4. By Fact 50, the area of $\triangle AED$ is $\dfrac{2^2\sqrt{3}}{4} = \dfrac{4\sqrt{3}}{4} = \sqrt{3}$. Then the area of the shaded region is $4 - \sqrt{3}$.

3. **(C)** Use Tactic 6: don't do more than you have to. In particular, don't solve for *x*. Here
   $$5x + 13 = 31 \Rightarrow 5x = 18 \Rightarrow 5x + 31 = 18 + 31 = 49 \Rightarrow \sqrt{5x + 31} = \sqrt{49} = 7$$

4. **150** This is a relatively simple ratio, but use Tactic 7 and make sure you get the units right. You need to know that there are 100 cents in a dollar and 16 ounces in a pound.
   $$\frac{price}{weight} : \frac{6 \text{ dollars}}{2.25 \text{ pounds}} = \frac{600 \text{ cents}}{36 \text{ ounces}} = \frac{x \text{ cents}}{9 \text{ ounces}}$$

   Now cross-multiply and solve: $36x = 5400 \Rightarrow x = 150$.

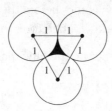

5. **(D)** Use Tactic 4 and add some lines: connect the centers of the three circles to form an equilateral triangle whose sides are 2. Now use Tactic 5 and find the shaded area by subtracting the area of the three sectors from the area of the triangle, which is $\dfrac{2^2\sqrt{3}}{4} = \sqrt{3}$ (Fact 50). Each sector is $\dfrac{1}{6}$ of a circle of radius 1. Together the three sectors form $\dfrac{1}{2}$ of such a circle, so their total area is $\dfrac{1}{2}\pi(1)^2 = \dfrac{\pi}{2}$. Finally, subtract: the area of the shaded region is $\sqrt{3} - \dfrac{\pi}{2}$.

6. **(C)** Use Tactic 8. Systematically list all the factors of 30, either individually or in pairs: 1, 30, 2, 15, 3, 10, 5, 6. Of the 8 factors, 4 are even and 4 are odd. The columns are equal (C).

7. **(A)** Use Tactic 8. Systematically list the numbers that contain the digit 1, writing as many as you need to see the pattern. Between 1 and 99 the digit 1 is used 10 times as the units digit (1, 11, 21, . . . , 91) and 10 times as the tens digit (10, 11, 12, . . . , 19) for a total of 20 times. From 200 to 299, there are 20 more times (the same 20 but preceded by 2). Finally, from 100 to 199 there are 20 more plus 100 numbers where the digit 1 is used in the hundreds place. The total is 20 + 20 + 20 + 100 = 160. Column A is greater.

8. **(C)** Use Tactic 6: don't do more than is necessary. You don't need to solve this system of equations; you don't need to know the values of a and b, only their average. Adding the two equations gives

$$6a + 6b = 30 \Rightarrow a + b = 5 \Rightarrow \dfrac{a+b}{2} = \dfrac{5}{2}$$

The columns are equal (C).

9. **(C)** Use Tactic 8. Systematically list all of the orders in which the marbles could be drawn. With 4 colors, there would ordinarily have been 24 orders, but since the first marble drawn was red, there are only 6 arrangements for the other 3 colors: BYG, BGY, YGB, YBG, GYB, GBY.

In 3 of these 6 the yellow comes before the blue, and in the other 3 the blue comes before the yellow. Therefore, the probability that the yellow marble will be removed before the blue marble is $\frac{3}{6} = \frac{1}{2} = .5$.

The columns are equal (C).

10. **(B)** The shaded sector is $\frac{45}{360} = \frac{1}{8}$ of the circle, so its area is $\frac{1}{8}$ of 12: $\frac{12}{8} = \frac{3}{2} = 1.5$. Since $\pi > 3$, $\frac{\pi}{2} > 1.5$. Column B is greater.

DISCRETE QUANTITATIVE QUESTIONS

About 20 of the 40 questions in the two math sections are what the ETS calls discrete quantitative questions. These questions are of three types:

- Multiple-choice questions
- Multiple-answer questions
- Numeric entry questions

Multiple-choice questions are just the standard multiple-choice questions that you are familiar with. Each one has five answer choices, exactly one of which is the correct answer. To get credit for a multiple-choice question you simply click on the oval in front of the one correct answer choice.

Multiple-answer questions are multiple-choice questions with a twist. These questions could have anywhere from 3 to 12 answer choices, any number of which could be correct, from just one to all of them. To alert you to the fact that there may be, and usually is, more than one correct answer, instead of an oval, a square appears in front of each answer choice. To get credit for a multiple-answer question, you must click on the square in front of each correct answer and leave blank the squares in front of each of the incorrect answers.

Numeric entry questions are the only questions on the test for which no answer choices are given. The answer to such a question may be positive or negative and may be an integer, decimal, or fraction. If the answer is negative, use the hyphen for the negative sign. To get credit for a numeric entry question you must use the keyboard to enter your answer into the box on the screen directly below the question. If in answering a question, you use the onscreen calculator and the digital readout is exactly the answer that you want to enter in the box, you can click on the calculator's TRANSFER DISPLAY bar and the readout will automatically appear in the box. Always enter the exact answer unless the question tells you to round your answer, in which case you must round it to the degree of accuracy asked for.

If the answer is to be entered as a fraction, there will be two boxes, and you are to enter the numerator in the upper box and the denominator in the lower box. Any answer equivalent to a correct answer earns full credit. If the correct answer to a question is 2.5, then 2.50 is equally acceptable, unless you were told to give the answer to the nearest tenth. Also, fractions do not have to be reduced: if the correct answer is $\frac{1}{2}$, then you would receive full credit for $\frac{3}{6}$ or $\frac{13}{26}$, or any other fraction equivalent to $\frac{1}{2}$.

The majority of discrete quantitative questions are of the multiple-choice variety, and all of the tactics discussed in this chapter apply to them. Some of the tactics also apply to multiple-answer questions and numeric entry questions.

The important strategies you will learn in this chapter help you answer many questions on the GRE. However, as invaluable as these tactics are, use them only when you need them. *If you know how to do a problem and are confident that you can do it accurately and reasonably quickly, JUST DO IT!*

As we have done throughout this book, on multiple-choice questions we will continue to label the five answer choices A, B, C, D, and E and to refer to them as such. On multiple-answer questions, the choices will be consecutively labeled A, B, C, etc., using as many letters as there are answer choices. Of course, when you take the GRE, these letters will not appear—there will simply be a blank oval in front of each of the answer choices. When we refer to Choice C—as we do, for example, in Tactic 9 (below)—we are simply referring to the third answer choice among the five presented.

Tactic 9: Test the Choices, Starting with C

Tactic 9, often called *backsolving*, is useful when you are asked to solve for an unknown and you understand what needs to be done to answer the question, but you want to avoid doing the algebra. The idea is simple: test the various choices to see which one is correct.

> **Note**
>
> On the GRE the answers to virtually all numerical multiple-choice questions are listed in either increasing or decreasing order. Consequently, in applying Tactic 9, *you should always start with the middle value* (what we call C). For example, assume that Choices A, B, C, D, and E are given in increasing order. Try (C). If it works, you've found the answer. If (C) doesn't work, you should now know whether you need to test a larger number or a smaller one, and that information permits you to eliminate two more choices. If (C) is too small, you need a larger number, so (A) and (B) are out; if (C) is too large, you can eliminate (D) and (E), which are even larger.

Examples 14 and 15 illustrate the proper use of Tactic 9.

EXAMPLE 14

If the average (arithmetic mean) of 2, 7, and x is 12, what is the value of x?

Ⓐ 9   Ⓑ 12   Ⓒ 21   Ⓓ 27   Ⓔ 36

SOLUTION

Use Tactic 9. Test Choice C: $x = 21$.

- Is the average of 2, 7, and 21 equal to 12?

- No: $\dfrac{2+7+21}{3} = \dfrac{30}{3} = 10$, which is *too small*.

- Eliminate (C); also, since, for the average to be 12, x must be *greater* than 21, eliminate (A) and (B).

- Try Choice D: $x = 27$. Is the average of 2, 7, and 27 equal to 12?

- Yes: $\dfrac{2+7+27}{3} = \dfrac{36}{3} = 12$. The answer is D.

Every problem that can be solved using Tactic 9 can be solved directly, usually in less time. Therefore, we stress: *if you are confident that you can solve a problem quickly and accurately, just do so.*

EXAMPLE 15

If the sum of five consecutive odd integers is 735, what is the largest of these integers?

Ⓐ 155   Ⓑ 151   Ⓒ 145   Ⓓ 143   Ⓔ 141

SOLUTION

Use Tactic 9. Test Choice C: 145.

- If 145 is the largest of the five integers, the integers are 145, 143, 141, 139, and 137. Add them. The sum is 705.
- Since 705 is too small, eliminate (C), (D), and (E).
- If you noticed that the amount by which 705 is too small is 30, you should realize that each of the five numbers needs to be increased by 6; therefore, the largest is 151 (B).
- If you didn't notice, just try 151, and see that it works.

This solution is easy, and it avoids having to set up and to solve the required equation:

$$n + (n + 2) + (n + 4) + (n + 6) + (n + 8) = 735$$

Tactic 10: **Replace Variables with Numbers**

Mastery of Tactic 10 is critical for anyone developing good test-taking skills. This tactic can be used whenever the five choices involve the variables in the question. There are three steps:

1. Replace each letter with an easy-to-use number.

2. Solve the problem using those numbers.

3. Evaluate each of the five choices with the numbers you picked to see which choice is equal to the answer you obtained.

Examples 16–17 illustrate the proper use of Tactic 10.

EXAMPLE 16

If a is equal to b multiplied by c, which of the following is equal to b divided by c?

(A) $\dfrac{a}{bc}$ (B) $\dfrac{ab}{c}$ (C) $\dfrac{a}{c}$ (D) $\dfrac{a}{c^2}$ (E) $\dfrac{a}{bc^2}$

SOLUTION

- Pick three easy-to-use numbers that satisfy $a = bc$: for example, $a = 6, b = 2, c = 3$.
- Solve the problem with these numbers: $b \div c = \dfrac{b}{c} = \dfrac{2}{3}$.

- Check each of the five choices to see which one is equal to $\frac{2}{3}$:

- (A) $\dfrac{a}{bc} = \dfrac{6}{(2)(3)} = 1$: NO. (B) $\dfrac{ab}{c} = \dfrac{(6)(3)^1}{3_1} = 6$: NO.

  (C) $\dfrac{a}{c} = \dfrac{6}{3} = 2$: NO. (D) $\dfrac{a}{c^2} = \dfrac{6}{3^2} = \dfrac{6}{9} = \dfrac{2}{3}$: YES!

  Still check (E): $\dfrac{a}{bc^2} = \dfrac{6}{2(3^2)} = \dfrac{6}{2(3^2)} = \dfrac{6}{18} = \dfrac{1}{3}$: NO.
- The answer is (D).

EXAMPLE 17

If the sum of four consecutive odd integers is s, then, in terms of s, what is the greatest of these integers?

(A) $\dfrac{s-12}{4}$ (B) $\dfrac{s-6}{4}$ (C) $\dfrac{s+6}{4}$ (D) $\dfrac{s+12}{4}$ (E) $\dfrac{s+16}{4}$

SOLUTION

- Pick four easy-to-use consecutive odd integers: say, 1, 3, 5, 7. Then s, their sum, is 16.
- Solve the problem with these numbers: the greatest of these integers is 7.
- When $s = 16$, the five choices are $\dfrac{s-12}{4} = \dfrac{4}{4}$, $\dfrac{s-6}{4} = \dfrac{10}{4}$, $\dfrac{s+6}{4} = \dfrac{22}{4}$,

  $\dfrac{s+12}{4} = \dfrac{28}{4}$, $\dfrac{s+16}{4} = \dfrac{32}{4}$.

- Only $\dfrac{28}{4}$, Choice D, is equal to 7.

Of course, Examples 16 and 17 can be solved without using Tactic 10 *if your algebra skills are good.*

The important point is that, if you are uncomfortable with the correct algebraic solution, you can use Tactic 10 and *always* get the right answer.

Example 18 is somewhat different. You are asked to reason through a word problem involving only variables. Most students find problems like these mind-boggling. Here, the use of Tactic 10 is essential.

Helpful Hint

Replace the letters with numbers that are easy to use, not necessarily ones that make sense. *It is perfectly OK to ignore reality.* A school can have five students, apples can cost $10 each, trains can go 5 miles per hour or 1000 miles per hour—it doesn't matter.

EXAMPLE 18

If a school cafeteria needs c cans of soup each week for each student, and if there are s students in the school, for how many weeks will x cans of soup last?

(A) $\dfrac{cx}{s}$ (B) $\dfrac{xs}{c}$ (C) $\dfrac{s}{cx}$ (D) $\dfrac{x}{cs}$ (E) csx

---

SOLUTION

- Replace c, s, and x with three easy-to-use numbers. If a school cafeteria needs 2 cans of soup each week for each student, and if there are 5 students in the school, how many weeks will 20 cans of soup last?
- Since the cafeteria needs $2 \times 5 = 10$ cans of soup per week, 20 cans will last for 2 weeks.
- Which of the choices equals 2 when $c = 2$, $s = 5$, and $x = 20$?
- The five choices become: $\dfrac{cx}{s} = 8$, $\dfrac{xs}{c} = 50$, $\dfrac{s}{cx} = \dfrac{1}{8}$, $\dfrac{x}{cs} = 2$, $csx = 200$. The answer is (D).

Tactic 11: Choose an Appropriate Number

Tactic 11 is similar to Tactic 10 in that we pick convenient numbers. However, here no variable is given in the problem. Tactic 11 is especially useful in problems involving fractions, ratios, and percents.

> **Helpful Hint**
>
> In problems involving fractions, the best number to use is the least common denominator of all the fractions. In problems involving percents, the easiest number to use is 100.

EXAMPLE 19

At Central High School each student studies exactly one foreign language. Three-fifths of the students take Spanish, and one-fourth of the remaining students take Italian. If all of the others take French, what <u>percent</u> of the students take French?

Ⓐ 10   Ⓑ 15   Ⓒ 20   Ⓓ 25   Ⓔ 30

SOLUTION

The least common denominator of $\frac{3}{5}$ and $\frac{1}{4}$ is 20, so assume that there are 20 students at Central High. (Remember that the numbers you choose don't have to be realistic.) Then the number of students taking Spanish is 12 $\left(\frac{3}{5} \text{ of } 20\right)$. Of the remaining 8 students, 2 $\left(\frac{1}{4} \text{ of } 8\right)$ take Italian. The other 6 take French. Finally, 6 is 30% of 20. The answer is (E).

EXAMPLE 20

From 1994 to 1995 the sales of a book decreased by 80%. If the sales in 1996 were the same as in 1994, by what percent did they increase from 1995 to 1996?

Ⓐ 80%   Ⓑ 100%   Ⓒ 120%   Ⓓ 400%   Ⓔ 500%

SOLUTION

Use Tactic 11, and assume that 100 copies were sold in 1994 (and 1996). Sales dropped by 80 (80% of 100) to 20 in 1995 and then increased by 80, from 20 back to 100, in 1996. The percent increase was

$$\frac{\text{actual increase}}{\text{original amount}} \times 100\% = \frac{80}{20} \times 100\% = 400\% \text{ (D)}$$

Tactic 12: **Add Equations**

When a question involves two equations, either add them or subtract them. If there are three or more equations, add them.

> **Helpful Hint**
>
> Very often, answering a question does not require you to solve the equations. Remember Tactic 6: *Do not do any more than is necessary.*

EXAMPLE 21

If $3x + 5y = 14$ and $x - y = 6$, what is the average of x and y?

Ⓐ 0   Ⓑ 2.5   Ⓒ 3   Ⓓ 3.5   Ⓔ 5

SOLUTION

Add the equations:

$$3x + 5y = 14$$
$$+ \quad x - y = 6$$
$$\overline{4x + 4y = 20}$$

Divide each side by 4:

$$x + y = 5$$

The average of x and y is their sum divided by 2:

$$\frac{x+y}{2} = 2.5$$

The answer is (B).

EXAMPLE 22

If $a - b = 1$, $b - c = 2$, and $c - a = d$, what is the value of d?

Ⓐ −3   Ⓑ −1   Ⓒ 1   Ⓓ 3
Ⓔ It cannot be determined from the information given.

SOLUTION

Add the three equations:

$$a - b = 1$$
$$b - c = 2$$
$$+ \; c - a = d$$
$$\overline{}$$
$$0 = 3 + d \Rightarrow d = -3$$

The answer is (A).

Tactic 13: **Eliminate Absurd Choices, and Guess**

When you have no idea how to solve a problem, eliminate all the absurd choices and *guess* from among the remaining ones.

EXAMPLE 23

The average of 5, 10, 15, and x is 20. What is x?

Ⓐ 0   Ⓑ 20   Ⓒ 25   Ⓓ 45   Ⓔ 50

SOLUTION

If the average of four numbers is 20, and three of them are less than 20, the other one must be greater than 20. Eliminate A and B and guess. If you further realize that, since 5 and 10 are *a lot* less than 20, x will probably be *a lot* more than 20, you can eliminate (C), as well. Then guess either (D) or (E).

EXAMPLE 24

If 25% of 220 equals 5.5% of w, what is w?

Ⓐ 10   Ⓑ 55   Ⓒ 100   Ⓓ 110   Ⓔ 1000

SOLUTION

Since 5.5% of w equals 25% of 220, which is surely greater than 5.5% of 220, w must be *greater* than 220. Eliminate Choices A, B, C, and D. The answer *must* be (E)!

PRACTICE QUESTIONS

1. Judy is now twice as old as Adam but 6 years ago she was 5 times as old as he was. How old is Judy now?

   Ⓐ 10   Ⓑ 16   Ⓒ 20   Ⓓ 24   Ⓔ 32

2. If $a < b$ and c is the sum of a and b, which of the following is the positive difference between a and b?

   Ⓐ $2a - c$ Ⓑ $2b - c$ Ⓒ $c - 2b$ Ⓓ $c - a + b$ Ⓔ $c - a - b$

3. If w widgets cost c cents, how many widgets can you get for d dollars?

   Ⓐ $\dfrac{100dw}{c}$ Ⓑ $\dfrac{dw}{100c}$ Ⓒ $100cdw$ Ⓓ $\dfrac{dw}{c}$ Ⓔ cdw

4. If 120% of a is equal to 80% of b, which of the following is equal to $a + b$?

   Ⓐ $1.5a$ Ⓑ $2a$ Ⓒ $2.5a$ Ⓓ $3a$ Ⓔ $5a$

5. In the figure at the right, $WXYZ$ is a square whose sides are 12. AB, CD, EF, and GH are each 8, and are the diameters of the four semicircles. What is the area of the shaded region?

   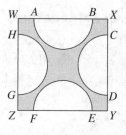

   Ⓐ $144 - 128\pi$ Ⓑ $144 - 64\pi$
   Ⓒ $144 - 32\pi$ Ⓓ $144 - 16\pi$ Ⓔ 16π

6. What is a divided by $a\%$ of a?

   Ⓐ $\dfrac{a}{100}$ Ⓑ $\dfrac{100}{a}$ Ⓒ $\dfrac{a^2}{100}$ Ⓓ $\dfrac{100}{a^2}$ Ⓔ $100a$

7. On a certain Russian-American committee, $\dfrac{2}{3}$ of the members are men, and $\dfrac{3}{8}$ of the men are Americans. If $\dfrac{3}{5}$ of the committee members are Russian, what fraction of the members are American women?

8. Nadia will be x years old y years from now. How old was she z years ago?

   (A) $x + y + z$ (B) $x + y - z$ (C) $x - y - z$

   (D) $y - x - z$ (E) $z - y - x$

9. If $12a + 3b = 1$ and $7b - 2a = 9$, what is the average (arithmetic mean) of a and b?

10. If $x\%$ of y is 10, which of the following is an expression for y in terms of x?

   (A) $\dfrac{10}{x}$ (B) $\dfrac{100}{x}$ (C) $\dfrac{1000}{x}$ (D) $\dfrac{x}{100}$ (E) $\dfrac{x}{10}$

Answer Key

1. **B**   3. **A**   5. **C**   7. $\dfrac{3}{20}$ 9. **0.5**

2. **B**   4. **C**   6. **B**   8. **C**   10. **C**

Answer Explanations

1. **(B)** Use Tactic 9: backsolve, starting with (C). If Judy is now 20, Adam is 10; 6 years ago, they would have been 14 and 4, which is less than 5 times as much. Eliminate C, D, and E, and try a smaller value. If Judy is now 16, Adam is 8; 6 years ago, they would have been 10 and 2. That's it; 10 is 5 times 2.

2. **(B)** Use Tactic 10. Pick simple values for a, b, and c. Let $a = 1$, $b = 2$, and $c = 3$. Then $b - a = 1$. Only $2b - c$ is equal to 1.

3. **(A)** Use Tactic 10: replaces variables with numbers. If 2 widgets cost 10 cents, then widgets cost 5 cents each; and for 3 dollars, you can get 60 widgets. Which of the choices equals 60 when $w = 2$, $c = 10$, and $d = 3$? Only $\dfrac{100dw}{c}$

4. **(C)** Use Tactic 11: choose appropriate numbers. Since 120% of 80 = 80% of 120, let $a = 80$ and $b = 120$. Then $a + b = 200$, and $200 \div 80 = 2.5$.

5. **(C)** If you don't know how to solve this, you must use Tactic 13: eliminate the absurd choices and guess. Which choices are absurd? Certainly, (A) and (B), both of which are negative. Also, since Choice D is about 94, which is much more than half the area of the square, it is much too large. Guess

between (C) (about 43) and (E) (about 50). If you remember that the way to find shaded areas is to subtract, guess (C): $144 - 32\pi$.

6. **(B)** Use Tactics 10 and 11: replace a by a number, and use 100 since the problem involves percents.

$$100 \div (100\% \text{ of } 100) = 100 \div 100 = 1$$

Test each choice; which ones equal 1 when $a = 100$? Only A and B: $\frac{100}{100} = 1$. Eliminate (C), (D), and (E); and test (A) and (B) with another value, 50, for a:

$$50 \div (50\% \text{ of } 50) = 50 \div (25) = 2$$

Now, only $\frac{100}{a}$ works: $\frac{100}{50} = 2$.

7. $\frac{3}{20}$ Use Tactic 11: choose appropriate numbers. The LCM of all the denominators is 120, so assume that the committee has 120 members. Then there are $\frac{2}{3} \times 120 = 80$ men and 40 women. Of the 80 men,

$30\left(\frac{3}{8} \times 80\right)$ are American. Since there are $72\left(\frac{3}{5} \times 120\right)$ Russians, there are $120 - 72 = 48$ Americans, of which 30 are men, so the other 18 are women. Finally, the fraction of American women is $\frac{18}{120} = \frac{3}{20}$.

8. **(C)** Use Tactic 10: replace x, y, and z with easy-to-use numbers.

Assume Nadia will be 10 in 2 years. How old was she 3 years ago? If she will be 10 in 2 years, she is 8 now and 3 years ago was 5. Which of the choices equals 5 when $x = 10$, $y = 2$, and $z = 3$? Only $x - y - z$.

9. **0.5** Use Tactic 12, and add the two equations:

$$10a + 10b = 10 \Rightarrow a + b = 1 \Rightarrow \frac{a+b}{2} = \frac{1}{2} \text{ or } 0.5$$

10. **(C)** Use Tactics 10 and 11. Since 100% of 10 is 10, let $x = 100$ and $y = 10$. When $x = 100$, Choices C and E are each 10. Eliminate Choices A, B, and D, and try some other numbers:

50% of 20 is 10. Of (C) and (E), only $\frac{1000}{x} = 20$ when $x = 50$.

QUANTITATIVE COMPARISON QUESTIONS

About 15 of the 40 questions on the two quantitative sections of the GRE are quantitative comparisons. Unless you took the SAT before 2005, it is very likely that you have never seen questions of this type and certainly never learned the correct strategies for answering them. Don't worry. In this chapter you will learn all of the necessary tactics. If you master them, you will quickly realize that quantitative comparisons are the easiest mathematics questions on the GRE and will wish that there were more than 15 of them.

Before the first quantitative comparison question appears on the screen, you will see these instructions.

> _**Directions:**_ In the following questions, there are two quantities, labeled Quantity A and Quantity B. You are to compare those quantities, taking into consideration any additional information given and decide which of the following statements is true:
>
> > Quantity A is greater.
> > Quantity B is greater.
> > The two quantities are equal.
> > It is impossible to determine which quantity is greater.
>
> _Note:_ The given information, if any, is centered above the two quantities. If a symbol appears more than once, it represents the same thing each time.

Before learning the different strategies for solving this type of question, let's clarify these instructions. In quantitative comparison questions there are two quantities, and it is your job to compare them. The correct answer to a quantitative comparison question is one of the four statements listed in the directions above. Of course, on the computer screen those choices will not be listed as A, B, C, and D. Rather, you will see an oval in front of each statement, and you will click on the oval in front of the statement you believe is true.

You should click on the oval in front of	if
Quantity A is greater.	Quantity A is greater *all the time, no matter what.*
Quantity B is greater.	Quantity B is greater *all the time, no matter what.*
The two quantities are equal.	The two quantities are equal *all the time, no matter what.*
It is impossible to determine which quantity is greater.	*The answer is not one of the first three choices.*

This means, for example, that *if you can find a single instance* when Quantity A is greater than Quantity B, then you can immediately eliminate two choices: the answer cannot be "Quantity B is greater," and the answer cannot be "The two quantities are equal." In order for the answer to be "Quantity B is greater," Quantity B would have to be greater *all the time*; but you know of one instance when it isn't. Similarly, since the quantities are not equal *all the time*, the answer can't be "The two quantities are equal." The correct answer, therefore, is either "Quantity A is greater" or "It is impossible to determine which quantity is greater." If it turns out that Quantity A *is* greater all the time, then that is the answer; if, however, you can find a single instance where Quantity A is not greater, the answer is "It is impossible to determine which quantity is greater."

By applying the tactics that you will learn in this chapter, you will probably be able to determine which of the choices is correct; if, however, after eliminating two of the choices, you still cannot determine which answer is correct, quickly guess between the two remaining choices and move on.

Helpful Hint

Right now, memorize the instructions for answering quantitative comparison questions. *When you take the GRE, dismiss the instructions for these questions immediately—do not spend even one second reading the directions (or looking at a sample problem).*

Before learning the most important tactics for handling quantitative comparison questions, let's look at two examples to illustrate the preceding instructions.

EXAMPLE 25

$$1 < x < 3$$

Quantity A	Quantity B
x^2	$2x$

○ Quantity A is greater.
○ Quantity B is greater.
○ The two quantities are equal.
○ It is impossible to determine which quantity is greater.

SOLUTION

Throughout, x represents the same thing — a number between 1 and 3. If x is 2, then x^2 and $2x$ are each 4, and *in this case* the two quantities are equal. We can, therefore, eliminate the first two choices: neither Quantity A nor Quantity B is greater *all the time*. However, in order for the correct answer to be "The two quantities are equal," the quantities would have to be equal *all the time*. Are they? Note that although 2 is the only *integer* between 1 and 3, it is not the only *number* between 2 and 3: x could be 1.1 or 2.5 or any of infinitely many other numbers. And in those cases the quantities are not equal [for example, $2.5^2 = 6.25$, whereas $2(2.5) = 5$]. The quantities are *not* always equal, and so the correct answer is the fourth choice: It is impossible to determine which quantity is greater.

EXAMPLE 26

p and q are primes
$$p + q = 12$$

Quantity A	Quantity B
p	8

○ Quantity A is greater.
○ Quantity B is greater.
○ The two quantities are equal.
○ It is impossible to determine which quantity is greater.

SOLUTION

Since 5 and 7 are the only primes whose sum is 12, p could be 5 or 7. In either case, p is less than 8, and so Quantity B is greater, *all the time*. Note that although $1 + 11 = 12$, p cannot be 11, because 1 is not a prime.

Note

To simplify the discussion, throughout the rest of this chapter, in the explanations of the answers to all sample questions and in the Model Tests, the four answer choices will be referred to as A, B, C, and D, respectively. For example, we will write

The correct answer is **B**.

rather than

The correct answer is: Quantity B is greater.

Tactic 14: **Replace Variables with Numbers**

Many problems that are hard to analyze because they contain variables become easy to solve when the variables are replaced by simple numbers.

Tactic 14 is the most important tactic for quantitative comparison questions. *Be sure to master it!*

Most quantitative comparison questions contain variables. When those variables are replaced by simple numbers such as 0 and 1, the two quantities become much easier to compare.

EXAMPLE 27

$$a < b < c < d$$

Quantity A	Quantity B
ab	cd

SOLUTION

- Replace a, b, c, and d with easy-to-use numbers that satisfy the condition $a < b < c < d$: for example, $a = 1$, $b = 2$, $c = 5$, $d = 10$.
- Evaluate the two quantities: $ab = (1)(2) = 2$, and $cd = (5)(10) = 50$.
- Therefore, *in this case*, Quantity B is greater.
- Does that mean that (B) is the correct answer? Not necessarily. Quantity

B is greater this time, but will it be greater **every single time, no matter what?**

- What it does mean is that neither (A) nor (C) could possibly be the answer: Quantity A can't be greater **every single time, no matter what**, because it isn't greater *this* time; and the quantities aren't equal **every single time, no matter what**, because they aren't equal *this* time.

The correct answer, therefore, is either (B) or (D); and in the few seconds that it took you to plug in 1, 2, 5, and 10 for *a, b, c,* and *d,* you were able to eliminate two of the four choices. If you could do nothing else, you should now guess.

But, of course, *you can and will do something else.* You will try some other numbers. But *which* numbers? Since the first numbers you chose were positive, try some negative numbers this time.

Let *a* = –5, *b* = –3, *c* = –2, and *d* = –1.

- Evaluate: *ab* = (–5)(–3) = 15 and *cd* = (–2)(–1) = 2.
- Therefore, *in this case,* Quantity A is greater.
- Quantity B is *not* greater all the time. (B) is *not* the correct answer.
- The answer is (D).

Here are some guidelines for deciding which numbers to use when applying Tactic 14.

1. **The very best numbers to use first are 1, 0, and –1.**

2. **Often, fractions between 0 and 1 are useful.**

3. **Occasionally, "large" numbers such as 10 or 100 can be used.**

4. **If there is more than one variable, it is permissible to replace each with the same number.**

5. **If a variable appears more than once in a problem, it must be replaced by the same number each time.**

6. **Do not impose any conditions not specifically stated.** In particular, do not assume that variables must represent integers. For example, 3 is not the only number that satisfies 2 < *x* < 4 (2.1, 3.95, and π all work). The expression *a* < *b* < *c* < *d* does not mean that *a, b, c, d* are *integers*, let alone *consecutive* integers (which is why we didn't choose 1, 2, 3, and 4 in Example 14), nor does it mean that any or all of these variables are *positive*.

When you replace the variables in a quantitative comparison question with numbers, remember:

If Quantity A is ever greater than Quantity B, eliminate (B) and (C)—the answer must be (A) or (D).

If Quantity B is ever greater than Quantity A, eliminate (A) and (C)—the answer must be (B) or (D).

If Quantities A and B are ever equal, eliminate (A) and (B)—the answer must be (C) or (D).

Practice applying Tactic 14 to these examples.

EXAMPLE 28

$$m > 0 \text{ and } m \neq 1$$

Quantity A	Quantity B
m^2	m^3

SOLUTION

Use Tactic 14. Replace m with numbers satisfying $m > 0$ and $m \neq 1$.

	Quantity A	Quantity B	Compare	Eliminate
Let $m = 2$.	$2^2 = 4$	$2^3 = 8$	(B) is greater.	(A) and (C)
Let $m = \dfrac{1}{2}$.	$\left(\dfrac{1}{2}\right)^2 = \dfrac{1}{4}$	$\left(\dfrac{1}{2}\right)^3 = \dfrac{1}{8}$	(A) is greater.	(B)

The answer is (D).

EXAMPLE 29

Quantity A	Quantity B
$w + 10$	$w - 11$

SOLUTION

Use Tactic 14. There are no restrictions on w, so use the best numbers: 1, 0, –1.

	Quantity A	Quantity B	Compare	Eliminate
Let $w = 1$.	$1 + 10 = 11$	$1 - 11 = -10$	(A) is greater.	(B) and (C)
Let $w = 0$.	$0 + 10 = 10$	$0 - 11 = -11$	(A) is greater.	
Let $w = -1$.	$-1 + 10 = 9$	$-1 - 11 = -12$	(A) is greater.	

Guess (A). We let w be a positive number, a negative number, and 0. Each time Quantity A was greater. That's not proof, but it justifies an educated guess.

Tactic 15: Choose an Appropriate Number

This is just like Tactic 14. We are replacing a variable with a number, but the variable isn't mentioned in the problem.

EXAMPLE 30

Every band member is either 15, 16, or 17 years old.
One-third of the band members are 16, and
twice as many band members are 16 as 15.

Quantity A

The number of
17-year-old band
members

Quantity B

The total number of
15- and 16-year-old
band members

SOLUTION

If the first sentence of Example 28 had been "There are n students in the school band, all of whom are 15, 16, or 17 years old," the problem would have been identical to this one. Using Tactic 14, you could have replaced n with an easy-to-use number, such as 6, and solved: $\frac{1}{3}(6) = 2$ are 16 years old; then 1 is 15, and the remaining 3 are 17. The answer is (C).

EXAMPLE 31

Abe, Ben, and Cal divided a cash prize.

Abe took 50% of the money and spent $\frac{3}{5}$ of what he took.

Ben took 40% of the money and spent $\frac{3}{4}$ of what he took.

Quantity A	Quantity B
The amount that Abe spent	The amount that Ben spent

SOLUTION

Use Tactic 15. Assume the prize was $100. Then Abe took $50 and spent $\frac{3}{\overset{1}{5}}(\overset{10}{\$50}) = \$30$. Ben took $40 and spent $\frac{3}{\overset{1}{4}}(\overset{10}{\$40}) = \$30$.

The answer is (C).

Tactic 16: **Make the Problem Easier: Do the Same Thing to Each Quantity**

In solving a quantitative comparison problem, you can always add the same number to each column or subtract the same number from each column. You can multiply or divide each side of an equation or inequality by the same number, *but in the case of <u>inequalities</u> you can do this only if the number is positive.* Since you don't know whether the quantities are equal or unequal, you cannot multiply or divide by a variable *unless you know that it is positive.* If each of the quantities are positive, you may square them or take their square roots.

Here are three examples on which to practice Tactic 16.

EXAMPLE 32

Quantity A	Quantity B
$\frac{1}{3} + \frac{1}{4} + \frac{1}{9}$	$\frac{1}{9} + \frac{1}{3} + \frac{1}{5}$

SOLUTION

Cancel (subtract) $\frac{1}{3}$ and $\frac{1}{9}$ from each quantity:

$$\frac{\cancel{1}}{\cancel{3}} + \frac{1}{4} + \frac{\cancel{1}}{\cancel{9}} \qquad\qquad \frac{\cancel{1}}{\cancel{9}} + \frac{\cancel{1}}{\cancel{3}} + \frac{1}{5}$$

Since $\frac{1}{4} > \frac{1}{5}$, the answer is (A).

EXAMPLE 33

a is a negative number

Quantity A	Quantity B
a^2	$-a^2$

SOLUTION

Add a^2 to each quantity:

$$a^2 + a^2 = 2a^2 \qquad\qquad\qquad -a^2 + a^2 = 0$$

Since a is negative, $2a^2$ is positive. The answer is (A).

EXAMPLE 34

Quantity A	Quantity B
$\dfrac{\sqrt{20}}{2}$	$\dfrac{5}{\sqrt{5}}$

SOLUTION

Square each quantity:

$$\left(\frac{\sqrt{20}}{2}\right)^2 = \frac{20}{4} = 5 \qquad\qquad \left(\frac{5}{\sqrt{5}}\right)^2 = \frac{25}{5} = 5$$

The answer is (C).

Tactic 17: **Ask "Could They Be Equal?" and "Must They Be Equal?"**

Tactic 17 is most useful when one quantity contains a variable and the other contains a number. In this situation ask yourself, "Could they be equal?" If the answer is "yes," eliminate (A) and (B), and then ask, "Must they be equal?" If the second answer is "yes," then (C) is correct; if the second answer is "no," then choose (D). When the answer to "Could they be equal?" is "no," we usually know right away what the correct answer is.

Let's look at a few examples:

EXAMPLE 35

The sides of a triangle are 3, 4, and x.

Quantity A	Quantity B
x	5

SOLUTION

Could they be equal? Could $x = 5$? Of course. That's the all-important 3-4-5 right triangle. Eliminate (A) and (B). Must they be equal? Must $x = 5$? The answer is "no." Actually, x can be any number satisfying the inequality $1 < x < 7$.

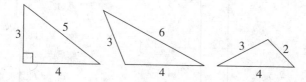

EXAMPLE 36

Bank A has 10 tellers and bank B has 20 tellers.
Each bank has more female tellers than male tellers.

Quantity A	Quantity B
The number of female tellers at bank A	The number of female tellers at bank B

SOLUTION

Could they be equal? Could the number of female tellers be the same in both banks? No. More than half (i.e., more than 10) of bank B's 20 tellers are female, but bank A has only 10 tellers in all. The answer is (B).

EXAMPLE 37

Quantity A	Quantity B
The perimeter of a rectangle whose area is 21	20

SOLUTION

Could they be equal? Could a rectangle whose area is 21 have a perimeter of 20? Yes, if its length is 7 and its width is 3: 7 + 3 + 7 + 3 = 20. Eliminate (A) and (B). Must they be equal? If you're *not* sure, guess between (C) and (D).

There are other possibilities—lots of them; here are a 7 × 3 rectangle and a few others:

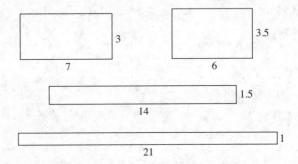

Tactic 18: **Don't Calculate: Compare**

Avoid unnecessary calculations. You don't have to determine the exact values of Quantities A and B; you just have to compare them.

These are problems on which poor test-takers waste time doing arithmetic and good test-takers think! Practicing Tactic 18 will help you become a good test-taker.

Now, test your understanding of Tactic 18 by solving these problems.

EXAMPLE 38

Quantity A	Quantity B
The number of years	The number of years
from 1492 to 1929	from 1429 to 1992

SOLUTION

The subtraction is easy enough, but why do it? The dates in Quantity B start earlier and end later than those in Quantity A. Clearly, they span more years. You don't need to know how many years. Quantity B is greater.

EXAMPLE 39

Quantity A	Quantity B
$43^2 + 27^2$	$(43 + 27)^2$

SOLUTION

For *any* positive numbers a and b, $(a + b)^2 > a^2 + b^2$. You should do the calculations only if you don't know this fact. Quantity B is greater.

EXAMPLE 40

Howie earned a 75 on each of his first three math tests
and an 80 on the fourth and fifth tests.

Quantity A	Quantity B
Howie's average	Howie's average
after four tests	after five tests

SOLUTION

Remember that you want to know which average is higher, *not* what the averages are. After four tests Howie's average is clearly less than 80, so an 80 on the fifth test had to *raise* his average. Quantity B is greater.

PRACTICE QUESTIONS

1.

$$a < 0$$

Quantity A	Quantity B
$4a$	a^4

2.

$$x > 0$$

Quantity A	Quantity B
$10x$	$\dfrac{10}{x}$

3.

$$ab < 0$$

Quantity A	Quantity B
$(a + b)^2$	$a^2 + b^2$

4.

Quantity A	Quantity B
$99 + 299 + 499$	$103 + 305 + 507$

5.

Quantity A	Quantity B
The area of a circle whose radius is 17	The area of a circle whose diameter is 35

6.

Line ℓ goes through (1, 1) and (5, 2).
Line m is perpendicular to ℓ.

Quantity A	Quantity B
The slope of line ℓ	The slope of line m

7.

x, y, and z are three consecutive integers
between 300 and 400.

Quantity A	Quantity B
The average (arithmetic mean) of x and z	The average (arithmetic mean) of x, y, and z

8.

$$x + y = 5$$
$$y - x = -5$$

Quantity A	Quantity B
y	0

9.

Stores A and B sell the same television set.
The regular price at store A is 10% less
than the regular price at store B.

Quantity A	Quantity B
The price of the television set when store A has a 10% off sale	The price of the television set when store B has a 20% off sale

10.

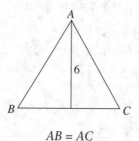

$$AB = AC$$

Quantity A	Quantity B
The area of $\triangle ABC$	3

Answer Key

1. **B**	3. **B**	5. **B**	7. **C**	9. **A**
2. **D**	4. **B**	6. **A**	8. **C**	10. **D**

Answer Explanations

1. **(B)** Use Tactic 14. Replace a with numbers satisfying $a < 0$.

	Quantity A	Quantity B	Compare	Eliminate
Let $a = -1$.	$4(-1) = -4$	$(-1)^4 = 1$	B is greater.	A and C
Let $a = -2$.	$4(-2) = -8$	$(-2)^4 = 16$	B is greater.	

Choose (B). Note $4a$ is negative; a^4 is positive.

2. **(D)** Use Tactic 14. When $x = 1$, the quantities are equal; when $x = 2$, they aren't.

3. **(B)** Use Tactic 16.

	Quantity A	Quantity B
Expand Quantity A:	$(a + b)^2 =$	$a^2 + b^2$
	$a^2 + 2ab + b^2$	

Subtract $a^2 + b^2$
from each quantity: 2ab 0

Since it is given that $ab < 0$, then $2ab < 0$.

4. **(B)** Use Tactic 18: don't calculate; compare. Each of the three numbers in Quantity B is greater than the corresponding number in Quantity A. Quantity B is greater.

5. **(B)** Again, use Tactic 18: don't calculate the two areas; compare them. The circle in Quantity A has a radius of 17, and so its diameter is 34. Since the circle in Quantity B has a larger diameter, its area is greater.

6. **(A)** Again, use Tactic 18: don't calculate either slope. Quickly, make a rough sketch of line ℓ, going through (1, 1) and (5, 2), and draw line m perpendicular to it. Line ℓ has a positive slope (it slopes upward), whereas line m has a negative slope. Quantity A is greater.

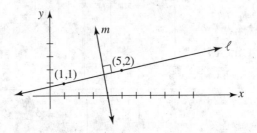

7. **(C)** Use Tactic 14: replace x, y, and z with three consecutive integers between 300 and 400—say, 318, 319, and 320, and just calculate to find the averages.

Quantity A: $\dfrac{318 + 320}{2} = \dfrac{638}{2} = 319$.

Quantity B: $\dfrac{318 + 319 + 320}{3} = \dfrac{957}{3} = 319$.

8. **(C)** Use Tactic 17. Could $y = 0$? In each equation, if $y = 0$, then $x = 5$, so *y can* equal 0. Eliminate (A) and (B), and either guess between (C) and (D) or try to continue. Must $y = 0$? Yes; when you have two equations in two variables, there is only one solution, so nothing else is possible.

9. **(A)** Use Tactic 15: choose an appropriate number. *The best number to use in percent problems is 100*, so assume that the regular price of the television in store *B* is 100 (the units don't matter). Since 10% of 100 is 10, the regular price in store *A* is $100 - 10 = 90$.

Quantity A: 10% of 90 is 9, so the sale price in store A is $90 - 9 = 81$.

Quantity B: 20% of 100 is 20, so the sale price in store B is $100 - 20 = 80$.

10. **(D)** Use Tactic 17. Could the area of $\triangle ABC = 3$? Since the height is 6, the area would be 3 only if the base were 1: $\frac{1}{2}(1)(6) = 3$. Could $BC = 1$? Sure (see the figure). Must the base be 1? Of course not. Neither quantity is *always* greater, and the two quantities are not *always* equal (D).

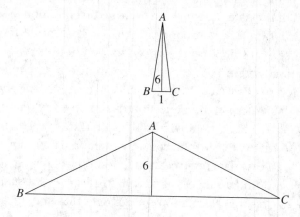

DATA INTERPRETATION QUESTIONS

Three of the 20 questions in each quantitative section of the GRE are data inter-pretation questions. As their name suggests, these questions are always based on the information that is presented in some form of a graph or a chart. Occasionally, the data are presented in a chart or table, but much more often, they are presented graphically. The most common types of graphs are line graphs, bar graphs, and circle graphs. It is also possible, but much less likely, that the data are presented in a *scatter plot*.

In each section, the data interpretation questions are three consecutive ques-tions, say Questions 14, 15, and 16, all of which refer to the same set of graphs or charts.

When the first data interpretation question appears, either the graphs will be on the left-hand side of the screen, and the question will be on the right-hand side, or the graphs will be at the top of the screen and the question will be below them. It is possible, but unlikely, that you will have to scroll down in order to see all of the data. After you answer the first question, a second ques-tion will replace it on the right-hand side (or the bottom) of the screen; the graphs, of course, will still be on the screen for you to refer to.

The tactics discussed in this section can be applied to any type of data, no matter how they are displayed. In the practice exercises at the end of the sec-tion, there are data interpretation questions based on every type of graph that could appear on the GRE. Carefully, read through the answer explanations for each exercise, so that you learn the best way to handle each type of graph.

Infrequently, an easy data interpretation question will require only that you read the graph and find a numerical fact that is displayed. Usually, however, you will have to do some calculation on the data that you are analyzing. In harder questions, you may be given hypothetical situations and asked to make inferences based on the information provided in the given graphs.

Most data interpretation questions are multiple-choice questions, but some could be multiple-answer or numeric entry questions. They are never quanti-tative comparisons.

The four questions that follow will be used to illustrate the tactics that you should use in answering data interpretation questions. Remember, however, that on the GRE there will always be exactly three questions that refer to a par-ticular graph or set of graphs.

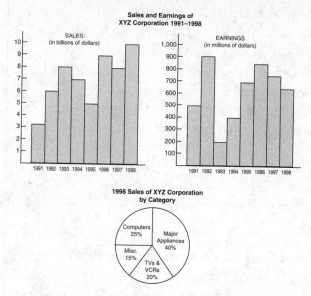

Sales and Earnings of
XYZ Corporation 1991–1998

1998 Sales of XYZ Corporation
by Category

1. What is the average (arithmetic mean) in billions of dollars of the sales of XYZ Corporation for the period 1991–1998?

Ⓐ 5.5   Ⓑ 6.0   Ⓒ 7.0   Ⓓ 8.0   Ⓔ 8.5

2. For which year was the percentage increase in earnings from the previous year the greatest?

Ⓐ 1992   Ⓑ 1993   Ⓒ 1994   Ⓓ 1995   Ⓔ 1996

3. Which of the following statements can be deduced from the data in the given charts and circle graph?

Indicate *all* such statements.

A̲ Sales of major appliances in 1998 exceeded total sales in 1991.

B̲ Earnings for the year in which earnings were greatest were more than sales for the year in which sales were lowest.

C̲ If in 1998, the sales of major appliances had been 10% less, and the sales of computers had been 10% greater, the sales of major appliances would have been less than the sales of computers.

4. What was the ratio of earnings to sales in 1993?

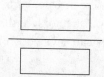

Tactic 19: First Read the Titles

When the first data interpretation question appears on the screen, do not even read it! Before you attempt to answer a data interpretation question, take 15 or 30 seconds to study the graphs. Try to get a general idea about the information that is being displayed.

Observe that the bar graphs on which Questions 1–4 are based present two different sets of data. The bar graph on the left-hand side provides information about the sales of XYZ Corporation, and the right-hand graph provides information about the corporation's earnings. Also, note that whereas sales are given in billions of dollars, earnings are given in millions of dollars. Finally, the circle graph gives a breakdown by category of the sales of XYZ Corporation for one particular year.

Tactic 20: Don't Confuse Percents and Numbers

Many students make mistakes on data interpretation questions because they don't distinguish between absolute numbers and percents. Although few students would look at the circle graph shown and think that XYZ Corporation sold 25 computers in 1998, many would mistakenly think that it sold 15% more major appliances than computers.

The problem is particularly serious when the questions involve percent increases or percent decreases. In Question 2 you are not asked for the year in which the increase in earnings from the previous year was the greatest. You are asked for the year in which the percent increase in earnings was the greatest. A quick glance at the right-hand graph reveals that the greatest increase occurred from 1991 to 1992 when earnings jumped by $400 million. However, when we solve this problem in the discussion of Tactic 21, you will see that Choice A is not the correct answer.

> **Note**
> Since many data interpretation questions involve percents, you should study facts 25 and 26 on page 106, and be sure to review the tactics for solving percent problems. In particular, always try to use the number 100 or 1000, since it is so easy to mentally calculate percents of powers of 10.

Tactic 21: Whenever Possible, Estimate

Even though you have an on-screen calculator when you take the GRE, you will not be expected to do complicated or lengthy calculations. Often, thinking and using some common sense can save you considerable time. For example, it may seem that in order to get the correct answer to Question 2, you have to calculate five different percents. In fact, you only need to do one calculation, and that one you can do in your head!

Just looking at the Earnings bar graph, it is clear that the only possible answers are 1992, 1994, and 1995, the three years in which there was a significant increase in earnings from the year before. From 1993 to 1994 expenditures doubled, from $200 million to $400 million—an increase of 100%. From 1991 to 1992 expenditures increased by $400 million (from $500 million to $900 million), but that is less than a 100% increase (we don't care how much less). From 1994 to 1995 expenditures increased by $300 million (from $400 million to $700 million); but again, this is less than a 100% increase. The answer is (C).

Tactic 22: Do Each Calculation Separately

As in all multiple-answer questions, Question 3 requires you to determine which of three separate statements is true. The key is to work with the statements individually.

To determine whether or not Statement A is true, look at both the Sales bar graph and the circle graph. In 1998, total sales were $10 billion, and sales of major appliances accounted for 40% of the total: 40% of $10 billion = $4 billion. This exceeds the $3 billion total sales figure for 1991, so Statement A is true.

In 1992, the year in which earnings were greatest, earnings were $900 million. In 1991, the year in which sales were lowest, sales were $3 billion, which is much greater than $900 million. Statement B is false.

In 1998, sales of major appliances were $4 billion. If they had been 10% less, they would have been $3.6 billion. That year, sales of computers were $2.5 billion (25% of $10 billion). If computer sales had increased by 10%, sales would have been $2.75 billion. Statement C is false.

The answer is A.

Tactic 23: Use Only the Information Given

You must base your answer to each question only on the information in the given charts and graphs. It is unlikely that you have any preconceived notion as to the sales of XYZ Corporation, but you might think that you know the population of the United States for a particular year or the percent of women currently in the workplace. If your knowledge contradicts any of the data presented in the graphs, ignore what you know. First of all, you may be mistaken; but more important, the data may refer to a different, unspecified location or year. In any event, *always* base your answers on the given data.

Tactic 24: **Always Use the Proper Units**

In answering Question 4, observe that earnings are given in millions, while sales are in billions. If you answer too quickly, you might say that in 1993 earnings were 200 and sales were 8, and conclude that the desired ratio is $\frac{200}{8} = \frac{25}{1}$.

You will avoid this mistake if you keep track of units: earnings were 200 *million dollars*, whereas sales were 8 *billion* dollars. The correct ratio is

$$\frac{200{,}000{,}000}{8{,}000{,}000{,}000} = \frac{2}{80} = \frac{1}{40}$$

Enter 1 or 2 in the box for the numerator and 40 or 80 in the box for the denominator, respectively.

Remember, fractions do not have to be reduced to lowest terms.

Tactic 25: **Be Sure That Your Answer Is Reasonable**

Before confirming your answer, take a second to be sure that it is reasonable. For example, in Question 4, from the logic of the situation, you should realize that earnings can't exceed sales. The desired ratio, therefore, must be less than 1. If you use the wrong units (see Tactic 24), your initial thought might be to enter $\frac{25}{1}$. By testing your answer for reasonableness, you will realize that you made a mistake.

Remember that if you don't know how to solve a problem, you should always guess. Before guessing, however, check to see if one or more of the choices are unreasonable. If so, eliminate them. For example, if you forget how to calculate a percent increase, you would have to guess at Question 2. But before guessing wildly, you should at least eliminate Choice B, since from 1992 to 1993 earnings decreased.

Tactic 26: **Try to Visualize the Answer**

Because graphs and tables present data in a form that enables you to readily see relationships and to make quick comparisons, you can often avoid doing any calculations. Whenever possible, use your eye instead of your computational skills.

For example, to answer Question 1, rather than reading the sales figures in the bar graph on the left for each of the eight years, adding them, and then dividing by 8, visualize the situation. Where could you draw a horizontal line across the graph so that there would be the same amount of gray area above the line as white area below it? Imagine a horizontal line drawn through the 7 on the vertical axis. The portions of the bars above the line for 1993 and 1996–1998 are just about exactly the same size as the white areas below the line for 1991, 1992, and 1994. The answer is (C).

PRACTICE QUESTIONS

On the GRE there will always be exactly two questions based on any set of graphs. Accordingly, in the tests in this book, there are two pairs of data interpretation questions, each pair referring to a different set of graphs.

Questions 1–2 refer to the following graphs.

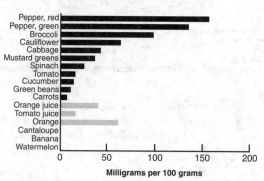

Source: U.S. Department of Agriculture.

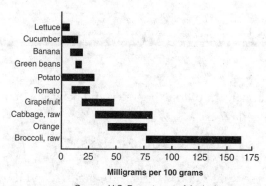

Source: U.S. Department of Agriculture.

1. What is the ratio of the amount of Vitamin C in 500 grams of orange to the amount of Vitamin C in 500 grams of orange juice?

   (A) 4:7   (B) 1:1   (C) 7:4   (D) 2:1   (E) 4:1

2. How many grams of tomato would you have to eat to be certain of getting more Vitamin C than you would get by eating 100 grams of raw broccoli?

   (A) 300   (B) 500   (C) 750   (D) 1200   (E) 1650

Questions 3–4 refer to the following graphs.

Percentage of students who reported spending time on homework
and watching television

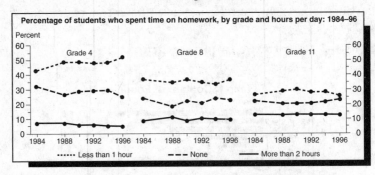

Percentage of students who spent time on homework, by grade and hours per day: 1984–96

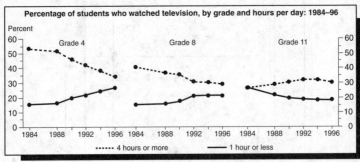

Percentage of students who watched television, by grade and hours per day: 1984–96

SOURCE: U.S. Department of Education.

3. In 1996, what percent of fourth-graders did between 1 and 2 hours of homework per day?

Ⓐ 5%   Ⓑ 15%   Ⓒ 25%   Ⓓ 40%   Ⓔ 55%

4. If in 1984 there were 2,000,000 eleventh-graders, and if between 1984 and 1996 the number of eleventh-graders increased by 10%, then approximately how many fewer eleventh-graders watched 1 hour or less of television in 1996 than in 1984?

Ⓐ 25,000   Ⓑ 50,000   Ⓒ 75,000   Ⓓ 100,000   Ⓔ 150,000

Questions 5–6 refer to the following graph.

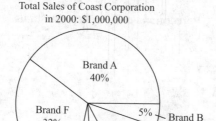

Total Sales of Coast Corporation
in 2000: $1,000,000

5. If the above circle graph were drawn to scale, then which of the following is closest to the difference in the degree measurements of the central
   angle of the sector representing Brand C and the central angle of the
   sector representing Brand D?

   (A) 5°
   (B) 12°
   (C) 18°
   (D) 25°
   (E) 43°

6. The total sales of Coast Corporation in 2005 were 50% higher than
   in 2000. If the dollar value of the sales of Brand A was 25% higher
   in 2005 than in 2000, then the sales of Brand A accounted for what
   percentage of total sales in 2005?

   (A) 20%
   (B) 25%
   (C) $33\frac{1}{3}$%
   (D) 40%
   (E) 50%

Questions 7–8 refer to the following graph.

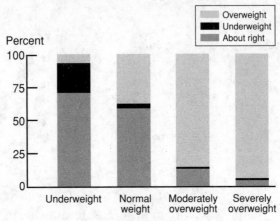

Perceptions of Body Weight Status

Perceived compared with actual weight status of adult females.

Source: U.S. Department of Agriculture.

7. To the nearest 5%, what percent of underweight adult females perceive themselves to be underweight?

 %

8. The members of which of the four groups had the least accurate perception of their body weight?

Ⓐ Underweight

Ⓑ Normal weight

Ⓒ Moderately overweight

Ⓓ Severely overweight

Ⓔ It cannot be determined from the information given in the graph.

Questions 9–10 refer to the following tables.

Residents of New York City pay both New York State and New York City tax. Residents of New York State who live and work outside of New York City pay only New York State tax.

Tax Rate Schedules for 1979											
New York State						**City of New York**					
Taxable Income						Taxable Income					
over	but not over		Amount of Tax			over	but not over		Amount of Tax		
$ 0	$1,000			2%	of taxable income	$ 0	$1,000			0.9%	of taxable income
1,000	3,000	$20 plus	3%	of excess over	$1,000	1,000	3,000	$ 9 plus	1.4%	of excess over	$1,000
3,000	5,000	80 plus	4%	of excess over	3,000	3,000	5,000	37 plus	1.8%	of excess over	3,000
5,000	7,000	160 plus	5%	of excess over	5,000	5,000	7,000	73 plus	2.0%	of excess over	5,000
7,000	9,000	260 plus	6%	of excess over	7,000	7,000	9,000	113 plus	2.3%	of excess over	7,000
9,000	11,000	380 plus	7%	of excess over	9,000	9,000	11,000	159 plus	2.5%	of excess over	9,000
11,000	13,000	520 plus	8%	of excess over	11,000	11,000	13,000	209 plus	2.7%	of excess over	11,000
13,000	15,000	680 plus	9%	of excess over	13,000	13,000	15,000	263 plus	2.9%	of excess over	13,000
15,000	17,000	860 plus	10%	of excess over	15,000	15,000	17,000	321 plus	3.1%	of excess over	15,000
17,000	19,000	1,060 plus	11%	of excess over	17,000	17,000	19,000	383 plus	3.3%	of excess over	17,000
19,000	21,000	1,280 plus	12%	of excess over	19,000	19,000	21,000	449 plus	3.5%	of excess over	19,000
21,000	23,000	1,520 plus	13%	of excess over	21,000	21,000	23,000	519 plus	3.8%	of excess over	21,000
23,000		1,780 plus	14%	of excess over	23,000	23,000	25,000	595 plus	4.0%	of excess over	23,000
						25,000		675 plus	4.3%	of excess over	25,000

9. In 1979 how much tax would a resident of New York State who lived and worked outside New York City have paid on a taxable income of $16,100?

   Ⓐ $34   Ⓑ $110   Ⓒ $352   Ⓓ $970   Ⓔ $1322

10. In 1979, how much more total tax would a resident of New York City who had a taxable income of $36,500 pay, compared to a resident of New York City who had a taxable income of $36,000?

   Ⓐ $21.50   Ⓑ $43   Ⓒ $70   Ⓓ $91.50   Ⓔ $183

Answer Key

1. **C**	3. **B**	5. **C**	7. **25**	9. **D**
2. **E**	4. **E**	6. **C**	8. **A**	10. **D**

Answer Explanations

1. **(C)** According to the graph on the left, there are approximately 70 milligrams of vitamin C in 100 grams of orange and 40 milligrams in the same amount of orange juice. This is a ratio of 70:40 = 7:4. Since the question refers to the same amount of orange and orange juice (500 grams), the ratio is unchanged.

2. **(E)** From the graph on the right, you can see that by eating 100 grams of raw broccoli, you could receive as much as 165 milligrams of vitamin C. Since 100 grams of tomato could have as little as 10 milligrams of vitamin C, you would have to eat 1650 grams of tomato to be sure of getting 165 milligrams of vitamin C.

3. **(B)** From the top graph, we see that among fourth-graders in 1996:

   25% did no homework;
   55% did less than 1 hour;
    5% did more than 2 hours.

   This accounts for 85% of the fourth-graders; the other 15% did between 1 and 2 hours of homework per day.

4. **(E)** In 1984, approximately 540,000 eleventh-graders watched television 1 hour or less per day (27% of 2,000,000). By 1996, the number of eleventh-graders had increased by 10% to 2,200,000, but the percent of them who watched television 1 hour or less per day decreased to about 18%: 18% of 2,200,000 is 396,000. This is a decrease of 144,000, or approximately 150,000.

5. **(C)** The central angle of the sector representing Brand C is 12% of 360°:

   $(0.12) \times 360° = 43.2°$

   The central angle of the sector representing Brand D is 7% of 360°.

   $(0.7) \times 360° = 25.2°$

   Finally, $43.2° - 25.2° = 18°$

   **Note this can be done in one step by noticing that the percentage difference between Brands C and D is 5% and 5% of 360 is $(0.05) \times 380 = 18$.

6. **(C)** Since total sales in 2000 were $1,000,000, in 2005 sales were $1,500,000 (a 50% increase).

   In 2000, sales of Brand A were $400,000 (40% of $1,000,000).

   In 2005 sales of Brand A were $500,000 (25% or $\frac{1}{4}$ more than in 2000).

   Finally, $500,000 is $\frac{1}{3}$ or $33\frac{1}{3}$% of $1,500,000.

7. **25** The bar representing underweight adult females who perceive themselves to be underweight extends from about 70% to about 95%, a range of approximately 25%.

8. **(A)** Almost all overweight females correctly considered themselves to be overweight; and more than half of all females of normal weight correctly considered themselves "about right." But nearly 70% of underweight adult females inaccurately considered themselves "about right."

9. **(D)** Referring only to the New York State table, we see that the amount of tax on a taxable income between $15,000 and $17,000 was $860 plus 10% of the excess over $15,000. Therefore, the tax on $16,100 is $860 plus 10% of $1,100: $860 + $110 = $970.

10. **(D)** According to the tables, each additional dollar of taxable income over $25,000 was subject to a New York State tax of 14% and a New York City tax of 4.3%, for a total tax of 18.3%. Therefore, an additional $500 in taxable income would have incurred an additional tax of $0.183 \times 500 = \$91.50$.

Test Yourself: Two Practice Tests

7

This chapter contains two full-length practice tests. The format of each test is identical to the computer-delivered GRE that you will take, in that it has exactly the same number of verbal, quantitative, and writing questions that an actual test has. Within each section, there is also exactly the same breakdown of question types. For example, in the verbal sections there are the same number of sentence completions and reading questions as on a real test; in each quantitative section there are two data interpretation questions and 7 or 8 quantitative comparisons; and there are two writing tasks in the analytical writing section. Directions will appear only the first time a given type of question is introduced in each section; after that, only the type of question will appear.

After taking the test, score your answers and evaluate your results. (Be sure also to read the answer explanations for questions you answered incorrectly and questions you answered correctly but found difficult.)

SIMULATE TEST CONDITIONS

To best simulate actual test conditions, find a quiet place to work. Have a stop watch or a clock handy so that you can keep perfect track of the time. Go through each section by answering the questions in the order in which they appear. If you don't know the answer to a question, guess (making an educated guess, if possible) and move on. Do not leave out any question. If you have some time left over at the end of a section, return to a question that you were unsure of. Knowing how much time you have for each section and how many questions there are, try to pace yourself so that you have time to finish each section in the time allowed. Do not spend too much time on any one question. Again, if you get stuck, just guess and go on to the next question.

ANSWER SHEET—MODEL TEST 1

Section 2—Verbal Reasoning

1 Ⓐ Ⓑ Ⓒ Ⓓ Ⓔ Ⓕ
2 Ⓐ Ⓑ Ⓒ Ⓓ Ⓔ Ⓕ
3 Ⓐ Ⓑ Ⓒ Ⓓ Ⓔ Ⓕ
4 Ⓐ Ⓑ Ⓒ Ⓓ Ⓔ Ⓕ
5 Ⓐ Ⓑ Ⓒ Ⓓ Ⓔ Ⓕ
6 Ⓐ Ⓑ Ⓒ Ⓓ Ⓔ
7 Ⓐ Ⓑ Ⓒ Ⓓ Ⓔ
8 Ⓐ Ⓑ Ⓒ Ⓓ Ⓔ

9 Ⓐ Ⓑ Ⓒ Ⓓ Ⓔ
10 Ⓐ Ⓑ Ⓒ Ⓓ Ⓔ
11 Ⓐ Ⓑ Ⓒ Ⓓ Ⓔ Ⓕ
12 Ⓐ Ⓑ Ⓒ Ⓓ Ⓔ Ⓕ
13 Ⓐ Ⓑ Ⓒ Ⓓ Ⓔ Ⓕ Ⓖ Ⓗ Ⓘ
14 Ⓐ Ⓑ Ⓒ Ⓓ Ⓔ Ⓕ
15 Ⓐ Ⓑ Ⓒ Ⓓ Ⓔ Ⓕ Ⓖ Ⓗ Ⓘ
16 Ⓐ Ⓑ Ⓒ Ⓓ Ⓔ

17 Ⓐ Ⓑ Ⓒ Ⓓ Ⓔ
18 Ⓐ Ⓑ Ⓒ Ⓓ Ⓔ
19 Ⓐ Ⓑ Ⓒ Ⓓ Ⓔ
20 Ⓐ Ⓑ Ⓒ Ⓓ

Section 3—Quantitative Ability

1 Ⓐ Ⓑ Ⓒ Ⓓ
2 Ⓐ Ⓑ Ⓒ Ⓓ
3 Ⓐ Ⓑ Ⓒ Ⓓ
4 Ⓐ Ⓑ Ⓒ Ⓓ
5 Ⓐ Ⓑ Ⓒ Ⓓ
6 Ⓐ Ⓑ Ⓒ Ⓓ
7 Ⓐ Ⓑ Ⓒ Ⓓ
8 Ⓐ Ⓑ Ⓒ Ⓓ
9 Ⓐ Ⓑ Ⓒ Ⓓ Ⓔ

10

11

12 Ⓐ Ⓑ Ⓒ Ⓓ Ⓔ
13 Ⓐ Ⓑ Ⓒ Ⓓ
14 Ⓐ Ⓑ Ⓒ Ⓓ Ⓔ
15 Ⓐ Ⓑ Ⓒ Ⓓ Ⓔ
16 Ⓐ Ⓑ Ⓒ
17 Ⓐ Ⓑ Ⓒ Ⓓ Ⓔ
18 Ⓐ Ⓑ Ⓒ
19 Ⓐ Ⓑ Ⓒ Ⓓ Ⓔ
20 Ⓐ Ⓑ Ⓒ Ⓓ Ⓔ

ANSWER SHEET—MODEL TEST 1

Section 4—Verbal Reasoning

1 Ⓐ Ⓑ Ⓒ Ⓓ Ⓔ Ⓕ
2 Ⓐ Ⓑ Ⓒ Ⓓ Ⓔ Ⓕ
3 Ⓐ Ⓑ Ⓒ Ⓓ Ⓔ Ⓕ
4 Ⓐ Ⓑ Ⓒ Ⓓ Ⓔ Ⓕ
5 Ⓐ Ⓑ Ⓒ Ⓓ Ⓔ Ⓕ
6 Ⓐ Ⓑ Ⓒ Ⓓ Ⓔ
7 Ⓐ Ⓑ Ⓒ Ⓓ Ⓔ
8 Ⓐ Ⓑ Ⓒ Ⓓ Ⓔ

9 Ⓐ Ⓑ Ⓒ Ⓓ Ⓔ
10 Ⓐ Ⓑ Ⓒ Ⓓ Ⓔ
11 Ⓐ Ⓑ Ⓒ Ⓓ Ⓔ
12 Ⓐ Ⓑ Ⓒ Ⓓ Ⓔ Ⓕ
13 Ⓐ Ⓑ Ⓒ Ⓓ Ⓔ Ⓕ
14 Ⓐ Ⓑ Ⓒ Ⓓ Ⓔ Ⓕ
15 Ⓐ Ⓑ Ⓒ Ⓓ Ⓔ Ⓕ
16 Ⓐ Ⓑ Ⓒ Ⓓ Ⓔ Ⓕ

17 Ⓐ Ⓑ Ⓒ Ⓓ Ⓔ
18 Ⓐ Ⓑ Ⓒ Ⓓ Ⓔ
19 Ⓐ Ⓑ Ⓒ Ⓓ Ⓔ
20 Ⓐ Ⓑ Ⓒ Ⓓ Ⓔ

Section 5—Quantitative Ability

1 Ⓐ Ⓑ Ⓒ Ⓓ
2 Ⓐ Ⓑ Ⓒ Ⓓ
3 Ⓐ Ⓑ Ⓒ Ⓓ
4 Ⓐ Ⓑ Ⓒ Ⓓ
5 Ⓐ Ⓑ Ⓒ Ⓓ
6 Ⓐ Ⓑ Ⓒ Ⓓ
7 Ⓐ Ⓑ Ⓒ Ⓓ
8 Ⓐ Ⓑ Ⓒ Ⓓ Ⓔ
9 Ⓐ Ⓑ Ⓒ Ⓓ Ⓔ

10 Ⓐ Ⓑ Ⓒ Ⓓ Ⓔ Ⓕ
11 Ⓐ Ⓑ Ⓒ Ⓓ Ⓔ
12 Ⓐ Ⓑ Ⓒ Ⓓ Ⓔ

13 ☐

14 Ⓐ Ⓑ Ⓒ Ⓓ Ⓔ

15 Ⓐ Ⓑ Ⓒ Ⓓ Ⓔ
16 Ⓐ Ⓑ Ⓒ Ⓓ Ⓔ

17 ☐

18 Ⓐ Ⓑ Ⓒ Ⓓ Ⓔ

19 ☐

20 Ⓐ Ⓑ Ⓒ Ⓓ Ⓔ

Model Test 1

SECTION 1—ANALYTICAL WRITING

Time —60 minutes
2 Writing Tasks

Task 1: Analyze an Issue

30 MINUTES

Directions: In 30 minutes, compose an essay on the topic below. You may not write on any other topic.

The topic is presented in a one- to two-sentence quotation commenting on an issue of general concern. Your essay may support, refute, or qualify the views expressed in the quotation. Whatever you write, however, must be relevant to the issue under discussion, and you must support your viewpoint with reasons and examples derived from your studies and/or experience.

If you will be taking the computer-delivered test, write your essay using a word-processing program with its spelling and grammar checker turned off. If you will be taking the paper-delivered test, write your essay on lined paper using a #2 pencil.

Faculty members from various institutions will evaluate your essay, judging it on the basis of your skill in the following areas:

- ☑ Coverage of each of the elements in the task instructions
- ☑ Analysis of the statement's implications
- ☑ Organization and articulation of your ideas
- ☑ Use of relevant examples and arguments to support your case
- ☑ Handling of the mechanics, grammar, and usage of standard written English

Issue Task

"We venerate loyalty—to our schools, employers, institutions, friends—as a virtue. Loyalty, however, can be at least as detrimental an influence as it can be a beneficial one."

Compose an essay that identifies how greatly you concur (or differ) with the statement provided, describing in detail the rationale for your argument. As you build and provide evidence for your argument, include examples that demonstrate circumstances in which the statement could (or could not) be valid. Be sure to explain the impact these examples have on your argument.

Task 2: Analyze an Argument

30 MINUTES

Directions: In 30 minutes, prepare a critical analysis of an argument expressed in a short paragraph, following the specific task instructions provided. You may not offer an analysis of any other argument.

Be sure to support your analysis with evidence (reasons and/or examples) but **do not present your personal views on the topic**. Your job is to analyze the elements of an argument, not to support or contradict that argument.

If you will be taking the computer-delivered test, write your essay using a word-processing program with its spelling and grammar checker turned off. If you will be taking the paper-delivered test, write your essay on lined paper using a #2 pencil.

Faculty members from various institutions will evaluate your essay, judging it on the basis of your skill in the following areas:

- ☑ Coverage of each of the elements in the task instructions
- ☑ Identification and assessment of the argument's main elements
- ☑ Organization and articulation of your thoughts
- ☑ Use of relevant examples and arguments to support your case
- ☑ Handling of the mechanics, grammar, and usage of standard written English

Argument Task

The following appeared in a petition presented by Classen University students to the school's administration.

"The purpose of higher education is to prepare students for the future, but Classen students are at a serious disadvantage in the competition for post-college employment due to the University's burdensome breadth requirements. Classen's job placement rate is substantially lower than placement rates of many top-ranked schools. Classen students would be more attractive to employers if they had more time to take advanced courses in their specialty, rather than being required to spend fifteen percent of their time at Classen taking courses outside of their subject area. We demand, therefore, that the University abandon or drastically cut back on its breadth requirements."

Compose an essay that identifies the questions that must be answered before reaching a conclusion about whether the prediction and the argument supporting it make sense. In writing your essay you should describe the impact that the answers to these questions would have on your assessment of the prediction.

SECTION 2—VERBAL REASONING

Time —30 minutes
20 Questions

> **Directions:** For each of the following sentences, select the **two** answers of the six choices given that, when substituted in the sentence, both logically complete the sentence as a whole **and** create sentences that are equivalent to one another in meaning.

Questions 1–5

1. It seems ironic that the preacher's sermon, intended to reconcile the feuding brothers, served only to _____ them further.

   [A] intimidate

   [B] estrange

   [C] avenge

   [D] arbitrate

   [E] commiserate

   [F] disaffect

2. In recent years, the British seem to have become _____ Americanisms: even members of Parliament fall into baseball metaphors, although very few Britons understand the rules of the game.

   [A] critical of

   [B] indifferent to

   [C] enamored of

   [D] aggrieved by

   [E] tired of

   [F] hooked on

3. The general was such a contrarian that, at times when it appeared that the only sane action would be to _____, he became all the more determined to fight to the bitter end.

    A capitulate

    B remonstrate

    C exonerate

    D submit

    E repeat

    F resist

4. Some critics of the administration maintained that it was _____ of the White House to describe its proposal to reduce welfare payments to single parents as "tough love": the plan, in their opinion, while decidedly tough, was not loving at all.

    A witty

    B accurate

    C disingenuous

    D diplomatic

    E mendacious

    F salient

5. A perfectionist is someone who feels _____ when he makes even the most minuscule of errors.

    A vexation

    B hostility

    C indifference

    D chagrin

    E condemnation

    F bafflement

<u>Directions:</u> The next questions are based on the content of the following passage. Read the passage and then determine the best answer choice for each question. Base your choice on what this passage *states* directly or *implies*, not on any information you may have gained elsewhere.

For each of Questions 6–10, select *one* answer choice unless otherwise instructed.

Questions 6–10 are based on the following passage.

There can be no doubt that the emergence of the Negro writer in the post-war period stemmed, in part, from the fact that he was inclined to exploit the opportunity to write about himself. It was more than that, how-
Line ever. The movement that has variously been called the "Harlem Renais-
(5) sance," the "Black Renaissance," and the "New Negro Movement" was essentially a part of the growing interest of American literary circles in the immediate and pressing social and economic problems. This growing inter-est coincided with two developments in Negro life that fostered the growth of the New Negro Movement. These two factors, the keener realization of
(10) injustice and the improvement of the capacity for expression, produced a crop of Negro writers who constituted the "Harlem Renaissance."

The literature of the Harlem Renaissance was, for the most part, the work of a race-conscious group. Through poetry, prose, and song, the writers cried out against social and economic wrongs. They protested against seg-
(15) regation and lynching. They demanded higher wages, shorter hours, and better conditions of work. They stood for full social equality and first-class citizenship. The new vision of social and economic freedom that they had did not force them to embrace the several foreign ideologies that sought to sink their roots in some American groups during the period.

(20) The writers of the Harlem Renaissance, bitter and cynical as some of them were, gave little attention to the propaganda of the socialists and com-munists. The editors of the *Messenger* ventured the opinion that the New Negro was the "product of the same world-wide forces that have brought into being the great liberal and radical movements that are now seizing the
(25) reins of power in all the civilized countries of the world." Such forces may have produced the New Negro, but the more articulate of the group did not resort to advocating the type of political action that would have subverted American constitutional government. Indeed, the writers of the Harlem Ren-aissance were not so much revolting against the system as they were
(30) protesting its inefficient operation. In this approach they proved as charac-teristically American as any writers of the period.

6. Which of the following is implied by the statement that the writers of the Harlem Renaissance "were not so much revolting against the system as they were protesting its inefficient operation" (lines 29–30)?

Ⓐ Black writers played only a minor part in protesting the injustices of the period.

Ⓑ Left to itself, the system was certain to function efficiently.

Ⓒ Black writers in general were not opposed to the system as such.

Ⓓ In order for the system to operate efficiently, blacks must seize the reins of power in America.

Ⓔ Black writers were too caught up in aesthetic questions to identify the true nature of the conflict.

7. With which of the following statements regarding the writers of the Harlem Renaissance would the author most likely agree?

Ⓐ They needed to increase their commitment to international solidarity.

Ⓑ Their awareness of oppression caused them to reject American society.

Ⓒ They transformed their increasing social and political consciousness into art.

Ⓓ Their art suffered from their overinvolvement in political crusades.

Ⓔ Their detachment from their subject matter lessened the impact of their work.

8. The information in the passage suggests that the author is most likely

Ⓐ a historian concerned with presenting socially conscious black writers of the period as loyal Americans

Ⓑ a literary critic who questions the conclusions of historians about the Harlem Renaissance

Ⓒ an educator involved in fostering creative writing programs for minority youths

Ⓓ a black writer of fiction bent on discovering new facts about his literary roots

Ⓔ a researcher with questions about the validity of his sources

9. Which of the following statements best describes the organization of lines 20–28) of the passage ("The writers . . . constitutional government")?

   (A) The author cites an authority supporting a previous statement and then qualifies the original statement to clarify its implications.

   (B) The author makes a point, quotes an observation apparently contradicting that point, and then resolves the inconsistency by limiting the application of his original statement.

   (C) The author makes a negative comment and then modifies it by rephrasing his original comment to eliminate its negative connotations.

   (D) The author summarizes an argument, quotes an observation in support of that argument, and then advances an alternative hypothesis to explain potential contradictions in that argument.

   (E) The author states a thesis, quotes a statement relevant to that thesis, and then presents two cases, both of which corroborate the point of the original statement.

10. The passage supplies information for answering which of the following questions?

   (A) What factors led to the stylistic improvement in the literary work of black writers in the post-war period?

   (B) Who were the leading exponents of protest literature during the Harlem Renaissance?

   (C) Why were the writers of the Harlem Renaissance in rebellion against foreign ideological systems?

   (D) How did black writers in the post-war period define the literary tradition to which they belonged?

   (E) With what specific socioeconomic causes did the black writers of the post-war period associate themselves?

Directions: Each of the following sentences or groups of sentences contains one, two, or three blanks. These blanks signify that a word or set of words has been left out. Below each sentence are columns of words or sets of words. For each blank, pick the *one* word or set of words from the corresponding column that best completes the text.

11. Like the theory of evolution, the big-bang model of the universe's formation has undergone modification and (i) _____, but it has (ii) _____ all serious challenges.

Blank (i)	Blank (ii)
Ⓐ refinement	Ⓓ resisted
Ⓑ evaluation	Ⓔ acknowledged
Ⓒ refutation	Ⓕ misdirected

12. A rigid and conventional thinker, he lacked both the (i) _____ to adapt to changing conditions and the (ii) _____ to be innovative.

Blank (i)	Blank (ii)
Ⓐ volatility	Ⓓ creativity
Ⓑ refinement	Ⓔ discipline
Ⓒ flexibility	Ⓕ impertinence

13. Perugino's initial fame brought him considerable wealth and prestige, if not (i) _____ glory: some years after having been lauded as the most famous artist in Italy, his reputation having suffered a decline, Perugino was (ii) _____ by the acerbic Michelangelo as an artistic (iii) _____.

Blank (i)	Blank (ii)	Blank (iii)
Ⓐ mundane	Ⓓ derided	Ⓖ virtuoso
Ⓑ enduring	Ⓔ claimed	Ⓗ bumpkin
Ⓒ ephemeral	Ⓕ emulated	Ⓘ precursor

14. Rather than portraying Joseph II as a radical reformer whose reign was strikingly (i) _____, the play *Amadeus* depicts him as (ii) _____ thinker, too wedded to orthodox theories of musical composition to appreciate an artist of Mozart's genius.

Blank (i)	Blank (ii)
Ⓐ dissipated	Ⓓ a revolutionary
Ⓑ enlightened	Ⓔ an iconoclastic
Ⓒ placid	Ⓕ a doctrinaire

15. Some critics maintain that fixed poetic forms, which require a specific number of lines and syllables, invite and may even (i) _____ wordiness; when no such (ii) _____ exists, the poet can easily spot and (iii) _____ superfluities.

Blank (i)	Blank (ii)	Blank (iii)
Ⓐ curtail	Ⓓ constraint	Ⓖ foster
Ⓑ encourage	Ⓔ lyricism	Ⓗ brandish
Ⓒ juxtapose	Ⓕ subterfuge	Ⓘ eliminate

16. A university training enables a graduate to see things as they are, to go right to the point, to disentangle a twisted _____ of thought.

Ⓐ line
Ⓑ lack
Ⓒ mass
Ⓓ plethora
Ⓔ skein

Directions: The next questions are based on the content of the following passage. Read the passage and then determine the best answer choice for each question. Base your choice on what this passage *states directly* or *implies*, not on any information you may have gained elsewhere.

For each of Questions 17–20, select one answer choice unless otherwise instructed.

Questions 17–19 are based on the following passage.

As the works of dozens of women writers have been rescued from what E. P. Thompson calls "the enormous condescension of posterity," and con-sidered in relation to each other, the lost continent of the female tradition
Line has risen like Atlantis from the sea of English literature. It is now becoming
(5) clear that, contrary to Mill's theory, women have had a literature of their own all along. The woman novelist, according to Vineta Colby, was "really neither single nor anomalous," but she was also more than a "register and spokesman for her age." She was part of a tradition that had its origins before her age, and has carried on through our own.
(10) Many literary historians have begun to reinterpret and revise the study of women writers. Ellen Moers sees women's literature as an international movement, "apart from, but hardly subordinate to the mainstream: an under-current, rapid and powerful. This 'movement' began in the late eighteenth century, was multinational, and produced some of the greatest literary works
(15) of two centuries, as well as most of the lucrative pot-boilers." Patricia Meyer Spacks, in *The Female Imagination*, finds that "for readily discernible histori-cal reasons women have characteristically concerned themselves with mat-ters more or less peripheral to male concerns, or at least slightly skewed from them. The differences between traditional female preoccupations and
(20) roles and male ones make a difference in female writing." Many other critics are beginning to agree that when we look at women writers collectively we can see an imaginative continuum, the recurrence of certain patterns, themes, problems, and images from generation to generation.

17. In the second paragraph of the passage the author's attitude toward the literary historians cited can best be described as one of

(A) irony
(B) ambivalence
(C) disparagement
(D) receptiveness
(E) awe

**Directions:** For the following question, consider each of the choices separately and select _all_ that apply.

18. The passage supplies information for answering which of the following questions?

    A Does the author believe the female literary tradition to be richer in depth than its masculine counterpart?

    B Which literary historian maintains that the female literary tradition transcends national boundaries?

    C Does Moers share Mill's concern over the ephemeral nature of female literary renown?

    D What patterns, themes, images, and problems recur sufficiently in the work of women writers to belong to the female imaginative continuum?

    E Did Mill acknowledge the existence of a separate female literary tradition?

19. In the first paragraph, the author fails to make use of which of the following literary techniques?

    Ⓐ extended metaphor
    Ⓑ enumeration and classification
    Ⓒ classical allusion
    Ⓓ direct quotation
    Ⓔ comparison and contrast

Directions: For the following question, consider each of the choices separately and select *all* that apply.

Question 20 is based on the following passage.

In 1798 Thomas Malthus wrote "An Essay on the Principle of Population," in which he postulates that food supply never can keep pace with the rate of increase in human population. Increase the supply of food, Malthus argues, and population will rise to meet this increase. This, he asserts, means that the race between population and resources can never be truly won by any sociocultural system. Therefore, some measure of social inequality is inevitable in all human societies.

20. Which of the following statements, if true, would tend to undermine Malthus's argument?

[A] The rate of population increase has begun to decline in Northern Europe, but the food supply has not diminished.

[B] In many nations, the increase in human population has far outstripped the food-producing capacity.

[C] Human population growth may be limited by the use of contraception.

[D] For many ethnic and religious groups, artificial control of conception is morally unacceptable.

SECTION 3—QUANTITATIVE ABILITY

Time —35 minutes
20 Questions

Directions: In each of Questions 1–8, there are two quantities—Quantity A and Quantity B. You are to compare those quantities, taking into consideration any additional information given. The correct answer to such a question is

Ⓐ Quantity A is greater.
Ⓑ Quantity B is greater.
Ⓒ The two quantities are equal.
Ⓓ It is impossible to determine which quantity is greater.

Note: The given information, if any, is always centered above the two quantities. In any question, if a symbol or letter appears more than once, it represents the same thing each time.

1.

Quantity A	Quantity B
The sum of the positive divisors of 19	The product of the positive divisors of 19

2.

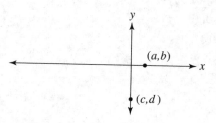

Quantity A	Quantity B
$a + b$	$c + d$

3.

Quantity A	Quantity B
$5(r + t)$	$5r + t$

4.

Quantity A	Quantity B
The average (arithmetic mean) of all the positive multiples of 5 less than 26	The average (arithmetic mean) of all the positive multiples of 7 less than 26

5.

c and d are positive

$$\frac{1}{c} = 1 + \frac{1}{d}$$

Quantity A	Quantity B
c	d

6.

A number is a *palindrome* if it reads exactly the same from right to left as it does from left to right. For example, 959 and 24742 are palindromes.

Quantity A	Quantity B
The probability that a three-digit number chosen at random is a palindrome	$\dfrac{1}{10}$

7.

Jack and Jill each bought the same TV set
using a 10% off coupon. Jack's cashier took
10% off the price and then added 8.5% sales
tax. Jill's cashier first added the tax and then
took 10% off the total price.

Quantity A	Quantity B
The amount	The amount
Jack paid	Jill paid

8.

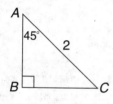
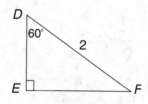

Quantity A	Quantity B
The area of	The area of
△ABC	△DEF

Directions: Questions 9–20 have three different formats. Unless a question has its own directions that specifically state otherwise, each question has five answer choices, exactly one of which is correct.

9. If it is now June, what month will it be 400 months from now?

   (A) January
   (B) April
   (C) June
   (D) October
   (E) December

Directions: The answer to the following question is a fraction. Enter the numerator in the upper box and the denominator in the lower box.

10. If $\frac{5}{9}$ of the members of the school chorus are boys, what is the ratio of girls to boys in the chorus?

$$\frac{\boxed{}}{\boxed{}}$$

Directions: For the following question, enter your answer in the box.

11. What is the volume of a cube whose total surface area is 54?

$$6x^2 = 54$$
$$x^2 = 9$$
$$x = 3$$

$$V = x^3$$
$$= 27$$

$$\boxed{27}$$

12. If A is 25 kilometers east of B, which is 12 kilometers south of C, which is 9 kilometers west of D, how far is it, in kilometers, from A to D?

Ⓐ 20

Ⓑ $5\sqrt{34}$

Ⓒ $5\sqrt{41}$

Ⓓ $10\sqrt{13}$

Ⓔ 71

Directions: For the following question, consider each of the choices separately and select *all* that apply.

13. The math scores of all the students who took the SAT in January 2015 formed a normal distribution with a mean of 500 and a standard deviation of 100. Which of the following statements must be true?

Indicate *all* such statements.

A Fewer than 4% of the students scored above 700.

B More students scored between 500 and 550 than between 600 and 700.

C More than 80% of the students scored above 400.

D If a student is chosen at random, the probability that his or her math score is less than 600 is greater than $\frac{4}{5}$.

Questions 14–16 refer to the following graphs.

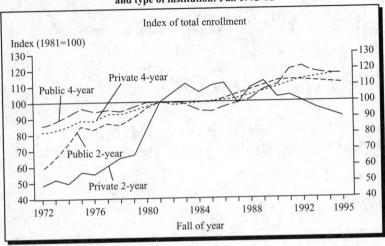

Total enrollment in higher education institutions, by control and type of institution: Fall 1972–95

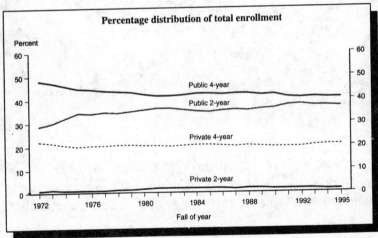

SOURCE: U.S. Department of Education.

14. In 1995 the number of students enrolled in public institutions of higher education was approximately how many times the number of students enrolled in private institutions of higher education?

   Ⓐ 2

   Ⓑ 2.5

   Ⓒ 3

   Ⓓ 3.5

   Ⓔ 4

15. If the total enrollment in institutions of higher education in 1972 was 5,000,000, approximately how many students were enrolled in private 4-year institutions in 1995?

    (A) 1,000,000
    (B) 1,100,000
    (C) 1,250,000
    (D) 1,500,000
    (E) 1,650,000

> **Directions:** For the following question, consider each of the choices separately and select *all* that apply.

16. Based on the information in the two graphs, which of the following statements are true?

Indicate *all* such statements.

    [A] The number of students enrolled in private 2-year institutions was approximately the same in 1981 and 1987.
    [B] The percentage of students enrolled in private 2-year institutions was approximately the same in 1981 and 1987.
    [C] From 1972 to 1995, the percentage of college students who were enrolled in 2-year institutions rose by more than 25%.

17. Which of the following expresses the area of a circle in terms of C, its circumference?

(A) $\dfrac{C^2}{4\pi}$

(B) $\dfrac{C^2}{2\pi}$

(C) $\dfrac{\sqrt{C}}{2\pi}$

(D) $\dfrac{C\pi}{4}$

(E) $\dfrac{C}{4\pi}$

Directions: For the following question, consider each of the choices separately and select *all* that apply.

18. If the lengths of two of the sides of a triangle are 9 and 10, which of the following could be the length of the third side?

Indicate *all* such lengths.

[A] 1

[B] 11

[C] 21

19. If p pencils cost c cents at the same rate, how many pencils can be bought for d dollars?

    (A) cdp

    (B) $100\ cdp$

    (C) $\dfrac{dp}{100c}$

    (D) $\dfrac{100cd}{p}$

    (E) $\dfrac{100dp}{c}$

20. If 3 children are chosen at random from a group of 5 boys and 5 girls, what is the probability that the 3 children chosen are all boys?

    (A) $\dfrac{1}{15}$

    (B) $\dfrac{1}{12}$

    (C) $\dfrac{1}{5}$

    (D) $\dfrac{1}{3}$

    (E) $\dfrac{1}{2}$

SECTION 4—VERBAL REASONING

Time —30 minutes
20 Questions

Directions: For each of the following sentences, select the **two** answers of the six choices given that, when substituted in the sentence, both logically complete the sentence as a whole **and** create sentences that are equivalent to one another in meaning.

Questions 1–5

1. From papayas in Hawaii to canola in Canada, the spread of pollen or seeds from genetically engineered plants is evolving from _____ scientific worry into a significant practical problem.

   A a toxic

   B a theoretical

   C a radical

   D an abstract

   E an overblown

   F an analogous

2. When facts are _____ and data hard to come by, even scientists occasionally throw aside the professional pretense of objectivity and tear into each other with shameless appeals to authority and arguments that are unabashedly ad hominem.

   A elusive

   B established

   C demonstrable

   D ineluctable

   E uncertain

   F relevant

3. You may wonder how the expert on fossil remains is able to trace descent through teeth, which seem _____ pegs upon which to hang whole ancestries.

   A novel

   B reliable

   C flimsy

   D specious

   E inadequate

   F academic

4. During the military takeover, the constitution was not abolished, but some of its clauses temporarily were _____ as the armed forces took over the administration.

   A suspended

   B notarized

   C under construction

   D put in abeyance

   E left undefined

   F widely promulgated

5. Woolf _____ conventional notions of truth: in her words, one cannot receive from any lecture "a nugget of pure truth" to wrap up between the pages of one's notebook and keep on the mantelpiece forever.

   A anticipates

   B articulates

   C makes light of

   D mocks

   E pays heed to

   F puts up with

Directions: The next questions are based on the content of the following passage. Read the passage and then determine the best answer choice for each question. Base your choice on what the passages *state directly* or *imply*, not on any information you may have gained elsewhere.

For each of Questions 6–10, select one answer choice unless otherwise instructed.

Question 6 is based on the following passage.

Contemporary literary scholars have come to discard the once-conventional image of English theater in the time of Elizabeth I as an anomalous literary wonder, a sudden flowering of creativity rooted not in the dramatic traditions of England but the theater of ancient Greece and Rome. While acknowledging the debt of the Elizabethan playwrights to the dramas of Terence, Plautus, and Seneca, and to the *Poetics* of Aristotle, the majority of theater scholars today regard Elizabethan drama as being organically related to traditional English drama, above all to the medieval cycles of mystery and morality plays.

Directions: For the following question, consider each of the choices separately and select *all* that apply.

6. Which of the following is NOT consistent with the passage above?

 A Theater historians have significantly altered their views of the origins of Elizabethan drama.

 B England had a native dramatic tradition antedating the Elizabethan era.

 C Although Elizabethan drama deals with English subject matter, it derives its form and method solely from classical Greek and Roman theater.

 D Once envisioned as a historical and literary anomaly, Elizabethan drama now is interpreted as part of a historical continuum.

 E Modern theater scholars view Elizabethan drama as a direct offshoot of Greek and Roman dramatic traditions.

Question 7 is based on the following passage.

The current trend toward specialization in nearly all occupational groups is exactly the opposite of what the educational system needs. World problems today are so diverse, complex, and interrelated that only the generalist stands a chance of understanding the broad picture. Unless our schools stress a truly broad, liberal education, the world will crumble around us as we each expertly perform our own narrow function.

7. Which of the following, if true, would weaken the conclusion drawn above?

(A) Many of the world's problems can be solved only by highly specialized experts working on specific problems.

(B) Relatively few generalists are needed to coordinate the work of the many specialists.

(C) Specialization does not necessarily entail losing the ability to see the broad picture.

(D) Increasingly complex problems require a growing level of technical expertise that can be acquired only through specialization.

(E) Even the traditional liberal education is becoming more highly specialized today.

Questions 8–10 are based on the following passage.

Given the persistent and intransigent nature of the American race system, which proved quite impervious to black attacks, Du Bois in his speeches and writings moved from one proposed solution to another, and the salience
Line of various parts of his philosophy changed as his perceptions of the needs
(5) and strategies of black America shifted over time. Aloof and autonomous in his personality, Du Bois did not hesitate to depart markedly from whatever was the current mainstream of black thinking when he perceived that the conventional wisdom being enunciated by black spokesmen was proving inadequate to the task of advancing the race. His willingness to seek differ-
(10) ent solutions often placed him well in advance of his contemporaries, and this, combined with a strong-willed, even arrogant personality made his career as a black leader essentially a series of stormy conflicts.

Thus Du Bois first achieved his role as a major black leader in the controversy that arose over the program of Booker T. Washington, the most promi-
(15) nent and influential black leader at the opening of the twentieth century. Amidst the wave of lynchings, disfranchisement, and segregation laws,

Washington, seeking the good will of powerful whites, taught blacks not to protest against discrimination, but to elevate themselves through industrial education, hard work, and property accumulation; then, they would ulti-
(20) mately obtain recognition of their citizenship rights. At first Du Bois agreed with this gradualist strategy, but in 1903 with the publication of his most influential book, *Souls of Black Folk*, he became the chief leader of the onslaught against Washington that polarized the black community into two wings—the "conservative" supporters of Washington and his "radical"
(25) critics.

8. Which of the following statements about W. E. B. Du Bois does the passage best support?

    (A) He sacrificed the proven strategies of earlier black leaders to his craving for political novelty.

    (B) Preferring conflict to harmony, he followed a disruptive course that alienated him from the bulk of his followers.

    (C) He proved unable to change with the times in mounting fresh attacks against white racism.

    (D) He relied on the fundamental benevolence of the white population for the eventual success of his movement.

    (E) Once an adherent of Washington's policies, he ultimately lost patience with them for their inefficacy.

9. It can be inferred that, in comparison with W. E. B. Du Bois, Booker T. Washington could not be described as

    (A) submissive to the majority

    (B) concerned with financial success

    (C) versatile in adopting strategies

    (D) traditional in preaching industry

    (E) respectful of authority

10. The author's attitude towards Du Bois's departure from conventional black policies can best be described as

    (A) skeptical

    (B) derisive

    (C) shocked

    (D) approving

    (E) resigned

**Directions:** Each of the following sentences or groups of sentences contains one, two, or three blanks. These blanks signify that a word or set of words has been left out. Below each sentence are columns of words or sets of words. For each blank, pick the one word or set of words from the corresponding column that best completes the text.

11. As any visitor to Claude Monet's final home at Giverny can _____, Japanese prints were the artist's passion: his home overflows with works by Hiroshige, Utamaro, and other Japanese masters.

Ⓐ	portray
Ⓑ	attest
Ⓒ	contest
Ⓓ	rectify
Ⓔ	invalidate

12. Breaking with established musical traditions, Stravinsky was (i) _____ composer whose (ii) _____ works infuriated the traditionalists of his day.

Blank (i)		Blank (ii)	
Ⓐ	a derivative	Ⓓ	hackneyed
Ⓑ	an uncontroversial	Ⓔ	heterodox
Ⓒ	an iconoclastic	Ⓕ	euphonious

13. While the disease is in (i) _____ state it is almost impossible to determine its existence by (ii) _____.

Blank (i)
Ⓐ a critical
Ⓑ a latent
Ⓒ an overt

Blank (ii)
Ⓓ postulate
Ⓔ methodology
Ⓕ observation

14. The paleontologist's (i) _____ orthodoxy meant that the evidence he had so painstakingly gathered would inevitably be (ii) _____ by his more conventional colleagues.

Blank (i)
Ⓐ break with
Ⓑ dependence on
Ⓒ reputation for

Blank (ii)
Ⓓ considered
Ⓔ contested
Ⓕ classified

15. An essential purpose of the criminal justice system is to enable purgation to take place; that is, to provide a (i) _____ by which a community expresses its collective (ii) _____ the transgression of the criminal.

Blank (i)
Ⓐ catharsis
Ⓑ disclaimer
Ⓒ prototype

Blank (ii)
Ⓓ empathy with
Ⓔ indifference to
Ⓕ outrage at

16. In a classic example of scholarly (i) _____, the poet and scholar A. E. Housman once assailed a German rival for relying on manuscripts "as a drunkard relies on lampposts, for support rather than (ii) _____."

Blank (i)
Ⓐ productivity
Ⓑ invective
Ⓒ detachment

Blank (ii)
Ⓓ stability
Ⓔ illumination
Ⓕ credibility

Directions: The next questions are based on the content of the following passage. Read the passage and then determine the best answer choice for each question. Base your choice on what the passages *state directly* or *imply*, not on any information you may have gained elsewhere.

For each of Questions 17–20, select one answer choice unless otherwise instructed.

Question 17 is based on the following passage.

Exquisitely adapted for life in one of Earth's harshest environments, polar bears can survive for 20 years or more on the Arctic Circle's glacial ice. At home in a waste where temperatures reach minus 50 degrees Fahrenheit,
Line these largest members of the bear family are a striking example of natural
(5) selection at work. With two layers of fur over a subcutaneous layer of blubber, polar bears are well adapted to resist heat loss. Their broad, snowshoe-like paws and sharp, curved claws enable them to traverse the ice with ease. Formidable hunters, these monarchs of the icy waste even possess the capacity to scent prey from a distance of 20 miles.

17. In the context of the passage's final sentence, "capacity" most nearly means

  (A) faculty
  (B) stature
  (C) dimensions
  (D) spaciousness
  (E) intelligence

Questions 18–20 are based on the following passage.

At night, schools of prey and predators are almost always spectacularly illuminated by the bioluminescence produced by the microscopic and larger plankton. The reason for the ubiquitous production of light by the microor-

Line ganisms of the sea remains obscure, and suggested explanations are
(5) controversial. It has been suggested that light is a kind of inadvertent by-product of life in transparent organisms. It has also been hypothesized that the emission of light on disturbance is advantageous to the plankton in making the predators of the plankton conspicuous to their predators! Unquestionably, it does act this way. Indeed, some fisheries base the detec-
(10) tion of their prey on the bioluminescence that the fish excite. It is difficult, however, to defend the thesis that this effect was the direct factor in the original development of bioluminescence, since the effect was of no advan-tage to the individual microorganism that first developed it. Perhaps the luminescence of a microorganism also discourages attack by light-avoiding
(15) predators and is of initial survival benefit to the individual. As it then becomes general in the population, the effect of revealing plankton preda-tors to their predators would also become important.

18. The primary topic of the passage is which of the following?

  (A) The origin of bioluminescence in plankton predators
  (B) The disadvantages of bioluminescence in microorganisms
  (C) The varieties of marine bioluminescent life forms
  (D) Symbiotic relationships between predators and their prey
  (E) Hypotheses on the causes of bioluminescence in plankton

19. The author mentions the activities of fisheries in order to provide an example of

  (A) how ubiquitous the phenomenon of bioluminescence is coastally
  (B) how predators do make use of bioluminescence in locating their prey
  (C) how human intervention imperils bioluminescent microorganisms
  (D) how nocturnal fishing expeditions are becoming more and more widespread
  (E) how limited bioluminescence is as a source of light for human use

20. The passage provides an answer to which of the following questions?

  (A) What is the explanation for the phenomenon of bioluminescence in marine life?
  (B) Does the phenomenon of plankton bioluminescence have any practical applications?
  (C) Why do only certain specimens of marine life exhibit the phenomenon of bioluminescence?
  (D) How does underwater bioluminescence differ from atmospheric bioluminescence?
  (E) What are the steps that take place as an individual microorganism becomes bioluminescent?

SECTION 5—QUANTITATIVE ABILITY

Time —35 minutes
20 Questions

Directions: In each of Questions 1–7, there are two quantities—Quantity A and Quantity B. You are to compare those quantities, taking into consideration any additional information given. The correct answer to such a question is

Ⓐ Quantity A is greater.
Ⓑ Quantity B is greater.
Ⓒ The two quantities are equal.
Ⓓ It is impossible to determine which quantity is greater.

Note: The given information, if any, is always centered above the two quantities. In any question, if a symbol or letter appears more than once, it represents the same thing each time.

1.

Quantity A	Quantity B
$\dfrac{1}{\pi}$	$\dfrac{1}{\sqrt{10}}$

2.

n is an odd positive integer
$700 < n < 800$

Quantity A	Quantity B
The number of the prime factors of n	The number of prime factors of $2n$

3.

$$x < y$$

Quantity A	Quantity B
The average (arithmetic mean) of x and y	The average (arithmetic mean) of x, y, and y

4.

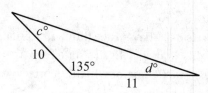

Quantity A	Quantity B
c	d

5.

$$0 < a < b$$

Quantity A	Quantity B
$a\%$ of $\dfrac{1}{b}$	$b\%$ of $\dfrac{1}{a}$

6.

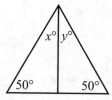

Quantity A	Quantity B
x	y

7.

Line *l* passes through
$$\left(-\sqrt{2},\sqrt{3}\right) \text{ and } \left(\sqrt{2},-\sqrt{3}\right).$$

Line *m* is perpendicular to line *l*.

Quantity A	Quantity B
The slope of *l*	The slope of *m*

Directions: Questions 8–20 have three different formats. Unless a question has its own directions that specifically state otherwise, each question has five answer choices, exactly one of which is correct.

8. In the figure below, what is the average (arithmetic mean) of the measures of the five angles?

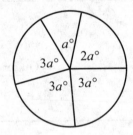

Ⓐ 36
Ⓑ 45
Ⓒ 60
Ⓓ 72
Ⓔ 90

9. Camille's average on her 6 math tests this marking period is 75. Fortunately for Camille, her teacher drops each student's lowest grade, and this raises her average to 85. What was her lowest grade?

Ⓐ 20
Ⓑ 25
Ⓒ 30
Ⓓ 40
Ⓔ 50

Directions: For Questions 10 and 11, consider each of the choices separately and select *all* that apply.

10. If the area of a rectangle is 40, which of the following could be the perimeter of the rectangle?

    Indicate *all* such areas.

    A 20

    B 40

    C 200

    D 400

    E 2,000

    F 4,000

11. Which of the following is an equation of a line that is perpendicular to the line whose equation is $2x + 3y = 4$?

    Indicate *all* such equations.

    A $3x + 2y = 4$

    B $3x - 2y = 4$

    C $2x - 3y = 4$

    D $4 - 3x = -2y$

    E $4 + 2x = 3y$

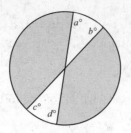

12. In the figure above, the diameter of the circle is 20 and the area of the shaded region is 80π. What is the value of $a + b + c + d$?

Ⓐ 144
Ⓑ 216
Ⓒ 240
Ⓓ 270
Ⓔ 288

Directions: The answer to the following question is a fraction. Enter the numerator in the upper box and the denominator in the lower box.

13. Each integer from 1 to 50 whose units digit is a 3 is written on a slip of paper and placed in a box. If two slips of paper are drawn at random, what is the probability that both the numbers picked are prime?

Questions 14–16 refer to the following graph.

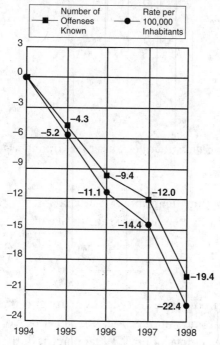

Motor Vehicle Theft in the U.S.
Percent Change from 1994 to 1998

Source: U.S. Department of Justice,
Federal Bureau of Investigation.

14. If 1,000,000 vehicles were stolen in 1994, how many were stolen in 1996?

  (A) 889,000
  (B) 906,000
  (C) 940,000
  (D) 1,094,000
  (E) 1,100,000

15. By what percent did the number of vehicles stolen decrease from 1997 to 1998?

  (A) 7.4%
  (B) 8.0%
  (C) 8.4%
  (D) 12.0%
  (E) 19.4%

16. To the nearest percent, by what percent did the population of the United States increase from 1994 to 1998?

Ⓐ 1%

Ⓑ 2%

Ⓒ 3%

Ⓓ 4%

Ⓔ 5%

Directions: For the following question enter your answer in the box.

17. If the average (arithmetic mean) of v, w, x, y, and z is 12.3, and the average of v and w is 45.6, what is the average of x, y, and z?

18. At Tyler High School, there are twice as many girls than boys on the yearbook staff. At one staff meeting, the percentage of girls attending was twice the percentage of boys. What percent of those attending were boys?

Ⓐ 20

Ⓑ 25

Ⓒ 30

Ⓓ 33

Ⓔ 50

Directions: For the following question enter your answer in the box.

19. If four boys can shovel a driveway in two hours, how many minutes would it take five boys to shovel that driveway? (Assume that each boy works at the same rate.)

$$\boxed{}\ \text{minutes}$$

20. In 1950 Roberto was four times as old as Juan. In 1955, Roberto was three times as old as Juan. How old was Roberto when Juan was born?

Ⓐ 5
Ⓑ 10
Ⓒ 20
Ⓓ 30
Ⓔ 40

MODEL TEST 1 ANSWER KEY

Section 1—Analytical Writing

The Analytical Writing sections are scored holistically, in accordance with the following guidelines.

First, estimate your score on the Issue Essay by using the following rubric.

	Argument	Support	Structure	Fluency	Conventions
6	Presents a clear and perceptive argument that responds to the specific task instructions	Provides strong reasoning and/or examples to fully support its thesis	Is focused and very well organized and has logical and skillful transitions between ideas	Expresses ideas clearly and fluently, with sophisticated word choice and varied sentence structure	Displays impressive command of the grammar, usage, and mechanics of standard written English
5	Presents a clear and thoughtful argument that responds to the specific task instructions	Provides logical reasoning and/or appropriate examples to support its thesis	Is focused and well organized and has logical transitions between ideas	Expresses ideas effectively, with appropriate word choice and varied sentence structure	Displays solid command of the grammar, usage, and mechanics of standard written English
4	Presents a clear argument that adequately responds to the specific task instructions	Provides adequate reasoning and/or examples to support its thesis	Is reasonably well focused and organized	Expresses ideas effectively, with appropriate word choice	Displays command of the grammar, usage, and mechanics of standard written English
3	Presents an argument that is somewhat unclear or that does not clearly respond to the specific task instructions	Makes unsupported claims or has limited relevant examples to support its thesis	Is minimally focused and/or organized	Is somewhat unclear due to incorrect word choice or sentence structure	Includes infrequent major or frequent minor errors in grammar, usage, and/or mechanics
2	Presents an argument that is unclear or fails to address the specific task instructions	Provides nearly no relevant examples or reasons to support its thesis	Is unfocused and/or disorganized	Is unclear due to frequent incorrect word choice or sentence structure	Includes significant errors in grammar, usage, and/or mechanics that render its meaning unclear
1	Presents an argument that demonstrates severely limited understanding of the topic	Provides little to no examples or reasoning that are related to the assigned topic	Is extremely disorganized or excessively short	Is very unclear due to pervasive incorrect word choice or sentence structure	Includes pervasive errors in grammar, usage, and/or mechanics that render it indecipherable
0	Addresses a topic other than the one assigned, is written in a language other than English, is nothing more than the words in the topic and/or task instructions, is nothing more than random characters, is not legible.				

As you examine the rubric you will notice that all of the scores below four are shaded gray. The reason for this is that ETS, the maker of the GRE, states that essays scoring below four display **one or more** of the characteristics listed in the shaded area. In other words, if your essay displays even one characteristic listed in the shaded area, that low score will determine your overall score. If all of your essay's characteristics are found in the boxes above the shaded area, your score should be the average of the five scores (for argument, support, structure, fluency, and writing conventions).

Scoring the Issue Essay

Using the Issue Essay rubric, check the box in each column that best describes your work. If each of the boxes you have checked is above the shaded area, add those five scores together and calculate their average.

Example:

Argument	4
Support	4
Structure	5
Fluency	4
Conventions	4
Total	21

The average is 4.2, rounded down to a likely score of 4.

If, however, **any** of your scores fall into the shaded area of the rubric, the lowest score marked will be your final score.

Next, estimate your score on the Argument Essay by using the following rubric.

	Argument	Support	Structure	Fluency	Conventions
6	Pinpoints the elements of the argument at issue and evaluates them with great insight	Provides detailed and persuasive support for its main points	Expresses ideas clearly and is very well organized, with logical and clear transitions between ideas	Expresses ideas clearly and fluently, with sophisticated word choice and varied sentence structure	Displays impressive command of the grammar, usage, and mechanics of standard written English
5	Pinpoints the elements of the argument at issue and evaluates them thoughtfully	Provides thoughtful and persuasive support for its main points	Expresses ideas clearly and is well organized, with suitable transitions between ideas	Expresses ideas effectively, with appropriate word choice and varied sentence structure	Displays solid command of the grammar, usage, and mechanics of standard written English
4	Identifies the elements of the argument at issue and evaluates them, but may include less relevant points	Provides sufficient, though possibly uneven, support for its main points	Expresses ideas reasonably clearly and is organized, but transitions between ideas are inadequate or absent	Expresses ideas effectively, with appropriate word choice	Displays command of the grammar, usage, and mechanics of standard written English
3	Fails to distinguish or evaluate the most relevant elements of the argument, though some relevant aspects may be discussed	Provides support that is sometimes irrelevant to its main points	Expresses ideas with little depth and/or organizes them illogically	Is somewhat unclear due to incorrect word choice or sentence structure	Includes infrequent major or frequent minor errors in grammar, usage, and/or mechanics
2	Fails to evaluate the argument using logic, but may provide the writer's personal views on the topic	Provides support that is generally irrelevant to its main points	Expresses ideas inadequately and organizes them illogically	Is unclear due to frequent incorrect word choice or sentence structure	Includes significant errors in grammar, usage, and/or mechanics that render its meaning unclear
1	Fails to demonstrate any grasp of the argument at issue	Provides no support for its main points	Is extremely disorganized or excessively short	Is very unclear due to pervasive incorrect word choice or sentence structure	Includes pervasive errors in grammar, usage, and/or mechanics that render it indecipherable
0	Addresses a topic other than the one assigned, is written in a language other than English, is nothing more than the words in the topic and/or task instructions, is nothing more than random characters, is not legible.				

Scoring the Argument Essay

Using the Argument Essay rubric, check the box in each column that best describes your work. If each of the boxes you have checked is above the shaded area, add those five scores together and calculate their average.

Calculating Your Overall Score

To determine your overall Analytical Writing score, add the scores for both essays (Issue and Argument) together and divide by 2. The overall score is given in half-point increments, so you should round up to the nearest half point when calculating this score. As an example, if you earn a score of 5 on the Issue Essay and a score of 4.5 on the Argument Essay, your overall Analytical Writing score will be 4.75, rounded up to 5.

Section 2—Verbal Reasoning

1. **B, F**	6. **C**	11. **A, D**	16. **E**
2. **C, F**	7. **C**	12. **C, D**	17. **D**
3. **A, D**	8. **A**	13. **B, D, H**	18. **B, E**
4. **C, E**	9. **B**	14. **B, F**	19. **B**
5. **A, D**	10. **E**	15. **B, D, I**	20. **A, C**

Section 3—Quantitative Ability

1. **A**	6. **C**	11. **27**	16. **A, B, C**
2. **A**	7. **C**	12. **A**	17. **A**
3. **D**	8. **A**	13. **A, B, C, D**	18. **B**
4. **A**	9. **D**	14. **D**	19. **E**
5. **B**	10. **4/5**	15. **E**	20. **B**

Section 4—Verbal Reasoning

1. **B, D**	6. **C, E**	11. **B**	16. **B, E**
2. **A, E**	7. **E**	12. **C, E**	17. **A**
3. **C, E**	8. **E**	11. **B, F**	18. **E**
4. **A, D**	9. **C**	14. **A, E**	19. **B**
5. **C, D**	10. **D**	15. **A, F**	20. **B**

Section 5—Quantitative Ability

1. **A**	6. **D**	11. **B, D**	16. **D**
2. **B**	7. **B**	12. **E**	17. **−9.9**
3. **B**	8. **D**	13. **3/5**	18. **A**
4. **A**	9. **B**	14. **B**	19. **96**
5. **B**	10. **B, C, D, E, F**	15. **C**	20. **D**

ANSWER EXPLANATIONS

Section 1—Analytical Writing

PROMPT #1

"We venerate loyalty—to our schools, employers, institutions, friends—as a virtue. Loyalty, however, can be at least as detrimental an influence as it can be a beneficial one."

Compose an essay that identifies how greatly you concur (or differ) with the statement provided, describing in detail the rationale for your argument. As you build and provide evidence for your argument, include examples that demonstrate circumstances in which the statement could (or could not) be valid. Be sure to explain the impact these examples have on your argument.

SCORE 6 ISSUE ESSAY

In press coverage of the epidemic of violence in some urban area like Chicago, there is frequent reference to a "Code of the Streets" that counsels residents, "don't be a snitch." Law enforcement officials decry this loyalty as misguided and ultimately harmful, agreeing with those who argue that loyalty "can be as detrimental an influence as it can be a beneficial one." They are, of course, correct. Loyalty can be detrimental. Their error comes in failing to recognize that this observation applies to themselves as much as it does to the members of the community whose silence they criticize.

The "Code of the Streets" has an analog in the "Blue Code of Silence" that places loyalty to fellow police officers, right or wrong, above the interests and safety of the community. News stories abound with examples of incidents in which police officers describe events one way, only to have their stories contradicted by video evidence. It is not surprising that police officers who have behaved improperly might stretch the truth, or even concoct stories out of whole cloth, in order to avoid being held responsible for their actions. The actions of lawless police officers are a serious problem, but the loyalty of their brothers and sisters in blue is even more detrimental. The inability of the majority of law-abiding police officers to speak out against the misconduct of so-called bad apples undermines the legitimacy of law enforcement as a whole in many of the communities that need its help the most.

Though the "Code of the Streets" and the "Blue Code of Silence" demonstrate that loyalty can be detrimental, the solution is not to embrace disloyalty. It is, after all, difficult to imagine how valuing betrayal could lead to better consequences. The problem in these instances is not really loyalty per se, but a mistaken understanding of community. So long as police officers and members of the public feel that they are not members of one community, their loyalty will be misguided, focused on protecting their own (be they police officers or civilians) from threatening and lawless others (be they police officers or civilians). If we could break down this divide and accept that we are all members of the same community, our loyalty to that greater community would shatter both the "Code of the Streets" and the "Blue Code of Silence." When we learn to embrace our historic enemies as members of a single human community, rather than combatants from warring factions, loyalty will be a venerable virtue. Until that distant day, it will remain, as often as not, an abhorrent vice.

APPLYING THE RUBRIC

Argument	6
Support	6
Structure	5
Fluency	6
Conventions	6
Total	29

The average is 5.8, rounded up to a likely score of 6.

ARGUMENT The essay presents a clear and perceptive argument that loyalty can be as detrimental as it is beneficial. The writer does an especially good job of presenting instances in which loyalty can have consequences that fracture communities and threaten public safety. The argument is also quite sophisticated, proposing an additional factor that may cause loyalty to be harmful and suggesting that, absent that reason, loyalty might be a virtue.

SUPPORT The essay includes two strong examples of groups whose loyalty to their members does great harm to the larger community, though it focuses more deeply on a single group—police officers.

STRUCTURE The essay is well focused and does not stray from the task of proving its thesis. Its organization is clear, and transitions between paragraphs are logical.

FLUENCY The essay displays sophisticated and powerful vocabulary. Its sentence structure is varied throughout.

CONVENTIONS Outstanding. The essay includes no noticeable errors in grammar, usage, or mechanics.

SCORE 5 ISSUE ESSAY

Loyalty is considered a virtue in our culture, but where is the breaking point at which one decides that loyalty does more damage than good? Can loyalty be more detrimental than beneficial?

Recently, professional football player Colin Kaepernick came under fire from patriotic Americans for his decision to "take a knee" when the national anthem is played at NFL football games. Kaepernick cited the number of African-Americans killed by police as one of many examples that the United States does not value the lives of its African-American citizens. He questioned why he should demonstrate loyalty or patriotism to a country that treats some people as second-class citizens. Across America—especially on the internet—pundits, both professional and amateur, weighed in on the subject. Even among those who claimed to agree with his motivation, many took the stance that he was somehow still protesting in the "wrong" way. "He can be upset," they said, "but he's being unpatriotic, disrespectful, disloyal." Loyalty to country was seen as a virtue, and criticism, as un-American.

Interestingly enough, loyalty as a fan also became part of the debate around Kaepernick's protest. If Kaep's team, the 49ers, is "your" team, are you allowed to break ranks with them in protest of his disloyalty? Does that make you a fair-weather fan? Is it fair to the other players on the team if you, as a fan, jump ship because one player is doing something you don't like? Of course, if loyalty is hierarchical, loyalty to country must outweigh loyalty to team. The order of importance is God, country, family, and football (though some fans disagree with the order of the last two). This is the American way.

Or is it?

If a hallmark of American citizenship is freedom, is loyalty in the form of patriotism a virtue? Loyalty to our country, especially post-September 11, can be seen as a form of collective strength. But does blind allegiance to an ideal vision of what America could and should be require that we turn a blind eye to what America is? In other areas of life, we know that pretending that toxic behavior and attitudes are acceptable simply because we are loyal to those who engage in such behaviors cannot only be harmful to ourselves, but also to the perpetrator. Why isn't the same true of loyalty to country? If your child's school was harming children, would you allow it to continue out of loyalty to the institution? Or would your loyalty to the school end the second someone's child was in danger? Why, then, do we not have the same standard for the ill treatment of adults? If an institution is abusive, must we remain loyal despite the abuse because it could be worse elsewhere? Is "America—love it or leave it" the only acceptable response when our country fails to live up to its lofty goals? Is this a standard of loyalty we would live by when it came to any subject other than patriotism?

The answer to this question is clearly no. Loyalty can clearly be detrimental in so many circumstances. We would never stand by and let a teacher abuse students because of loyalty to the school. When Penn State was found guilty of covering up an employee's sexual abuse of children, the public was rightly horrified at the behavior of the individuals who knew about the abuse but remained silent as a result of their loyalty to the institution. Similarly, we do not expect victims of spousal abuse to remain with their abusers. We counsel them that their abusers do not deserve their loyalty, and that they must inform the authorities of their situation. We encourage them to testify against their abusers in court so that justice can be done. It is high time that we recognize that our country too can do wrong, and that it must be corrected and held accountable when it does so. Turning a blind eye to our nation's failures out of loyalty is harmful and wrong. When we see our nation behave unjustly, we should "take a knee" with Colin Kaepernick.

APPLYING THE RUBRIC

Argument	5
Support	6
Structure	5
Fluency	5
Conventions	5
Total	26

The average is 5.2, rounded down to a likely score of 5.

ARGUMENT   The essay presents a clear and thoughtful argument that loyalty, even loyalty to country, can be detrimental.

SUPPORT   The essay includes compelling examples that provide strong support for its thesis. The Penn State example is especially persuasive, demonstrating terrible consequences of remaining silent out of loyalty to an institution. The Colin Kaepernick example is engaging, while also demonstrating the complexity of choosing to criticize one's country.

STRUCTURE   The essay is generally well focused, though the Kaepernick/49ers story at the start runs a bit long, slightly obscuring the essay's thesis. Transitions between paragraphs are logical, and the thesis becomes crystal clear in the final paragraph.

FLUENCY   The ideas in the essay are clear, and its vocabulary use is appropriate and effective, if a bit colloquial at times. Sentence structure is varied.

CONVENTIONS   The essay demonstrates solid command of the grammar, usage, and mechanics of standard written English. There are few, if any, obvious errors.

SCORE 4 ISSUE ESSAY

I agree that loyalty is detrimental, especially blind loyalty. Loyalty should be conditional upon the other institution or person meeting certain standards. Loyalty is a virtue in that it is indicative of the faith that one person holds in the other. However, this faith should not be given without inhibition, but should be given on a merit basis.

I think blindly pledging loyalty to a political party can be detrimental. In pre-World War II Germany, Adolf Hitler's militant Nazism and charisma gained him a large following—large enough to place him at the head of Germany at the time and allowed him to lead the country to commit atrocious horrors upon Jews, homosexuals, the disabled, and other minorities not fitting into his vision for what Germany should look like. If people weren't so ready to blindly pledge loyalty but were more autonomous, perhaps concentration camps wouldn't have occurred, or perhaps not on the scale that they did.

Blindly giving loyalty to an employer can also have a dangerous outcome. Say, for example, there is a factory and the company running the factory knows of safety hazards, but doesn't report them to avoid the cost of fixing the safety hazards. The employees see the safety hazards too, but don't report them because of company loyalty. Worst-case scenario is that there could be a serious injury or worse if the danger goes unreported. This would all be because people were too loyal to go over the company's head and do something about the concern.

There are nevertheless benefits of loyalty. It can be good to feel as if you can rely on someone, and likewise for them be able to rely on you. It makes things predictable in that you know how things will run, assuming conditions run their course. However, that is not how it always is—sometimes events blindside us. For these unplanned and uncharacteristic events, loyalty not only can be, but should be, questioned. If a large enough and horrendous enough crime were committed by my friend, I definitely would question my loyalty to him or her. If I, however, decided instead to protect my guilty friend and hide this person, not only would I be obstructing justice (a crime unto itself) but I would also be hurting society by allowing a crime like this to go unpunished.

Loyalty is detrimental when it is blind and its continual questioning is beneficial to society.

```
┌──────────────────────────────────────────┐
│           APPLYING THE RUBRIC             │
│                                           │
│           Argument         5              │
│           Support          5              │
│           Structure        4              │
│           Fluency          4              │
│           Conventions      4              │
│                          ─────            │
│           Total           22              │
│                                           │
│  The average is 4.4, rounded down to a    │
│  likely score of 4.                       │
└──────────────────────────────────────────┘
```

ARGUMENT   The essay presents a clear argument that misplaced loyalty can lead to devastating consequences. Though the analysis could be more sophisticated, it admits some complexity to the issue, granting that loyalty can provide comfort and reliability.

SUPPORT   The essay includes two strong examples that provide strong support for its thesis. The third, contrasting example (the friend who commits a crime) is a bit muddled and underdeveloped.

STRUCTURE   The essay is reasonably well focused, though the transitions between paragraphs are abrupt. The conclusion is too short, and fails to adequately summarize the essay's arguments.

FLUENCY   The ideas in the essay are clear, and its vocabulary use is generally appropriate, with a few distracting errors. The essay sounds awkward in places, but it is generally effective despite this.

CONVENTIONS   The essay demonstrates adequate command of the grammar, usage, and mechanics of standard written English. There are several minor errors, but not enough to obscure meaning.

PROMPT #2

The following appeared in a petition presented by Classen University students to the school's administration.

"The purpose of higher education is to prepare students for the future, but Classen students are at a serious disadvantage in the competition for post-college employment due to the University's burdensome breadth requirements. Classen's job placement rate is substantially lower than placement rates of many top-ranked schools. Classen students would be more attractive to employers if they had more time to take advanced courses in their specialty, rather than being required to spend fifteen percent of their time at Classen taking courses outside of their subject area. We demand, therefore, that the University abandon or drastically cut back on its breadth requirements."

Compose an essay that identifies the questions that must be answered before reaching a conclusion about whether the prediction and the argument supporting it make sense. In writing your essay you should describe the impact that the answers to these questions would have on your assessment of the prediction.

SCORE 6 ARGUMENT ESSAY

As the technology sector of the US economy has burgeoned, the argument for increasing education in STEM subjects (Science, Technology, Engineering, and Math) and consequently decreasing time spent on the Humanities has grown popular. The students at Classen University echo this argument (that education should focus on preparing workers to meet the needs of the economy) in their petition demanding a decrease in the University's breadth requirements. Though their argument is a popular one, it is grounded on a number of questionable premises that bear further examination.

The Classen students start off on the wrong foot by making the unsubstantiated claim that "the purpose of higher education is to prepare students for the future." But is preparing students for the future truly higher education's sole purpose? If Classen's petitioning students are wrong about the answer to this question, their claim is flawed from the outset. While it is unarguable that preparing students for the future is *a* purpose of higher education, there is no consensus on a single, overriding purpose. Additionally, even if the students are correct that preparation for the future is the primary purpose of higher education, their focus on career preparation and employment is based on a very narrow view of that future. During the course of their lives these students will be citizens, community members, parents, and friends, not just workers. Perhaps a university education could and should prepare students for these roles as well.

Granting, for the sake of argument, that the purpose of higher education is to prepare students for employment, the students' case for decreasing breadth requirements is still weak because it fails to answer several additional important questions. The first among these is whether the top-ranked schools to which they compare Classen actually have fewer breadth requirements than Classen. If they do not, there is little reason to believe that decreasing Classen's breadth requirements will, in fact, improve the job placement rate of its graduates.

Another crucial question that remains unanswered by the students' petition is whether the demographics of the student body at Classen are similar to those of the student population of the top-ranked schools to which Classen is being compared. Are Classen's students as academically strong as those at these unnamed schools? Does Classen have a greater number of students for whom English is not their first language? Does Classen serve a student population with an unusually high percentage of students who are the first in their families to attend college? Do the students at the top-ranked schools come from wealthier families than do those at Classen? Because these factors all influence student success both in school and after graduation, answering the aforementioned questions is essential to evaluating whether Classen is indeed doing a poor job of preparing its graduates for employment.

Finally, even if the students are correct that Classen is doing a poor job of preparing its graduates for employment, it is not clear that decreasing breadth requirements is the solution to this problem. The students assert that graduates "would be more attractive to employers if they had more time to take advanced courses in their specialty," but they offer no evidence for this claim. What are employers looking for in potential employees? This question must be answered before an effective solution to the low job placement rate of Classen graduates can be crafted. If employers want to hire graduates with work experience, the solution may lie in a summer internship program. If they want employees with substantial advanced coursework in their specialty, the students' proposal may be sound. But if they require employees with a broad range of knowledge and the ability to attack problems flexibly and take different perspectives into account, more, rather than fewer, breadth requirements may be in order.

APPLYING THE RUBRIC	
Argument	6
Support	6
Structure	6
Fluency	6
Conventions	6
Total	30
The average is 6.	

ARGUMENT   The essay successfully pinpoints a number of problematic elements in the provided argument, explaining how its strength depends on the answers to several unanswered questions. The essay explicitly and thoughtfully describes the impact that these answers would have on the reliability of the students' argument.

SUPPORT The essay provides detailed and persuasive support for its main points, introducing a number of rival factors that might explain the poor job placement rate of Classen University students.

STRUCTURE The essay is well organized, expressing its position clearly and in a logical progression. Transitions between ideas are well executed, and the essay builds to a strong conclusion, suggesting that the best solution to Classen students' poor employment results may be the inverse of the plan advocated by the students.

FLUENCY The essay reads smoothly and uses sophisticated vocabulary. Sentence structure is varied.

CONVENTIONS Outstanding. The essay includes no noticeable errors in grammar, usage, or mechanics.

SCORE 5 ARGUMENT ESSAY

Classen students have presented a demand to their administration that breadth requirements be either drastically reduced or eliminated. In considering this demand, the University must evaluate two main points. First, do the students demonstrate an understanding of the purpose of a University education and know where breadth requirements fit into this purpose? Second, do the students make a clear case that the disadvantages that they attribute to the breadth requirements are in fact the sole reason for their lower job placement rates, and upon what do they base this case? Only with this information can the administration make a reasoned decision about whether to reduce or remove breadth requirements.

The students' assertion that "higher education is to prepare students for the future" is arguably a given. However, their definition of preparation for the future seems to be limited solely to job placement. However, while the university has a role to play in preparing for the work force, career preparation is not the sole purpose of higher education, and I suspect that nowhere in the mission statement of the school does the University state that its main focus is job training. Scholarship is important, both to individuals and to the greater culture. If it were not so, we could simply send students to various trade schools. While undergraduates should have opportunities to take advanced coursework in their fields, as the students assert, graduate school is the place to focus more intently on a particular field. While it may be frustrating for students to wade through other requirements before getting to that point, their frustration does not warrant scrapping the entire system.

Furthermore, the students have not considered or addressed the reality that breadth requirements are often instituted by schools because of feedback from employers—directly and culturally—that students are not socially or intellectually prepared for adult life. In other words, just as colleges admit students not solely on the basis of one skill or talent, so too do employers want employees with life skills, critical thinking skills, and other analytical skills in addition to the practical skills in their fields. Breadth requirements actually prepare students to do advanced work in their fields, by helping them learn how to learn, learn how to negotiate subjects with which they may be less familiar, and learn how to work with others whose strengths and interests lie in different areas than their own.

Even assuming that it's true that job placement is the sole goal of a college education (it isn't), the students have shown no evidence that Classen's lower job placement rate is the fault of breadth requirements. They are vague about "many top-ranked schools," without citing those schools, their course requirements, or their job placement rates. Perhaps the schools are top-ranked for other reasons, and those reasons are part of employers' motivation for hiring the students. In fact, what if some of the schools with higher job placement rates actually have more broad requirements? What if the very reason their graduates do better in the workforce is precisely because they experienced varied subject matter, teaching styles, and skills practice than do students who focus more exclusively within their own fields?

The simplicity of the Classen students' demands is actually exemplary of precisely why they need breadth requirements in the first place. Correlation is not causation (science classes teach that); their thesis is flawed (English classes teach that); the market needs varied skills (economics classes teach that); and their lack of understanding of greater socio-cultural influences on education means they are not considering the full extent of their demands (sociology classes teach that). Their demand statement is Freshman 101 level; they cannot use it to argue against the existence of Freshman 101 when they haven't passed the course yet.

APPLYING THE RUBRIC

Argument	5
Support	6
Structure	5
Fluency	5
Conventions	5
Total	26

The average is 5.2, rounded down to a likely score of 5.

ARGUMENT The essay successfully pinpoints two questions that must be answered in order to assess the argument in the Classen students' petition, and it evaluates their impact thoughtfully. If there is any weakness here it is only that the essay focuses somewhat more on the views of its author than it does on how different answers to the questions posed might lead to different conclusions about the strength of the students' argument.

SUPPORT The essay provides detailed support for its main points, especially in its exploration of other factors that might be driving Classen students' low job placement rate.

STRUCTURE The essay is well organized, with effective transitions between ideas. It could, however, be a bit clearer about which of the two questions it is addressing in each paragraph.

FLUENCY The essay expresses its ideas clearly, using appropriate vocabulary and varied sentence structure.

CONVENTIONS The essay displays solid command of the conventions of standard written English.

SCORE 4 ARGUMENT ESSAY

I disagree with this petition. I think that a well-rounded education is a beneficial one. When young, it is difficult to know what you want to do and having a requirement to take different classes in different disciplines can be good to allow students the opportunity to explore different disciplines. Furthermore, there are many factors at play for job placement and classes don't necessarily play that large of a part in that measurement. In addition, job placement isn't necessarily the only reason that people go to college.

First of all, taking different classes allows students to explore different topics of interest, all while fulfilling degree requirements. This is very beneficial to ensure that they truly do like what they plan to study for four years in the process of obtaining a bachelor's degree. Also, it is only fifteen percent of the classes, and that is less than a fifth so it is a very small percentage of classes that this petition is referring to.

Moreover, there are plenty of factors at play for getting jobs—classes just being one. We need to ask what factors are important in getting jobs to understand whether decreasing breadth requirements can help. There is a saying that "life isn't *what* you know but *who* you know," and there is definitely some truth to that. Networking is a very important skill that can't be learned in a class but is more taught through life. Furthermore, the petition is comparing job placements to other, larger and more prestigious universities where there are presumably larger budgets, more resources, and a more competitive student pool. All of these factors can change job placement rates. For example, larger and more prestigious companies might tend to prefer to higher from more prestigious universities. Though it's obviously not impossible to get positions at these firms, attending certain universities can arguably provide "leg up" to some individual students applying for certain positions at certain firms, thus affecting the job placement rates.

In addition, the petition begins with, "[the] purpose of higher education is to prepare students for the future," and I completely agree with this statement, but I measure future preparation in a different way. Preparedness for the future can't be quantitately measured through percentage of students landing jobs, or even how long these students last at these companies. Instead, being prepared for the future has more of a qualitative essence—it can't be measured through numerical evidence but is demonstrated by happiness and ability for students to meet any problems and struggles that life throws at them.

APPLYING THE RUBRIC

Argument	4
Support	5
Structure	4
Fluency	4
Conventions	4
Total	21

The average is 4.2, rounded down to a likely score of 4.

ARGUMENT The essay identifies and evaluates many elements of the argument provided, but its examination of questions that would need to be answered in order to evaluate the argument could be better. Only one of the essay's four paragraphs examines these questions, which are the main requirement of the task instructions.

SUPPORT The essay provides thoughtful and persuasive support for its main points.

STRUCTURE The essay expresses its ideas clearly and has adequate transitions (using words like "first of all" and "in addition." Despite this, the order in which the essay presents its points appears somewhat random, and the conclusion is abrupt.

FLUENCY The essay generally uses vocabulary effectively to express its ideas.

CONVENTIONS The essay generally displays command of the conventions of standard written English, despite the presence of a few minor errors that do not interfere with meaning.

Section 2—Verbal Reasoning

1. **(B)(F)** The verbs *estrange* and *disaffect* are synonyms; both mean to make unfriendly or to distance. The two words can be used interchangeably here. Think of "estranged couples" getting a divorce and "disaffected voters" leaving a political party.

2. **(C)(F)** Baseball metaphors are examples of Americanisms, American idioms enthusiastically embraced by Britons despite the British lack of understanding of the original context of these terms. The Britons are *hooked on* or *enamored of* them.

3. **(A)(D)** A contrarian is someone who takes a contrary view or action, one who makes decisions that contradict prevailing wisdom. Because he is a contrarian, the general is resolved to fight to the bitter end; clearly, the wise or sane course would be to *capitulate* or *submit*. Note that *submit* here is a synonym for yielding or giving in, not for asserting or proposing something.

4. **(C)(E)** If the plan, though tough, is not loving, then it certainly would not be *accurate* for the White House to describe it as tough love. It would not be particularly *witty* or *salient* (strikingly conspicuous) for the White House to do so. It might indeed have been *diplomatic* (tactful) for the White House to describe the plan as tough love. However, critics of the administration would be unlikely to put such a positive spin on the administration's description. Also, none of the other choices are synonyms for *diplomatic*. Only two choices remain: *disingenuous* and *mendacious*. To be disingenuous is to be insincere or untruthful. Likewise, to be mendacious is to be untruthful.

5. **(A)(D)** Perfectionists expect perfection of themselves. Therefore, when they make even tiny errors, they feel *vexation* (annoyance with themselves) and *chagrin* (annoyance mixed with humiliation).

6. **(C)** The fact that the writers were more involved with fighting problems in the system than with attacking the system itself suggests that fundamentally they *were not opposed to the* democratic system of government.

   Choice A is incorrect. The fact that the writers did not revolt against the system does not necessarily imply that they played a minor role in fighting abuses of the system.

   Choice B is incorrect. There is nothing in the statement that would imply that, *left to itself, the system was certain to function efficiently*.

Choice D is incorrect. There is nothing in the statement that would imply that *in order for the system to operate efficiently, blacks must seize the reins of power in America.*

Choice E is incorrect. There is nothing in the statement that would imply that *Black writers were too caught up in aesthetic questions to identify the true nature of the conflict.*

7. **(C)** In lines 4–7, the author mentions the growing interest in social and economic problems among the writers of the Harlem Renaissance. They used poetry, prose, and song to cry out against social and economic wrongs. Thus, they *transformed their increasing social and political consciousness into art.*

Choice A is incorrect. The author distrusts the foreign ideologies (lines 17–19) with their commitment to international solidarity.

Choice B is incorrect. The author states that the writers wished to contribute to American culture; they did not totally reject American society, but wished to improve it.

Choices D and E are incorrect. Neither is implied by the author.

8. **(A)** The author's evident concern to distinguish Negro writers from those who "embraced" socialist and communist propaganda (lines 17–19) suggest that he is a historian concerned with presenting these writers as loyal Americans.

Choice B is incorrect. The author touches on literature only in relationship to historical events.

Choices C, D, and E are incorrect. There is nothing in the passage to suggest any of these interpretations.

9. **(B)** The author makes the point that the writers essentially ignored socialist and communist propaganda. This point is apparently contradicted by the *Messenger* quote asserting that the same forces that produced socialism and communism *produced* the New Negro (and thus the new black writer). The author then *limits the application of his original* assertion by giving only qualified assent to that assertion ("Such forces *may* have produced the New Negro.").

10. **(E)** Choice E is answerable on the basis of this passage.

The passage cites the battles for better working conditions, desegregation, and social and political equality in which the black writers of the period were engaged. These were *specific socioeconomic causes* with which the writers associated themselves.

Choice A is unanswerable on the basis of this passage. The passage mentions an "improvement in the capacity for expression" in the period, but cites no factors leading to this stylistic improvement.

Choice B is unanswerable on the basis of this passage. The passage mentions no specific names.

Choice C is unanswerable on the basis of this passage. The passage states the writers did not "embrace the several foreign ideologies that sought to sink their roots" in America. However, it nowhere suggests that the writers were *in rebellion* against these foreign ideologies.

Choice D is unanswerable on the basis of this passage. No such information is supplied by the passage.

11. **(A)(D)** The author concedes that the big-bang theory has been changed somewhat: it has undergone *refinement* or polishing. However, he denies that its validity has been threatened seriously by any rival theories: it has *resisted* or defied all challenges.

   The use of the support signal *and* indicates that the first missing word is similar in meaning to "modification." The use of the contrast signal *but* indicates that the second missing word is contrary in meaning to "undergone modification."

12. **(C)(D)** Someone described as "rigid and conventional" would lack both the *flexibility* (adaptability) to adjust to changes and the *creativity* (inventiveness; imagination) to come up with new, innovative ideas.

13. **(B)(D)(H)** The phrases "some years after having been lauded" and "his reputation having suffered a decline" provide the key to unlocking this sentence. The subject here is the change in Perugino's reputation. In the beginning, he received wealth and status, but his fame did not last: he did not win *enduring* glory. Instead, Michaelangelo *derided* (ridiculed; mocked) him as an artistic *bumpkin* (clod; oaf).

14. **(B)(F)** The play *Amadeus* portrays Joseph II as "wedded to orthodox theories of musical composition." Thus, it depicts him as a *doctrinaire* thinker, dogmatic about which theories or doctrines he accepts. This view of Emperor Joseph is in contrast with his image as a reformer whose reign was impressively *enlightened* (liberal; civilized) for the period. The best way to attack this sentence is to complete the second blank first. Note that the second blank immediately precedes a long descriptive phrase that clarifies what kind of thinker Joseph II was.

15. **(B)(D)(I)** The adverb *even* (indeed) is used here as an intensive to stress something. Not only do fixed poetic forms *invite* wordiness, they may even *encourage* it. Because these fixed forms require the poet to write a specific number of lines or syllables, they place a *constraint* (limitation; restriction) on the poet. Without that constraint, the poet might have an easier time spotting and *eliminating* unnecessary syllables and words.

16. **(E)** One would have to disentangle a *skein* or coiled and twisted bundle of yarn. Note how the presence of the verb *disentangle*, which may be used both figuratively and literally, influences the writer's choice of words. In this case, while *line* is a possible choice, the word does not possess the connotations of twistings and tangled contortions that make *skein* a more suitable choice.

17. **(D)** The author opens the paragraph by stating that many literary critics have begun reinterpreting the study of women's literature. She then goes on to cite individual comments that support her assertion. Clearly, she is *receptive* or open to the ideas of these writers, for they and she share a common sense of the need to reinterpret their common field.

    Choices A and B are incorrect. The author cites the literary critics straightforwardly, presenting their statements as evidence supporting her thesis.

    Choice C is incorrect. The author does not *disparage* or belittle these critics. By quoting them respectfully she implicitly acknowledges their competence.

    Choice E is incorrect. The author quotes the critics as acknowledged experts in the field. However, she does not look on these critics with *awe* (an overwhelming feeling of reverence, admiration, or fear).

18. **(B)(E)** Choice B is answerable on the basis of the passage. According to lines 11–12, Ellen Moers "sees women's literature as an international movement," in other words, as a movement that *transcends national boundaries*.

    Likewise, Choice E is answerable on the basis of the passage. According to lines 5–6, Mill disbelieved in the idea that women "have had a literature of their own all along."

19. **(B)** The writer neither lists (*enumerates*) nor sorts (*classifies*) anything in the opening paragraph.

    Choice A is incorrect. The writer likens the female tradition to a lost continent and develops the metaphor by describing the continent "rising . . . from the sea of English literature."

Choice C is incorrect. The author refers or *alludes* to the classical legend of Atlantis.

Choice D is incorrect. The author quotes Colby and Thompson.

Choice E is incorrect. The author contrasts the revised view of women's literature with Mill's view.

20. **(A)(C)** The statement that "The rate of population increase has begun to decline in Northern Europe, but the food supply has not diminished" weakens Malthus's postulate that food supply cannot keep pace with the rate of increase of human population. Likewise, if "[h]uman population growth may be limited by the use of contraception," then it is possible that increasing the supply of food might not necessarily be followed by an increase in human population.

Section 3—Quantitative Ability

Two asterisks (**) indicate an alternative method of solving.

1. **(A)** The only positive divisors of 19 are 1 and 19. So Quantity A equals $1 + 19 = 20$, and Quantity B equals $1 \times 19 = 19$. Quantity A is greater.

2. **(A)** Since (a, b) is on the positive portion of the x-axis, a is positive and $b = 0$; so $a + b$ is positive. Also, since (c, d) is on the negative portion of the y-axis, $c = 0$ and d is negative; so $c + d$ is negative. Quantity A is greater.

3. **(D)** By the distributive law, Quantity A is $5r + 5t$. Subtracting $5r$ from each of Quantity A and Quantity B, we are left with $5t$ and t, respectively. So the two quantities are equal if $t = 0$ and unequal otherwise. Neither quantity is always greater, and the two quantities are not always equal (D).

4. **(A)** Quantity A: there are 5 positive multiples of 5 less than 26: 5, 10, 15, 20, 25; their average is 15, the middle one.

    Quantity B: there are 3 positive multiples of 7 less than 26: 7, 14, 21; their average is 14.

    Quantity A is greater.

5. **(B)** Since $\dfrac{1}{c} = 1 + \dfrac{1}{d}$, then $1 = \dfrac{1}{c} - \dfrac{1}{d} = \dfrac{d-c}{cd}$.

    Therefore, $d - c = cd$, which is positive since both c and d are positive. Then, $d - c$ is positive, and so $d > c$.

    Quantity B is greater.

6. **(C)** The simplest solution is to realize that there is one palindrome between 100 and 109 (101), one between 390 and 399 (393), one between 880 and 889 (888), and in general, one out of every 10 numbers. So the probability is $\frac{1}{10}$. The answer is (C).

   **The more direct solution is to count the number of 3-digit palindromes. Either systematically make a list and notice that there are 10 of them between 100 and 199, and 10 in each of the hundreds from the 100s to the 900s, for a total of 90; or use the counting principle: the hundreds digit can be chosen in any of 9 ways (any of the digits from 1 through 9), the tens digit in any of 10 ways (any of the digits from 0 through 9), and the units digit, since it must match the hundreds digit, can be chosen in only 1 way ($9 \times 10 \times 1 = 90$). Since there are 900 three-digit numbers, the probability is $\frac{90}{900} = \frac{1}{10}$.

7. **(C)** Let P = the price of the TV set. Then Jack paid $1.085(.90P)$, whereas Jill paid $.90(1.085P)$. The quantities are equal (C).

   **Choose a convenient number: assume the TV cost $100. Jack paid $90 plus $7.65 tax (8.5% of $90) for a total of $97.65. Jill's cashier rang up $100 plus $8.50 tax and then deducted $10.85 (10% of $108.50) for a final cost of $97.65.

8. **(A)** Quantity A: Since $\triangle ABC$ is a 45-45-90 right triangle whose hypotenuse is 2, the length of each leg is $\frac{2}{\sqrt{2}} = \sqrt{2}$, and the area is $\frac{1}{2}(\sqrt{2})(\sqrt{2}) = \frac{1}{2}(2) = 1$.

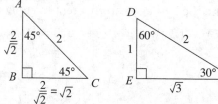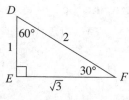

   Quantity B: Since $\triangle DEF$ is a 30-60-90 right triangle whose hypotenuse is 2, the shorter leg is 1, the longer leg is $\sqrt{3}$, and the area is $\frac{1}{2}(1)(\sqrt{3}) = \frac{\sqrt{3}}{2}$, which is less than 1 because $\sqrt{3}$ is less than 2.

   Quantity A is greater.

9. **(D)** Since 400 = 12 × 33 + 4, 100 months is 4 months more than 33 years. 33 years from June it will again be June, and 4 months later it will be October.

　　**Look for a pattern. Since there are 12 months in a year, after every 12 months it will again be June; i.e., it will be June after 12, 24, 36, 48, . . . , 120, . . . , 360 months. So, 396 (33 × 12) months from now, it will again be June. Count 4 more months to October.

10. $\frac{4}{5}$　Pick an easy-to-use number for the number of members of the chorus. Since $\frac{5}{9}$ of the members are boys, assume there are 9 members, 5 of whom are boys. Then the other 4 are girls, and the ratio of girls to boys is 4 to 5, or $\frac{4}{5}$.

11. **27**　Since the surface area of the cube is 54, the area of each of the six square faces is: 54 ÷ 6 = 9. Therefore, each edge is 3, and the volume is 3^3 = 27.

12. **(A)**　Draw a diagram. See the figure below on the left. Then form rectangle *BCDE* by drawing *DE* ⊥ *AB*, yielding the figure on the right

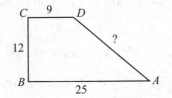 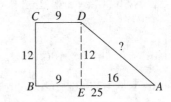

Then, *BE* = 9, *AE* = 16, and *DE* = 12. Finally, *DA* = 20, because right triangle *AED* is a 3-4-5 triangle in which each side is multiplied by 4. If you don't realize that, use the Pythagorean theorem to get *DA*:

$$(DA)^2 = (AE)^2 + (DE)^2 = 256 + 144 = 400 \Rightarrow DA = 20$$

13. **(A)(B)(C)(D)**

- In a normal distribution, 5% of the data lie outside of two standard deviations from the mean, in this case less than 300 and greater than 700. That 5% is equally divided: 2.5% below 300 and 2.5% above 700. Statement A is true.

- About 13.5% of the scores lie between one and two standard deviations above the mean (here, between 600 and 700). Of the 34% of the scores that are less than one standard deviation above the mean (between 500 and 600), well more than half (about 19%) are below 550. Statement B is true.

- About 16% of the scores are below 400. The other 84% are above 400. Statement C is true.

- This is essentially the same as Statement C. About 84% of the scores are below 600. Since 84% is greater than $\frac{4}{5}$, Statement D is true.

14. **(D)** From the bottom graph, we can estimate the percentage distribution of total enrollment to be:

Public 4-year	41%	Private 4-year	21%
Public 2-year	37%	Private 2-year	1%
Total public	78%	Total private	22%

$78 \div 22 \approx 3.5$, so there were 3.5 times as many students enrolled in public institutions as private ones.

15. **(E)** In 1972, enrollment in private 4-year institutions was approximately 1,100,000 (22% of the total enrollment of 5,000,000). By 1995, the index for private 4-year institutions had increased from 80 to 120, a 50% increase. Therefore, the number of private 4-year students enrolled in 1995 was approximately 1,650,000 (50% more than the 1,100,000 students enrolled in 1972).

16. **(A)(B)(C)**
    - From the top graph, we see that for every 100 students enrolled in private 2-year institutions in 1981, the number increased to about 110 in 1983, stayed between 105 and 110 until 1986, and then dropped back to 100 in 1987. Statement A is true.
    - From the bottom graph, we see that the percentage of students enrolled in 2-year private institutions remained constant at about 2% from 1981 to 1987. Statement B is true.
    -

	1972	1995
Public 2-year	28%	37%
Private 2-year	1%	1%
Total	29%	38%

    The percent increase from 29 to 38 is $\dfrac{\text{actual increase}}{\text{original amount}} \times 100\% =$

    $\dfrac{9}{29} \times 100\% = 31\%$, well more than 25%. Statement C is true.

17. **(A)** Since $C = 2\pi r$, then $r = \dfrac{C}{2\pi}$, and the area of the circle is

$$\pi r^2 = \pi \left(\dfrac{C}{2\pi} \right)^2 = \pi \left(\dfrac{C^2}{4\pi} \right) = \dfrac{C^2}{4\pi}$$

18. **(B)** By the triangle inequality,
    - The third side must be *less* than $9 + 10 = 19$. (C is false.)
    - The third side must be *greater* than $10 - 9 = 1$. (A is false.)
    - *Any* number between 1 and 19 could be the length of the third side. (B is true.)

19. **(E)** Since p pencils cost c cents, each pencil costs $\dfrac{c}{p}$ cents. By dividing the number of cents we have by $\dfrac{c}{p}$, we find out how many pencils we can buy.

Since d dollars equals $100d$ cents, we divide $100d$ by $\dfrac{c}{p}$, which is

equivalent to multiplying $100d$ by $\dfrac{p}{c}$: $100d \left(\dfrac{p}{c} \right) = \dfrac{100dp}{c}$.

You will probably prefer the alternative solution below.

**Replace the variables with numbers. Assume 2 pencils cost 10 cents. So, pencils cost 5 cents each or 20 for one dollar. So, for 3 dollars, we can buy 60 pencils. Which of the choices equals 60 when $p = 2$, $c = 10$, and $d = 3$? Only $\dfrac{100dp}{c}$.

20. **(B)** The probability that an event will occur is

$$\frac{\text{number of favorable outcomes}}{\text{total number of possible outcomes}}$$

Here, the number of favorable outcomes is the number of ways of choosing 3 of the 5 boys:

$$_5C_3 = \frac{5!}{3!2!} = \frac{5 \times 4(3 \times 2 \times 1)}{(3 \times 2 \times 1)(2 \times 1)} = 10$$

The total number of outcomes is the number of ways of choosing 3 of the 10 children:

$$_5C_3 = \frac{10!}{3!7!} = \frac{10 \times 9 \times 8(7 \times 6 \times 5 \times 4 \times 3 \times 2 \times 1)}{3 \times 2 \times 1(7 \times 6 \times 5 \times 4 \times 3 \times 2 \times 1)} = 120$$

The probability that the 3 children chosen are all boys is $\dfrac{10}{120} = \dfrac{1}{12}$.

Section 4—Verbal Reasoning

1. **(B)(D)** The spread of genetically engineered matter has become "a significant practical problem." Thus, it is no longer merely a *theoretical* (hypothetical; lacking practical application) or *abstract* worry.

2. **(A)(E)** Under certain circumstances scientists attack each other with *ad hominem* arguments (personal attacks) and shameless appeals to authority. When is this likely to occur? When facts are *established* or *demonstrable* or *ineluctable* (unavoidable) or *relevant*? Hardly. Under such circumstances they would rely on the facts to establish their case. It is when facts prove *elusive* (hard to pin down) or *uncertain* that they lose control and, in doing so, abandon their pretense of objectivity.

3. **(C)(E)** If "you may wonder" how the expert reaches his conclusions, it appears that it is questionable to rely on teeth for guidance in interpreting fossils. Choices C and E, *flimsy* and *inadequate*, create the element of doubt that the clause tries to develop. Choice D, *specious*, also creates an element of doubt; however, nothing in the context justifies the idea that the reasoning is specious or false.

Note that here you are dealing with an extended metaphor. Picture yourself hanging a heavy winter coat on a slim wooden peg. Wouldn't you worry that the peg might prove inadequate or flimsy?

4. **(A)(D)** If armed forces take over a country's administration, then that country is under military law rather than constitutional law. However, in this military takeover, the constitution has *not* been abolished or stamped out. Instead, some of its provisions merely have been *suspended* (rendered inoperative for a time) or *put in abeyance* (temporarily set aside).

5. **(C)(D)** The second clause presents an example of literary mockery or sarcastic jesting. The abstract idea of preserving a nugget of pure truth is appealing; the concrete example of setting it up on the mantelpiece *makes light of* or *mocks* the whole idea.

6. **(C)(E)** The passage asserts that literary scholars now *reject* the idea that Elizabethan drama has it roots in classical Greek and Roman drama. Therefore, it would be inconsistent with the passage to assert Statement C ("Although Elizabethan drama deals with English subject matter, it derives its form and method solely from classical Greek and Roman theater"). Likewise, it would be inconsistent with the passage to assert Statement E ("Modern theater scholars view Elizabethan drama as a direct offshoot of Greek and Roman dramatic traditions").

7. **(E)** Choice E does not weaken the argument, because the argument specifically calls for "a truly broad, liberal education." Choice E, however, merely refers to "the traditional liberal education," which is not necessarily the truly broad and liberal education the author has in mind.

   Choice A weakens the argument: it exposes the argument's failure to acknowledge that many specific problems may be solved by persons who don't understand the broad picture.

   Choice B weakens the argument: it exposes the assumption that because generalists are needed, *all* persons should be educated as generalists.

   Choice C weakens the argument: it exposes the false dichotomy between specialization and seeing the broad picture.

   Choice D weakens the argument: it attacks the implicit assumption that fewer specialists are needed.

8. **(E)** The last sentence points out that Du Bois originally agreed with Washington's program.

   Choice A is incorrect. Nothing in the passage suggests that Du Bois sacrificed effective strategies out of a desire to try something new.

   Choice B is incorrect. Du Bois gained in influence, effectively winning away large numbers of blacks from Washington's policies.

Choice C is incorrect. Du Bois's quickness to depart from conventional black wisdom when it proved inadequate to the task of advancing the race shows him to be well able to change with the times.

Choice D is incorrect. Washington, not Du Bois, is described as seeking the good will of powerful whites.

9. **(C)** The author does *not* portray Washington as versatile. Instead, he portrays Du Bois as versatile.

Choice A is incorrect. The author portrays Washington as submissive to the majority; he shows him teaching blacks not to protest.

Choice B is incorrect. The author portrays Washington as concerned with financial success; he shows him advocating property accumulation.

Choice D is incorrect. The author portrays Washington as traditional in preaching industry; he shows him advocating hard work.

Choice E is incorrect. The author portrays Washington as respectful of authority; he shows him deferring to powerful whites.

10. **(D)** Although the author points out that Du Bois's methods led him into conflicts, he describes Du Bois as "often . . . well in advance of his contemporaries" and stresses that his motives for departing from the mainstream were admirable. Thus, his attitude can best be described as *approving*.

11. **(B)** The fact that Monet's home was filled to overflowing with works by Japanese artists would be sufficient reason for someone to *attest* (declare; bear witness) that Japanese prints were Monet's passion.

12. **(C)(E)** The key phrase here is "Breaking with established musical traditions." Someone who breaks with traditions is by definition *iconoclastic* (unorthodox; radical; irreverent of tradition). The musical creations of an iconoclastic composer would most likely be *heterodox* or unorthodox as well.

13. **(B)(F)** A disease in a *latent* state has yet to manifest itself and emerge into view. Therefore it is almost impossible to determine its existence by *observation*.

The key phrase here is "almost impossible to determine its existence." By its very nature, it would *not* be almost impossible to determine the existence of a disease in its *critical* (acute) or *overt* (apparent; unconcealed) state.

14. **(A)(E)** The key phrase here is "his more conventional colleagues." The paleontologist described here is less conventional than his colleagues. What then is his relationship to orthodoxy (conventionality)? He has departed from conventional ways, has made a *break with* orthodoxy.

Therefore, his more conventional colleagues would *contest* (challenge) the evidence he has gathered.

15. **(A)(F)** Here the task is to determine the communal reaction to crime. The writer maintains that the criminal justice system of punishments allows the community to purge itself of its anger, its sense of *outrage* at the criminal's acts. Thus, it provides a *catharsis* or purgation for the community.

    It is unlikely that an essential purpose of the criminal justice system would be the provision of either a *disclaimer* (denial or disavowal, as in disavowing responsibility for a legal claim) or a *prototype* (model; exemplar).

16. **(B)(E)** The key word here is *assailed*. Housman is attacking his rival. Thus he is in the tradition of scholarly *invective* (vehement verbal attack), criticizing his foe for turning to manuscripts merely for confirmation or support of old theories and not for enlightenment or *illumination*. Again, note the use of figurative language, in this case the simile of the drunkard.

17. **(A)** The capacity of polar bears to scent prey at a great distance is their *faculty* or ability to do so. Note that *faculty* here is being used with a secondary meaning.

18. **(E)** The author first states that the reason for bioluminescence in underwater microorganisms is obscure and then proceeds to enumerate various hypotheses.

19. **(B)** The author does not deny that predators make use of bioluminescence in locating their prey. Instead, he gives an example of human predators (fishers) who are drawn to their prey (the fish that prey on plankton) by the luminescence of the plankton.

20. **(B)** As the previous answer makes clear, the phenomenon of plankton bioluminescence does have practical applications. It is a valuable tool for fisheries interested in increasing their catch of fish that prey on plankton.

Section 5—Quantitative Ability

Two asterisks (**) indicate an alternative method of solving.

1. **(A)** $\pi \approx 3.14$ and $\sqrt{10} \approx 3.16$. So $\pi < \sqrt{10}$.

   For any positive numbers a and b, if $a < b$, then $\frac{1}{a} > \frac{1}{b}$.

   So $\frac{1}{\pi} > \frac{1}{\sqrt{10}}$.

2. **(B)** It is irrelevant that $700 < n < 800$. Every factor of n is a factor of $2n$, but 2 is a prime factor of $2n$, which is not a factor of n (since n is odd). $2n$ has one more prime factor than n. Quantity B is greater.

3. **(B)** Since $x < y$, the average of x and y is less than y, so having another y raises the average. Quantity B is greater.
   ** Plug in the numbers: say $x = 2$ and $y = 4$.
   Quantity A: the average of 2 and 4 is 3.
   Quantity B: the average of 2, 4, and 4 is $10 \div 3 = 3.333$, which is more than 3; the second 4 raised the average.

4. **(A)** In any triangle, if one side is longer than a second side, the angle opposite the longer side is greater than the angle opposite the shorter side, so $c > d$. Quantity A is greater. (It is irrelevant that the third angle is 135°.)

5. **(B)**

   Quantity A: $a\%$ of $\dfrac{1}{b} = \dfrac{a}{100} \times \dfrac{1}{b} = \dfrac{a}{100b} = \dfrac{1}{100} \times \dfrac{a}{b}$

   Quantity B: $a\%$ of $\dfrac{1}{b} = \dfrac{b}{100} \times \dfrac{1}{a} = \dfrac{b}{100a} = \dfrac{1}{100} \times \dfrac{b}{a}$

   Since a and b are positive and $b > a$, $\dfrac{b}{a} > 1$, and $\dfrac{a}{b} < 1$.

   So Quantity B is greater.

6. **(D)** Could x and y be equal? Yes, the two small triangles could be right triangles, and x and y could each be 40. Must they be equal? No. On the GRE, diagrams are not necessarily drawn to scale. See the figure below, in which clearly $x < y$. Neither quantity is *always* greater, and the quantities are not *always* equal.

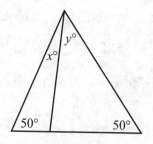

7. **(B)** Don't waste time using the slope formula; just make a quick sketch.

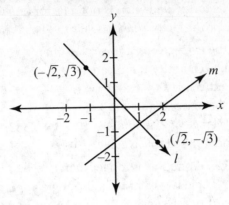

Note that l slopes downward, so its slope is negative, whereas m slopes upward, so its slope is positive. Quantity B is greater.

8. **(D)** The markings in the five angles are irrelevant. The sum of the five angles is 360°, and 360 ÷ 5 = 72.
   **If you solve the equation $a + 2a + 3a + 3a + 3a = 360$, you get that $12a = 360 \Rightarrow a = 30$, and so the degree measures of the five angles are 30, 60, 90, 90, and 90. You would then find that the average of those five numbers is 72; but all of that is a waste of time.

9. **(B)** On her six tests combined, Camille earned a total of $6 \times 75 = 450$ points. The total of her five best grades is $5 \times 85 = 425$ points, so her lowest grade was $450 - 425 = 25$.
   **Since Camille's average on her 5 best tests is 85, assume that those grades were each 85. Then each one has a deviation of 10 points above the average of 75, and the total deviation above 75 is $5 \times 10 = 50$ points. Therefore, her one bad grade must have been 50 points below 75.

10. **(B)(C)(D)(E)(F)** The perimeter of a rectangle whose area is 40 can be as large as we like (for example, if the length is 4,000 and the width is 0.01, the perimeter is 8,000.02). However, the perimeter is the smallest when the rectangle is a square, in which case each side is $\sqrt{40}$ and the perimeter is $4\sqrt{40}$. Since $\sqrt{40} > 6$, the perimeter is greater than $4 \times 6 = 24$.
   So Choice A, 20, is not possible. All of the other choices are possible.

11. **(B)(D)** Rewriting the equation of the given line, $2x + 3y = 4$, in slope-intercept form, we get that $y = -\frac{2}{3}x + \frac{4}{3}$. So the slope of the given line is $-\frac{2}{3}$.

The slope of any line perpendicular to that line must have a slope of $\frac{3}{2}$, the negative reciprocal of $-\frac{2}{3}$.

Rewrite each of the answer choices in slope-intercept form, and see which ones also have a slope of $\frac{3}{2}$.

A: $y = -\frac{3}{2}x + 2$

B: $y = \frac{3}{2}x - 2$

C: $y = \frac{2}{3}x - \frac{4}{3}$

D: $y = \frac{3}{2}x - 2$

E: $y = \frac{2}{3}x + \frac{4}{3}$

Only Choices B and D are the equations of lines whose slope is $\frac{3}{2}$.

12. **(E)** Since the diameter of the circle is 20, the radius is 10 and the area is 100π. Since the area of the shaded region is 80π, it is $\frac{80}{100} = \frac{4}{5}$ of the circle, and the white area is $\frac{1}{5}$ of the circle. So the sum of the measures of the two white central angles is $\frac{1}{5}$ of 360°, or 72°.

The sum of the measures of all six angles in the two triangles is 360°, so $a + b + c + d + 72 = 360 \Rightarrow a + b + c + d = \mathbf{288}$.

13. $\frac{3}{5}$ The five numbers are 3, 13, 23, 33, and 43, four of which are prime (all except 33). So the probability that the first number drawn is prime is $\frac{4}{5}$.

If the first number is prime, then three of the remaining four numbers are prime, and the probability is $\frac{3}{4}$ that the second number will be prime.

P(both numbers are prime) =

P(1st number is prime) $\times P$(2nd number is prime) = $\frac{4}{5} \times \frac{3}{4} = \frac{3}{5}$.

14. **(B)** From 1994 to 1996 there was a 9.4% decrease in the number of vehicles stolen. Since 9.4% of 1,000,000 = 94,000, the number of vehicles stolen in 1996 was 1,000,000 – 94,000 = 906,000. If you can't solve problems such as this, you have to guess. But since the number of stolen vehicles is clearly decreasing, be sure to eliminate Choices D and E first.

15. **(C)** For simplicity, assume that 1,000 vehicles were stolen in 1994. By 1997, the number had decreased by 12.0% to 880 (12% of 1000 = 120, and 1000 – 120 = 880); by 1998, the number had decreased 19.4% to 806 (19.4% of 1000 = 194 and 1000 – 194 = 806). So from 1997 to 1998, the number of vehicles stolen decreased by 74 from 880 to 806. This represents a decrease of $\frac{74}{880}$ = .084 = 8.4%.

16. **(D)** Simplify the situation by assuming that in 1994 the population was 100,000 and there were 1,000 vehicles stolen. As in the solution to Question 15, in 1998 the number of stolen vehicles was 806. At the same time, the number of thefts per 100,000 inhabitants decreased 22.4% from 1000 to 776. So if there were 776 vehicles stolen for every 100,000 inhabitants, and 806 cars were stolen, the number of inhabitants must have increased. To know by how much, solve the proportion:

$\frac{776}{100,000} = \frac{806}{x}$. Cross-multiplying, we get $776x = 80,600,000$.

So, $x = 103,800$. Then for every 100,000 inhabitants in 1994, there were 103,800 in 1998, an increase of 3.8%.

17. **–9.9**

- Since the average of the 5 numbers v, w, x, y, and z is 12.3, their sum is $5 \times 12.3 = 61.5$.

- Since the average of v and w is 45.6, their sum is $2 \times 45.6 = 91.2$.
- Then $x + y + z = 61.5 - 91.2 = -29.7$, and $\dfrac{x+y+z}{3} = \dfrac{-29.7}{3} = -9.9$.

18. **(A)** Even if you can do the algebra, this type of problem is easier if you plug in some easy-to-use numbers. Assume that there are 100 girls and 50 boys on staff and that 20% of the girls and 10% of the boys attended the meeting. Then, 20 girls and 5 boys were there, and 5 is 20% of 25, the total number attending.

    Of course, you *can* do this algebraically. If x represents the number of boys on staff, then $2x$ is the number of girls. If $y\%$ of the boys attended the meeting, then $2y\%$ of the girls did. So, the number of boys attending was $x\left(\dfrac{y}{100}\right) = \dfrac{xy}{100}$, whereas the number of girls attending was $2x\left(\dfrac{2y}{100}\right) = \dfrac{4xy}{100}$.

    Therefore, there were 4 times as many girls in attendance as boys: $\dfrac{4}{5}$ of those at the meeting were girls and $\dfrac{1}{5}$ or 20% were boys.

19. **96** Since 4 boys can shovel the driveway in 2 hours or $2 \times 60 = 120$ minutes, the job takes $4 \times 120 = 480$ boy-minutes to complete.

    Therefore, 5 boys will need $\dfrac{480 \text{ boy-minutes}}{5 \text{ boys}} = 96$ minutes.

20. **(D)** Make a table to determine Roberto's and Juan's ages. Let x represent Juan's age in 1950, and fill in the table as shown.

	1950	1955
Roberto	$4x$	$4x + 5$
Juan	x	$x + 5$

In 1955, Roberto was 3 times as old as Juan, so $4x + 5 = 3(x + 5) = 3x + 15$, and so $x = 10$. Therefore, in 1950, Juan was 10 and Roberto was 40. Because Roberto is 30 years older than Juan, Roberto was 30 when Juan was born.

ANSWER SHEET—MODEL TEST 2

Section 2—Verbal Reasoning

1 Ⓐ Ⓑ Ⓒ Ⓓ Ⓔ Ⓕ
2 Ⓐ Ⓑ Ⓒ Ⓓ Ⓔ Ⓕ
3 Ⓐ Ⓑ Ⓒ Ⓓ Ⓔ Ⓕ
4 Ⓐ Ⓑ Ⓒ Ⓓ Ⓔ Ⓕ
5 Ⓐ Ⓑ Ⓒ Ⓓ Ⓔ Ⓕ
6 Ⓐ Ⓑ Ⓒ Ⓓ Ⓔ Ⓕ
7 Ⓐ Ⓑ Ⓒ Ⓓ Ⓔ
8 Ⓐ Ⓑ Ⓒ Ⓓ Ⓔ

9 Ⓐ Ⓑ Ⓒ Ⓓ Ⓔ
10 Ⓐ Ⓑ Ⓒ Ⓓ Ⓔ
11 Ⓐ Ⓑ Ⓒ Ⓓ Ⓔ Ⓕ
12 Ⓐ Ⓑ Ⓒ Ⓓ Ⓔ Ⓕ
13 Ⓐ Ⓑ Ⓒ Ⓓ Ⓔ Ⓕ
14 Ⓐ Ⓑ Ⓒ Ⓓ Ⓔ Ⓕ
15 Ⓐ Ⓑ Ⓒ Ⓓ Ⓔ Ⓕ Ⓖ Ⓗ Ⓘ
16 Ⓐ Ⓑ Ⓒ Ⓓ Ⓔ

17 Ⓐ Ⓑ Ⓒ
18 Ⓐ Ⓑ Ⓒ Ⓓ Ⓔ
19 Ⓐ Ⓑ Ⓒ Ⓓ Ⓔ
20 Ⓐ Ⓑ Ⓒ Ⓓ Ⓔ

Section 3—Quantitative Ability

1 Ⓐ Ⓑ Ⓒ Ⓓ
2 Ⓐ Ⓑ Ⓒ Ⓓ
3 Ⓐ Ⓑ Ⓒ Ⓓ
4 Ⓐ Ⓑ Ⓒ Ⓓ
5 Ⓐ Ⓑ Ⓒ Ⓓ
6 Ⓐ Ⓑ Ⓒ Ⓓ
7 Ⓐ Ⓑ Ⓒ Ⓓ
8 Ⓐ Ⓑ Ⓒ Ⓓ
9 Ⓐ Ⓑ Ⓒ Ⓓ Ⓔ
10 Ⓐ Ⓑ Ⓒ Ⓓ Ⓔ

11

12 Ⓐ Ⓑ Ⓒ Ⓓ Ⓔ

13

14 Ⓐ Ⓑ Ⓒ Ⓓ Ⓔ
15 Ⓐ Ⓑ Ⓒ Ⓓ Ⓔ

16

17 Ⓐ Ⓑ Ⓒ Ⓓ Ⓔ
18 Ⓐ Ⓑ Ⓒ Ⓓ Ⓔ
19 Ⓐ Ⓑ Ⓒ Ⓓ Ⓔ

20

ANSWER SHEET—MODEL TEST 2

Section 4—Verbal Reasoning

1 Ⓐ Ⓑ Ⓒ Ⓓ Ⓔ Ⓕ
2 Ⓐ Ⓑ Ⓒ Ⓓ Ⓔ Ⓕ
3 Ⓐ Ⓑ Ⓒ Ⓓ Ⓔ Ⓕ
4 Ⓐ Ⓑ Ⓒ Ⓓ Ⓔ Ⓕ
5 Ⓐ Ⓑ Ⓒ Ⓓ Ⓔ Ⓕ
6 Ⓐ Ⓑ Ⓒ Ⓓ Ⓔ Ⓕ
7 Ⓐ Ⓑ Ⓒ Ⓓ Ⓔ
8 Ⓐ Ⓑ Ⓒ Ⓓ Ⓔ

9 Ⓐ Ⓑ Ⓒ Ⓓ Ⓔ
10 Ⓐ Ⓑ Ⓒ Ⓓ Ⓔ
11 Ⓐ Ⓑ Ⓒ Ⓓ Ⓔ Ⓕ
12 Ⓐ Ⓑ Ⓒ Ⓓ Ⓔ Ⓕ
13 Ⓐ Ⓑ Ⓒ Ⓓ Ⓔ Ⓕ
14 Ⓐ Ⓑ Ⓒ Ⓓ Ⓔ Ⓕ
15 Ⓐ Ⓑ Ⓒ Ⓓ Ⓔ
16 Ⓐ Ⓑ Ⓒ Ⓓ Ⓔ

17 Ⓐ Ⓑ Ⓒ Ⓓ Ⓔ
18 Ⓐ Ⓑ Ⓒ Ⓓ Ⓔ
19 Ⓐ Ⓑ Ⓒ Ⓓ Ⓔ
20 Ⓐ Ⓑ Ⓒ Ⓓ Ⓔ

Section 5—Quantitative Ability

1 Ⓐ Ⓑ Ⓒ Ⓓ
2 Ⓐ Ⓑ Ⓒ Ⓓ
3 Ⓐ Ⓑ Ⓒ Ⓓ
4 Ⓐ Ⓑ Ⓒ Ⓓ
5 Ⓐ Ⓑ Ⓒ Ⓓ
6 Ⓐ Ⓑ Ⓒ Ⓓ
7 Ⓐ Ⓑ Ⓒ Ⓓ
8 Ⓐ Ⓑ Ⓒ Ⓓ Ⓔ
9 Ⓐ Ⓑ Ⓒ Ⓓ Ⓔ

10 [   ]

11 Ⓐ Ⓑ Ⓒ Ⓓ Ⓔ
12 Ⓐ Ⓑ Ⓒ Ⓓ Ⓔ
13 Ⓐ Ⓑ Ⓒ Ⓓ Ⓔ

14 [   ]

15 Ⓐ Ⓑ Ⓒ Ⓓ Ⓔ

16 Ⓐ Ⓑ Ⓒ Ⓓ Ⓔ

17 [   ]

18 Ⓐ Ⓑ Ⓒ Ⓓ Ⓔ Ⓕ
19 Ⓐ Ⓑ Ⓒ Ⓓ Ⓔ
20 Ⓐ Ⓑ Ⓒ Ⓓ Ⓔ

Model Test 2

SECTION 1—ANALYTICAL WRITING

Time —60 minutes
2 Writing Tasks

Task 1: Analyze an Issue

30 MINUTES

<u>*Directions:*</u> In 30 minutes, compose an essay on the topic below. You may not write on any other topic.

The topic is presented in a one- to two-sentence quotation commenting on an issue of general concern. Your essay may support, refute, or qualify the views expressed in the quotation. Whatever you write, however, must be relevant to the issue under discussion, and you must support your viewpoint with reasons and examples derived from your studies and/or experience.

If you will be taking the computer-delivered test, write your essay using a word-processing program with its spelling and grammar checker turned off. If you will be taking the paper-delivered test, write your essay on lined paper using a #2 pencil.

Faculty members from various institutions will evaluate your essay, judging it on the basis of your skill in the following areas:

- ☑ Coverage of each of the elements in the task instructions
- ☑ Analysis of the statement's implications
- ☑ Organization and articulation of your ideas
- ☑ Use of relevant examples and arguments to support your case
- ☑ Handling of the mechanics, grammar, and usage of standard written English

Issue Task

"Public secondary school students should be required to pass a standardized national exit exam in order to receive a high school diploma."

Compose an essay that presents your opinion on the policy presented, explicating your rationale for this opinion. As you build and provide evidence for your argument, you must take into account the likely effects of applying the policy and describe the impact these potential effects have on your argument.

Task 2: Analyze an Argument

30 MINUTES

Directions: In 30 minutes, prepare a critical analysis of an argument expressed in a short paragraph, following the specific task instructions provided. You may not offer an analysis of any other argument.

Be sure to support your analysis with evidence (reasons and/or examples) but **do not present your personal views on the topic**. Your job is to analyze the elements of an argument, not to support or contradict that argument.

If you will be taking the computer-delivered test, write your essay using a word-processing program with its spelling and grammar checker turned off. If you will be taking the paper-delivered test, write your essay on lined paper using a #2 pencil.

Faculty members from various institutions will evaluate your essay, judging it on the basis of your skill in the following areas:

- ☑ Coverage of each of the elements in the task instructions
- ☑ Identification and assessment of the argument's main elements
- ☑ Organization and articulation of your thoughts
- ☑ Use of relevant examples and arguments to support your case
- ☑ Handling of the mechanics, grammar, and usage of standard written English

Argument Task

The following appeared in a letter to the editor in the journal *Health Matters*.

"Statistics gathered over the past three decades show that the death rate is higher among those who do not have jobs than among those with regular employment. Unemployment, just like heart disease and cancer, is a significant health issue. While many health care advocates promote increased government funding for medical research and public health care, it would be folly to increase government spending if doing so were to affect the nation's economy adversely and ultimately cause a rise in unemployment. A healthy economy means healthy citizens. Reining in government spending is, therefore, the best medicine."

Compose an essay that identifies the questions that must be answered before deciding whether the conclusion and the argument supporting it make sense. In writing your essay you should describe the impact that the answers to these questions would have on your assessment of the conclusion.

SECTION—2 VERBAL REASONING

Time —30 minutes
20 Questions

Directions: For each of the following sentences, select the **two** answers of the six choices given that, when substituted in the sentence, both logically complete the sentence as a whole **and** create sentences that are equivalent to one another in meaning.

Questions 1–6

1. Given the human tendency to suspect and disbelieve in processes that take place below the level of consciousness, it is unsurprising that many students of organizational development _____ the impact of the unconscious on business and political behavior and social dynamics.

   A intimate

   B acclaim

   C applaud

   D deny

   E gainsay

   F acknowledge

2. Although the young author had the reputation of being excessively taciturn, he seemed not at all _____ conversation.

   A inclined to

   B averse from

   C capable of

   D skilled at

   E opposed to

   F enamored of

3. To Mrs. Trollope, writing in the 1830s, nothing more clearly illustrated the _____ pervading "the land of the free" than the institution of slavery.

   A sanctimoniousness

   B conservatism

   C hypocrisy

   D rationality

   E liberality

   F orthodoxy

4. To someone as phlegmatic as Paul, it was a shock to find himself attracted to a woman so clearly his opposite in every way: a passionate activist, as _____ in her enthusiasms as in her dislikes.

   A dogmatic

   B ardent

   C haphazard

   D wholehearted

   E abstracted

   F mistaken

5. Soap operas and situation comedies, though given to distortion, are so derivative of contemporary culture that they are inestimable _____ the attitudes and values of our society in any particular decade.

   A contraventions of

   B antidotes to

   C indices of

   D prerequisites for

   E evidence of

   F determinants of

6. Slander is like counterfeit money: many people who would not coin it _____ without qualms.

    A hoard it

    B invest it

    C withdraw it

    D circulate it

    E spread it around

    F complain about it

Directions: The next questions are based on the content of the following passage. Read the passage and then determine the best answer choice for each question. Base your choice on what this passage *states directly* or *implies*, not on any information you may have gained elsewhere.

For each of Questions 7–10, select one answer choice unless otherwise instructed.

Questions 7–10 are based on the following passage.

With Meredith's *The Egoist* we enter into a critical problem that we have not yet before faced in these studies. That is the problem offered by a writer of recognizably impressive stature, whose work is informed by a muscular
Line intelligence, whose language has splendor, whose "view of life" wins our
(5) respect, and yet for whom we are at best able to feel only a passive appreciation which amounts, practically, to indifference. We should be unjust to Meredith and to criticism if we should, giving in to the inertia of indifference, simply avoid dealing with him and thus avoid the problem along with him. He does not "speak to us," we might say; his meaning is not a "meaning for
(10) us"; he "leaves us cold." But do not the challenge and the excitement of the critical problem as such lie in that ambivalence of attitude which allows us to recognize the intelligence and even the splendor of Meredith's work, while, at the same time, we experience a lack of sympathy, a failure of any enthusiasm of response?

7. According to the passage, the work of Meredith is noteworthy for its elements of

(A) sensibility and artistic fervor
(B) ambivalence and moral ambiguity
(C) tension and sense of vitality
(D) brilliance and linguistic grandeur
(E) wit and whimsical frivolity

8. Which of the following cannot be found in the author's discussion of Meredith?

(A) an indication of Meredith's customary effect on readers
(B) an enumeration of the admirable qualities in his work
(C) a selection of hypothetical comments at Meredith's expense
(D) an analysis of the critical ramifications of Meredith's effect on readers
(E) a refutation of the claim that Meredith evokes no sympathy

9. It can be inferred from the passage that the author finds the prospect of appraising Meredith's work critically to be

(A) counterproductive
(B) overly formidable
(C) somewhat tolerable
(D) markedly unpalatable
(E) clearly invigorating

10. It can be inferred from the passage that the author would be most likely to agree with which of the following statements about the role of criticism?

(A) Its prime office should be to make our enjoyment of the things that feed the mind as conscious as possible.
(B) It should be a disinterested endeavor to learn and propagate the best that is known and thought in the world.
(C) It should enable us to go beyond personal prejudice to appreciate the virtues of works antipathetic to our own tastes.
(D) It should dwell upon excellencies rather than imperfections, ignoring such deficiencies as irrelevant.
(E) It should strive both to purify literature and to elevate the literary standards of the reading public.

Directions: Each of the following sentences or groups of sentences contains one, two, or three blanks. These blanks signify that a word or set of words has been left out. Below each sentence are columns of words or sets of words. For each blank, pick the one word or set of words from the corresponding column that *best* completes the text.

11. Whereas off-Broadway theatre over the past several seasons has clearly (i) _____ a talent for experimentation and improvisation, one deficiency in the commercial stage of late has been its marked incapacity for (ii) _____.

Blank (i)	Blank (ii)
Ⓐ manifested	Ⓓ orthodoxy
Ⓑ lampooned	Ⓔ spontaneity
Ⓒ disavowed	Ⓕ burlesque

12. Although she had received many compliments for her (i) _____ in debate, at her inauguration as president of the student body she was surprisingly (ii) _____.

Blank (i)	Blank (ii)
Ⓐ candor	Ⓓ inarticulate
Ⓑ analysis	Ⓔ inattentive
Ⓒ fluency	Ⓕ inconsiderate

13. Even though their subjects and approaches are quite different, each of these filmmakers takes great care to (i) _____ a strong sense of place. In this way, they make their films intimate portraits of not only the characters but also the (ii) _____.

Blank (i)	Blank (ii)
Ⓐ reject	Ⓓ settings they emulate
Ⓑ impart	Ⓔ families they abandon
Ⓒ vitiate	Ⓕ spaces they inhabit

14. In England after 1600, small bass viols called division viols began to (i) _____ larger consort basses. They remained the dominant viol size until they (ii) _____ during the eighteenth century.

Blank (i)	Blank (ii)
Ⓐ impede	Ⓓ went out of fashion
Ⓑ displace	Ⓔ gained prominence
Ⓒ circumvent	Ⓕ achieved closure

15. The perpetual spinning of particles is much like that of a top, with one significant (i) _____: unlike the top, the particles have no need to be wound up, for (ii) _____ is one of their (iii) _____ properties.

Blank (i)	Blank (ii)
Ⓐ difference	Ⓓ circuitousness
Ⓑ correlation	Ⓔ rotation
Ⓒ result	Ⓕ collision

Blank (iii)
Ⓖ intrinsic
Ⓗ hypothetical
Ⓘ intangible

**Directions:** The passage below is followed by questions based on its content. Once you have read the passage, select the answer choice that _best_ answers each question. Answer all questions on the basis of what is _stated_ or _implied_ in the passage.

For each of Questions 16–20, select one answer choice unless otherwise instructed.

Questions 16–17 are based on the following passage.

How is a newborn star formed? For the answer to this question, we must look to the familiar physical concept of gravitational instability. It is a simple concept, long known to scientists, having been first recognized by Isaac Newton in the late 1600s.

(5)   Let us envision a cloud of interstellar atoms and molecules, slightly admixed with dust. This cloud of interstellar gas is static and uniform. Suddenly, something occurs to disturb the gas, causing one small area within it to condense. As this small area increases in density, becoming slightly denser than the gas around it, its gravitational field likewise increases

(10) somewhat in strength. More matter now is attracted to the area, and its gravity becomes even stronger; as a result, it starts to contract, in process increasing in density even more. This in turn further increases its gravity, so that it accumulates still more matter and contracts further still. And so the process continues, until finally the small area of gas gives birth to a

(15) gravitationally bound object, a newborn star.

16. It can be inferred from the passage that the author views the information contained within it as

Ⓐ controversial but irrefutable
Ⓑ speculative and unprofitable
Ⓒ uncomplicated and traditional
Ⓓ original but obscure
Ⓔ sadly lacking in elaboration

Directions: For the following question, consider each of the choices separately and select *all* that apply.

17. The author provides information that answers which of the following questions?

    A How does the small area's increasing density affect its gravitational field?

    B What causes the disturbance that changes the cloud from its original static state?

    C What is the end result of the gradually increasing concentration of the small area of gas?

Questions 18–20 are based on the following passage.

The Quechua world is submerged, so to speak, in a cosmic magma that weighs heavily upon it. It possesses the rare quality of being as it were interjected into the midst of antagonistic forces, which in turn implies a whole
Line body of social and aesthetic structures whose innermost meaning must be
(5) the administration of energy. This gives rise to the social organism known as the *ayllu*, the agrarian community that regulates the procurement of food. The *ayllu* formed the basic structure of the whole Inca empire.

The central idea of this organization was a kind of closed economy, just the opposite of our economic practices, which can be described as open.
(10) The closed economy rested on the fact that the Inca controlled both the production and consumption of food. When one adds to this fact the religious ideas noted in the Quechua texts cited by the chronicler Santa Cruz Pachacuti, one comes to the conclusion that in the Andean zone the margin of life was minimal and was made possible only by the system of magic the
(15) Quechua constructed through his religion.

Adversities, moreover, were numerous, for the harvest might fail at any time and bring starvation to millions. Hence the whole purpose of the Quechua administrative and ideological system was to carry on the arduous task of achieving *abundance* and staving off shortages. This kind of struc-
(20) ture presupposes a state of unremitting anxiety, which could not be resolved by action. The Quechua could not do so because his primordial response to problems was the use of magic, that is, recourse to the unconscious for the solution of external problems. Thus the struggle against the world was a struggle against the dark depths of the Quechua's own psyche, where the
(25) solution was found. By overcoming the unconscious, the outer world was also vanquished.

These considerations permit us to classify Quechua culture as absolutely static or, more accurately, as the expression of a mere state of being. Only in this way can we understand the refuge that it took in the germinative
(30) center of the cosmic *mandala* as revealed by Quechua art. The Quechua empire was nothing more than a *mandala*, for it was divided into four zones, with Cuzco in the center. Here the Quechua ensconced himself to contemplate the decline of the world as though it were caused by an alien and autonomous force.

18. The term "mandala" as used in the last paragraph most likely means

   (A) an agrarian community
   (B) a kind of superstition
   (C) a closed economic pattern
   (D) a philosophy or way of regarding the world
   (E) a figure composed of four divisions

19. The author implies that the Quechua world was

   (A) uncivilized
   (B) highly introspective
   (C) vitally energetic
   (D) free of major worries
   (E) well organized

20. With which of the following statements would the author most likely agree?

   (A) Only psychological solutions can remedy economic ills.
   (B) The Quechua were renowned for equanimity and unconcern.
   (C) The Quechua limited themselves to realizable goals.
   (D) Much of Quechua existence was harsh and frustrating.
   (E) Modern Western society should adopt some Quechua economic ideas.

SECTION 3—QUANTITATIVE ABILITY

Time —35 minutes
20 Questions

> **Directions:** In each of Questions 1–8, there are two quantities—Quantity A and Quantity B. You are to compare those quantities, taking into consideration any additional information given. The correct answer to such a question is
>
> (A) Quantity A is greater.
> (B) Quantity B is greater.
> (C) The two quantities are equal.
> (D) It is impossible to determine which quantity is greater.
>
> *Note:* The given information, if any, is always centered above the two quantities. In any question, if a symbol or letter appears more than once, it represents the same thing each time.

1.

m and n are positive integers
$$mn = 25$$

Quantity A	Quantity B
m	n

2.

Quantity A	Quantity B
65% of a	$\frac{2}{3}$ of a

3.

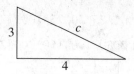

Quantity A	Quantity B
c	5

4.

$$a + b = 24$$
$$a - b = 25$$

Quantity A	Quantity B
b	0

5.

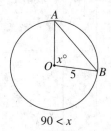

$$90 < x$$

Quantity A	Quantity B
The length of AB	7

6.

n	Frequency
1	4
2	5
3	2
4	3
5	6

The table above shows the frequency
distribution of the values of a variable, n.

Quantity A	Quantity B
The average (arithmetic mean) of the median and mode of the distribution	The range of the distribution

7.

List 1: 25, 50, 75, 100, 125

List 2: 50, 100, 150, 200, 250

Quantity A	Quantity B
The standard deviation of the data in List 1	The standard deviation of the data in List 2

8.

A school group charters three identical buses and occupies $\frac{4}{5}$ of the seats. After $\frac{1}{4}$ of the passengers leave, the remaining passengers use only two of the buses.

Quantity A	Quantity B
The fraction of the seats on the two buses that are now occupied	$\frac{9}{10}$

**Directions:** Questions 9–20 have three different formats. Unless a question has its own directions that specifically state otherwise, each question has five answer choices, exactly one of which is correct.

9. The Center City Little League is divided into d divisions. Each division has t teams, and each team has p players. How many players are there in the entire league?

    (A) $d + t + p$

    (B) dtp

    (C) $\dfrac{pt}{d}$

    (D) $\dfrac{dt}{p}$

    (E) $\dfrac{d}{pt}$

10. In 1980, the cost of p pounds of potatoes was d dollars. In 1990, the cost of $2p$ pounds of potatoes was $\dfrac{1}{2} d$ dollars. By what percent did the price of potatoes decrease from 1980 to 1990?

    (A) 25%
    (B) 50%
    (C) 75%
    (D) 100%
    (E) 400%

11. A number x is chosen at random from the set of positive integers less than 10. What is the probability that $\dfrac{9}{x} > x$?

12. A bag contains 3 red, 4 white, and 5 blue marbles. Jason begins removing marbles from the bag at random, one at a time. What is the least number of marbles he must remove to be sure that he has at least one of each color?

   (A) 3
   (B) 6
   (C) 8
   (D) 10
   (E) 12

13. Jordan has taken 5 math tests so far this semester. If he gets a 70 on his next test, it will lower the average (arithmetic mean) of his test scores by 4 points. What is his average now?

Questions 14–16 refer to the following graphs.

Adult education participation rates in the past 12 months: 1991 and 1995

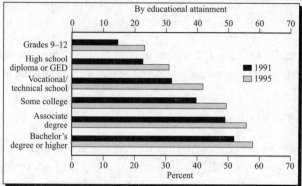

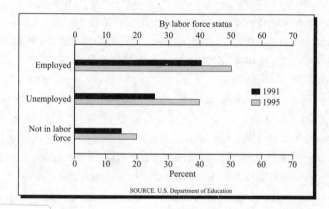

Directions: For the following question, consider each of the choices separately and select *all* that apply.

14. Which of the following is a valid conclusion from the graphs and the fact that the population of the United States was greater in 1995 than in 1991?

    Indicate *all* such conclusions.

    A In 1991, adults whose highest degree was at least a bachelor's were more than twice as likely to participate in adult education than those whose highest educational attainment was a high school diploma or GED (high school equivalency diploma).

    B On a percentage basis, from 1991 to 1995, the greatest increase in the adult education participation rate was among those adults whose highest educational attainment was grades 9–12, without earning a high school diploma.

    C In 1995, more people participated in adult education programs than in 1991.

    D From 1991 to 1995 the rate of participation in adult education among the groups represented in the graphs increased the least for those who attained at least a bachelor's degree.

    E In 1995, more adults with at least a bachelor's degree participated in adult education than did adults who attended some college but did not earn a college degree.

15. If, in the United States in 1995, there were 100 million employed adults and 40 million adults not in the labor force, then approximately what was the ratio of the number of employed adults participating in adult education to the number of people not in the labor force participating in adult education?

    (A) 5:4
    (B) 5:2
    (C) 10:3
    (D) 5:1
    (E) 6:1

Directions: For the following question, enter your answer in the box.

16. Assume that in 1996 the unemployment rate was 8%, meaning that 8 out of every 100 adults in the workforce were unemployed. What percentage of adults in the labor force participated in adult education? Round your answer to the nearest whole percent.

[   ] %

17. If a and b are the lengths of the legs of a right triangle whose hypotenuse is 10 and whose area is 20, what is the value of $(a + b)^2$?

    (A) 100
    (B) 120
    (C) 140
    (D) 180
    (E) 200

18. What is the average (arithmetic mean) of 3^{30}, 3^{60}, and 3^{90}?

    (A) 3^{60}
    (B) 3^{177}
    (C) $3^{10} + 3^{20} + 3^{30}$
    (D) $3^{27} + 3^{57} + 3^{87}$
    (E) $3^{29} + 3^{59} + 3^{89}$

19. The figure below consists of four semicircles in a large semicircle. If the small semicircles have radii of 1, 2, 3, and 4, what is the perimeter of the shaded region?

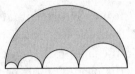

Ⓐ 10π

Ⓑ 20π

Ⓒ 40π

Ⓓ 60π

Ⓔ 100π

Directions: The answer to the following question is a fraction. Enter the numerator in the upper box and the denominator in the lower box.

20. If a and b are numbers such that when a is increased by 25% and b is decreased by 25%, the resulting numbers are equal. What is the ratio of a to b?

$$\frac{\boxed{}}{\boxed{}}$$

SECTION 4—VERBAL REASONING

Time —30 minutes
20 Questions

> **Directions:** For each of the following sentences, select the **two** answers of the six choices given that, when substituted in the sentence, both logically complete the sentence as a whole **and** create sentences that are equivalent to one another in meaning.

Questions 1–6

1. Ironically, the same mayor who preached _____ to his constituents was noted for his extravagance and his free-spending lifestyle.
   - [A] righteousness
   - [B] radicalism
   - [C] economy
   - [D] austerity
   - [E] repentance
   - [F] honesty

2. The portrait painter was disinclined to accept a commission unless she was assured of adequate _____ for the task.
   - [A] recompense
   - [B] illumination
   - [C] personnel
   - [D] remuneration
   - [E] equipment
   - [F] expertise

3. Beginning with the music and dance of the antebellum plantation, jazz, born from a slave culture, would eventually _____ a musical industry that African musicians would dominate for years to come.

  A preclude

  B spawn

  C withstand

  D advocate

  E disenfranchise

  F generate

4. To a sophisticated audience conversant with the wide range of contemporary literary criticism, this brief essay would have been seen as a _____ version of arguments rehearsed in much more detail elsewhere.

  A synoptic

  B perceptive

  C condensed

  D generic

  E censored

  F forensic

5. Among contemporary writers of fiction, Mrs. Woolf is _____ figure, in some ways as radical as James Joyce, in others no more modern than Jane Austen.

  A a curious

  B an introspective

  C a peripheral

  D a disinterested

  E an anomalous

  F a doctrinaire

6. Book publishing has long been _____ profession, partly because for younger editors the best way to win a raise or a promotion was to move on to another publishing house.

A an innovative

B a prestigious

C an itinerant

D a mobile

E a rewarding

F an insular

Directions: The passage below is followed by questions based on its content. Once you have read the passage, select the answer choice that _best_ answers each question. Answer all questions on the basis of what is _stated_ or _implied_ in the passage.

For each of Questions 7–9, select _one_ answer choice unless otherwise instructed.

Questions 7–9 are based on the following passage.

Mary Shelley herself was the first to point to her fortuitous immersion in the literary and scientific revolutions of her day as the source of her novel _Frankenstein_. Her extreme youth, as well as her sex, have contributed to the
Line   generally held opinion that she was not so much an author in her own right
(5)   as a transparent medium through which passed the ideas of those around her. "All Mrs. Shelley did," writes Mario Praz, "was to provide a passive reflection of some of the wild fantasies which were living in the air about her."
Passive reflections, however, do not produce original works of literature, and _Frankenstein_, if not a great novel, was unquestionably an original one.
(10)   The major Romantic and minor Gothic tradition to which it _should_ have belonged was to the literature of the overreacher: the superman who breaks through normal human limitations to defy the rules of society and infringe upon the realm of God. In the Faust story, hypertrophy of the individual will is symbolized by a pact with the devil. Byron's and Balzac's heroes; the
(15)   Wandering Jew; the chained and unchained Prometheus: all are overreachers, all are punished by their own excesses—by a surfeit of sensation, of experience, of knowledge and, most typically, by the doom of eternal life.

But Mary Shelley's overreacher is different. Frankenstein's exploration of the forbidden boundaries of human science does not cause the prolongation
(20) and extension of his own life, but the creation of a new one. He defies mortality not by living forever, but by giving birth.

7. The author quotes Mario Praz primarily in order to

(A) support her own perception of Mary Shelley's uniqueness

(B) illustrate recent changes in scholarly opinions of Shelley

(C) demonstrate Praz's unfamiliarity with Shelley's *Frankenstein*

(D) provide an example of the predominant critical view of Shelley

(E) contrast Praz's statement about Shelley with Shelley's own self-appraisal

8. The author of the passage concedes which of the following about Mary Shelley as an author?

(A) She was unaware of the literary and mythological traditions of the overreacher.

(B) She intentionally parodied the scientific and literary discoveries of her time.

(C) She was exposed to radical artistic and scientific concepts which influenced her work.

(D) She lacked the maturity to create a literary work of absolute originality.

(E) She was not so much an author in her own right as an imitator of the literary works of others.

9. According to the author, Frankenstein parts from the traditional figure of the overreacher in

(A) his exaggerated will

(B) his atypical purpose

(C) the excesses of his method

(D) the inevitability of his failure

(E) his defiance of the deity

Directions: Each of the following sentences or groups of sentences contains one, two, or three blanks. These blanks signify that a word or set of words has been left out. Below each sentence are columns of words or sets of words. For each blank, pick the *one* word or set of words from the corresponding column that *best* completes the text.

Questions 10–14

10. With units covering such topics as euthanasia, organ transplantation, and patient rights, the course *Religion, Ethics, and Medicine* explores the ways in which religious ideas and concepts _____ the practice of medicine and delivery of health care.

Ⓐ	inform
Ⓑ	obviate
Ⓒ	reiterate
Ⓓ	preclude
Ⓔ	deny

11. To the embittered ex-philanthropist, all the former recipients of his charity were (i) _____, as stingy with their thanks as they were wasteful of his (ii) _____.

Blank (i)		Blank (ii)	
Ⓐ	misers	Ⓓ	gratitude
Ⓑ	ingrates	Ⓔ	largesse
Ⓒ	prigs	Ⓕ	equanimity

12. For centuries, physicists have had good reason to believe in the principle of equivalence propounded by Galileo: it has (i) _____ many rigorous tests that (ii) _____ its accuracy to extraordinary precision.

Blank (i)	Blank (ii)
Ⓐ predicted	Ⓓ established
Ⓑ survived	Ⓔ compromised
Ⓒ postulated	Ⓕ equated

13. The actress had (i) _____ getting people to do things for her, and, to her delight, her new friends proved quite (ii) _____ in finding new ways to meet her needs.

Blank (i)	Blank (ii)
Ⓐ a knack for	Ⓓ assiduous
Ⓑ a disinclination for	Ⓔ dilatory
Ⓒ an indifference to	Ⓕ stoical

14. Although he did not consider himself (i) _____, he felt that the inconsistencies in her story (ii) _____ a certain degree of incredulity on his part.

Blank (i)	Blank (ii)
Ⓐ an apostate	Ⓓ intimated
Ⓑ a skeptic	Ⓔ dignified
Ⓒ a hypocrite	Ⓕ warranted

Directions: The passage below is followed by questions based on its content. Once you have read the passage, select the answer choice that *best* answers each question. Answer all questions on the basis of what is *stated* or *implied* in the passage.

For each of Questions 15–20, select *one* answer choice unless otherwise instructed.

Questions 15–17 are based on the following passage.

(The passage was written in the latter half of the 20th century.)

The coastlines on the two sides of the Atlantic Ocean present a notable parallelism: the easternmost region of Brazil, in Pernambuco, has a convexity that corresponds almost perfectly with the concavity of the African Gulf
Line of Guinea, while the contours of the African coastline between Rio de Oro
(5) and Liberia would, by the same approximation, match those of the Caribbean Sea.

Similar correspondences are also observed in many other regions of the Earth. This observation began to awaken scientific interest about sixty years ago, when Alfred Wegener, a professor at the University of Hamburg, used it
(10) as a basis for formulating a revolutionary theory in geological science.

According to Wegener, there was originally only one continent or land mass, which he called Pangaea. Inasmuch as continental masses are lighter than the base on which they rest, he reasoned, they must float on the substratum of igneous rock, known as sima, as ice floes float on the sea. Then
(15) why, he asked, might continents not be subject to drifting? The rotation of the globe and other forces, he thought, had caused the cracking and, finally, the breaking apart of the original Pangaea, along an extensive line represented today by the longitudinal submerged mountain range in the center of the Atlantic. While Africa seems to have remained static, the Americas
(20) apparently drifted toward the west until they reached their present position after more than 100 million years. Although the phenomenon seems fantastic, accustomed as we are to the concept of the rigidity and immobility of the continents, on the basis of the distance that separates them it is possible to calculate that the continental drift would have been no greater than
(25) two inches per year.

15. The primary purpose of the passage is to

Ⓐ describe the relative speed of continental movement
Ⓑ predict the future configuration of the continents
Ⓒ refute a radical theory postulating continental movement
Ⓓ describe the reasoning behind a geological theory
Ⓔ explain how to calculate the continental drift per year

16. It can be inferred from the passage that evidence for continental drift has been provided by the

Ⓐ correspondences between coastal contours
Ⓑ proof of an original solitary land mass
Ⓒ level of sima underlying the continents
Ⓓ immobility of the African continent
Ⓔ relative heaviness of the continental masses

17. The passage presents information that would answer which of the following questions?

Ⓐ In what ways do the coastlines of Africa and South America differ from one another?
Ⓑ How much lighter than the substratum of igneous rock below them are the continental masses?
Ⓒ Is the rotation of the globe affecting the stability of the present day continental masses?
Ⓓ According to Wegener's theory, in what direction have the Americas tended to move?
Ⓔ How does Wegener's theory account for the apparent immobility of the African continent?

Questions 18–20 are based on the following passage.

During the 1930s, National Association for the Advancement of Colored People (NAACP) attorneys Charles H. Houston, William Hastie, James M. Nabrit, Leon Ransom, and Thurgood Marshall charted a legal strategy
(Line) designed to end segregation in education. They developed a series of legal
(5) cases challenging segregation in graduate and professional schools. Houston believed that the battle against segregation had to begin at the highest academic level in order to mitigate fear of race mixing that could create even greater hostility and reluctance on the part of white judges. After establishing a series of favorable legal precedents in higher education,
(10) NAACP attorneys planned to launch an all-out attack on the separate-but-equal doctrine in primary and secondary schools. The strategy proved successful. In four major United States Supreme Court decisions precedents were established that would enable the NAACP to construct a solid legal foundation upon which the Brown case could rest: *Missouri ex rel. Gaines* v.
(15) *Canada, Registrar of the University of Missouri* (1938); *Sipuel* v. *Board of Regents of the University of Oklahoma* (1948); *McLaurin* v. *Oklahoma State Regents for Higher Education* (1950); and *Sweatt* v. *Painter* (1950).

In the Oklahoma case, the Supreme Court held that the plaintiff was entitled to enroll in the University. The Oklahoma Regents responded by sepa-
(20) rating black and white students in cafeterias and classrooms. The 1950 McLaurin decision ruled that such internal separation was unconstitutional. In the Sweatt ruling, delivered on the same day, the Supreme Court held that the maintenance of separate law schools for whites and blacks was unconstitutional. A year after Herman Sweatt entered the University of Texas law
(25) school, desegregation cases were filed in the states of Kansas, South Carolina, Virginia, and Delaware and in the District of Columbia asking the courts to apply the qualitative test of the Sweatt case to the elementary and secondary schools and to declare the separate-but-equal doctrine invalid in the area of public education.
(30) The 1954 *Brown* v. *Board of Education* decision declared that a classification based solely on race violated the 14th Amendment to the United States Constitution. The decision reversed the 1896 *Plessy* v. *Ferguson* ruling, which had established the separate-but-equal doctrine. The *Brown* decision more than any other case launched the "equalitarian revolution"
(35) in American jurisprudence and signalled the emerging primacy of equality as a guide to constitutional decisions; nevertheless, the decision did not end state sanctioned segregation. Indeed, the second *Brown* decision, known as *Brown II* and delivered a year later, played a decisive role in limiting the effectiveness and impact of the 1954 case by providing southern states with
(40) the opportunity to delay the implementation of desegregation.

18. According to the passage, Houston aimed his legislative challenge at the graduate and professional school level on the basis of the assumption that

   Ⓐ the greatest inequities existed at the highest academic and professional levels
   Ⓑ the separate-but-equal doctrine applied solely to the highest academic levels
   Ⓒ there were clear precedents for reform in existence at the graduate school level
   Ⓓ the judiciary would feel less apprehension at desegregation on the graduate level
   Ⓔ the consequences of desegregation would become immediately apparent at the graduate school level

19. Which of the following statements is most compatible with the principles embodied in *Plessy* v. *Ferguson* as described in the passage?

   Ⓐ Internal separation of whites and blacks within a given school is unconstitutional.
   Ⓑ Whites and blacks may be educated in separate schools so long as they offer comparable facilities.
   Ⓒ The maintenance of separate professional schools for blacks and whites is unconstitutional.
   Ⓓ The separate-but-equal doctrine is inapplicable to the realm of private education.
   Ⓔ Blacks may be educated in schools with whites whenever the blacks and whites have equal institutions.

20. The aspect of Houston's work most extensively discussed in the passage is its

   Ⓐ psychological canniness
   Ⓑ judicial complexity
   Ⓒ fundamental efficiency
   Ⓓ radical intellectualism
   Ⓔ exaggerated idealism

SECTION 5—QUANTITATIVE ABILITY

Time —35 minutes
20 Questions

Directions: In each of Questions 1–7, there are two quantities—Quantity A and Quantity B. You are to compare those quantities, taking into consideration any additional information given. The correct answer to such a question is

Ⓐ Quantity A is greater.
Ⓑ Quantity B is greater.
Ⓒ The two quantities are equal.
Ⓓ It is impossible to determine which quantity is greater.

Note: The given information, if any, is always centered above the two quantities. In any question, if a symbol or letter appears more than once, it represents the same thing each time.

1.

Quantity A	Quantity B
$(-8)^8$	$(-9)^9$

2.

$$a > 0$$

Quantity A	Quantity B
$\sqrt{a^{18}}$	$(a^2)(a^3)(a^4)$

3.

The price of a large pizza is 30% more than the price of a small pizza.

Quantity A	Quantity B
The price of a large pizza when it is on sale for 30% off	The price of a small pizza

4.

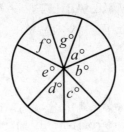

Quantity A	Quantity B
The average	50
(arithmetic mean)	
of a, b, c, d, e, f, and g	

5.

A palindrome is an integer that reads the same from left to right as from right to left (ignoring commas). For example, 22; 171; 3,003; and 18,481 are all palindromes.

Quantity A	Quantity B
The number of	The number of
5-digit palindromes	6-digit palindromes

6.

Quantity A	Quantity B
The area of an	The area of an
equilateral triangle	isosceles right
whose sides are 6	triangle whose
	legs are 6

7.

A bag contains four slips of paper, two of which have the number 1 written on them and two of which have the number –1 on them. Two of the slips are chosen at random.

Quantity A	Quantity B
The probability	The probability
that the product of	that the product of
the two numbers	the two numbers
chosen is –1	chosen is 1

Directions: Questions 8–20 have three different formats. Unless a question has its own directions that specifically state otherwise, each question has five answer choices, exactly one of which is correct.

8. John bought a $100 DVD player on sale at 8% off. How much did he pay including 8% sales tax?

   (A) $84.64
   (B) $92.00
   (C) $96.48
   (D) $99.36
   (E) $100.00

9. The sum of the lengths of all the edges of a cube is 3 feet. What is the volume, in cubic feet, of the cube?

   (A) $\dfrac{1}{64}$

   (B) $\dfrac{1}{8}$

   (C) $\dfrac{1}{4}$

   (D) 8

   (E) 27

Directions: For the following question, enter your answer in the box.

10. Mary read from the top of page 10 to the bottom of page 24 in 30 minutes. At this rate, how long, in minutes, will it take her to read from the top of page 25 to the bottom of page 50?

    ⬚ minutes

11. For how many positive integers $m \leq 100$ is $(m - 5)(m - 45)$ positive?

(A) 45

(B) 50

(C) 58

(D) 59

(E) 60

12. The magazine *Modern Crafts* published the instructions for making a circular mosaic whose diameter is 20 centimeters. Geraldine wants to use tiles of the same size as those listed in the magazine article to make a larger mosaic—one that is 30 centimeters in diameter. To have the correct number of tiles for her mosaic, by what factor must she multiply the number of tiles that were listed in the magazine's directions?

(A) 2.25

(B) 2.00

(C) 1.50

(D) 1.44

(E) 0.67

Directions: For the following question, consider each of the choices separately and select *all* that apply.

---

13. Every year between 70% and 85% of the students at Central High School attend the homecoming rally. If one year 1435 students attended the rally, which of the following could have been the number of students at Central High School that year?

Indicate *all* possible numbers of students.

A 1675

B 1775

C 1875

D 1975

E 2075

Questions 14–16 refer to the following graphs.

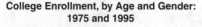

College Enrollment, by Age and Gender:
1975 and 1995

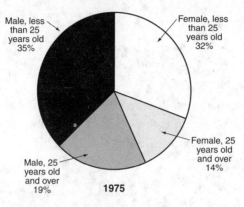

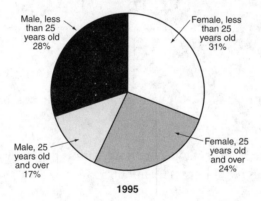

Source: U.S. Bureau of the Census, Current Population Survey.

Directions: For the following question, enter your answer in the box.

14. If there were 10,000,000 college students in 1975, how many more male
    students were there than female students?

15. In 1975, approximately what percent of female college students were at least 25 years old?

  Ⓐ 14%
  Ⓑ 30%
  Ⓒ 45%
  Ⓓ 69%
  Ⓔ 76%

16. If the total number of students enrolled in college was 40% higher in 1995 than in 1975, what is the ratio of the number of male students in 1995 to the number of male students in 1975?

  Ⓐ 5:6
  Ⓑ 6:7
  Ⓒ 7:6
  Ⓓ 6:5
  Ⓔ 7:5

Directions: For the following question, enter your answer in the box.

---

17. Eric can address 40 envelopes per hour. At this rate, how many envelopes can he address in 99 minutes?

  ☐

Directions: For the following question, consider each of the choices separately and select *all* that apply.

18. At Florence Pizza, the only slices of pizza available are plain and pepperoni, which cost $1.50 and $2.00, respectively. Small, medium, and large cups of soda cost $1.00, $1.50, and $1.75, respectively. Which of the following could be the total cost of two slices of pizza and two sodas? Indicate *all* such costs.

    A $5.00

    B $5.25

    C $6.00

    D $6.25

    E $7.00

    F $7.25

19. In a normal distribution, 68% of the scores lie within one standard deviation of the mean. If the SAT scores of all the high school juniors in Center City followed a normal distribution with a mean of 500 and a standard deviation of 100, and if 10,200 students scored between 400 and 500, approximately how many students scored above 600?

    Ⓐ 2,400
    Ⓑ 4,800
    Ⓒ 5,100
    Ⓓ 7,200
    Ⓔ 9,600

20. If $x + y = 10$, and $xy = 20$, what is the value of $\dfrac{1}{x} + \dfrac{1}{y}$?

(A) $\dfrac{1}{20}$

(B) $\dfrac{1}{15}$

(C) $\dfrac{1}{10}$

(D) $\dfrac{1}{2}$

(E) 2

MODEL TEST 2 ANSWER KEY

Section 1—Analytical Writing

The Analytical Writing sections are scored holistically, in accordance with the following guidelines.

First, estimate your score on the Issue Essay by using the following rubric.

	Argument	Support	Structure	Fluency	Conventions
6	Presents a clear and perceptive argument that responds to the specific task instructions	Provides strong reasoning and/or examples to fully support its thesis	Is focused and very well organized and has logical and skillful transitions between ideas	Expresses ideas clearly and fluently, with sophisticated word choice and varied sentence structure	Displays impressive command of the grammar, usage, and mechanics of standard written English
5	Presents a clear and thoughtful argument that responds to the specific task instructions	Provides logical reasoning and/or appropriate examples to support its thesis	Is focused and well organized and has logical transitions between ideas	Expresses ideas effectively, with appropriate word choice and varied sentence structure	Displays solid command of the grammar, usage, and mechanics of standard written English
4	Presents a clear argument that adequately responds to the specific task instructions	Provides adequate reasoning and/or examples to support its thesis	Is reasonably well focused and organized	Expresses ideas effectively, with appropriate word choice	Displays command of the grammar, usage, and mechanics of standard written English
3	Presents an argument that is somewhat unclear or that does not clearly respond to the specific task instructions	Makes unsupported claims or has limited relevant examples to support its thesis	Is minimally focused and/or organized	Is somewhat unclear due to incorrect word choice or sentence structure	Includes infrequent major or frequent minor errors in grammar, usage, and/or mechanics
2	Presents an argument that is unclear or fails to address the specific task instructions	Provides nearly no relevant examples or reasons to support its thesis	Is unfocused and/or disorganized	Is unclear due to frequent incorrect word choice or sentence structure	Includes significant errors in grammar, usage, and/or mechanics that render its meaning unclear
1	Presents an argument that demonstrates severely limited understanding of the topic	Provides little to no examples or reasoning that are related to the assigned topic	Is extremely disorganized or excessively short	Is very unclear due to pervasive incorrect word choice or sentence structure	Includes pervasive errors in grammar, usage, and/or mechanics that render it indecipherable
0	Addresses a topic other than the one assigned, is written in a language other than English, is nothing more than the words in the topic and/or task instructions, is nothing more than random characters, is not legible.				

As you examine the rubric you will notice that all of the scores below four are shaded gray. The reason for this is that ETS, the maker of the GRE, states that essays scoring below four display **one or more** of the characteristics listed in the shaded area. In other words, if your essay displays even one characteristic listed in the shaded area, that low score will determine your overall score. If all of your essay's characteristics are found in the boxes above the shaded area, your score should be the average of the five scores (for argument, support, structure, fluency, and writing conventions).

Scoring the Issue Essay

Using the Issue Essay rubric, check the box in each column that best describes your work. If each of the boxes you have checked is above the shaded area, add those five scores together and calculate their average.

Example:

Argument	4
Support	4
Structure	5
Fluency	4
Conventions	4
Total	21

The average is 4.2, rounded down to a likely score of 4.

If, however, **any** of your scores fall into the shaded area of the rubric, the lowest score marked will be your final score.

Next, estimate your score on the Argument Essay by using the following rubric.

	Argument	Support	Structure	Fluency	Conventions
6	Pinpoints the elements of the argument at issue and evaluates them with great insight	Provides detailed and persuasive support for its main points	Expresses ideas clearly and is very well organized, with logical and clear transitions between ideas	Expresses ideas clearly and fluently, with sophisticated word choice and varied sentence structure	Displays impressive command of the grammar, usage, and mechanics of standard written English
5	Pinpoints the elements of the argument at issue and evaluates them thoughtfully	Provides thoughtful and persuasive support for its main points	Expresses ideas clearly and is well organized, with suitable transitions between ideas	Expresses ideas effectively, with appropriate word choice and varied sentence structure	Displays solid command of the grammar, usage, and mechanics of standard written English
4	Identifies the elements of the argument at issue and evaluates them, but may include less relevant points	Provides sufficient, though possibly uneven, support for its main points	Expresses ideas reasonably clearly and is organized, but transitions between ideas are inadequate or absent	Expresses ideas effectively, with appropriate word choice	Displays command of the grammar, usage, and mechanics of standard written English
3	Fails to distinguish or evaluate the most relevant elements of the argument, though some relevant aspects may be discussed	Provides support that is sometimes irrelevant to its main points	Expresses ideas with little depth and/or organizes them illogically	Is somewhat unclear due to incorrect word choice or sentence structure	Includes infrequent major or frequent minor errors in grammar, usage, and/or mechanics
2	Fails to evaluate the argument using logic, but may provide the writer's personal views on the topic	Provides support that is generally irrelevant to its main points	Expresses ideas inadequately and organizes them illogically	Is unclear due to frequent incorrect word choice or sentence structure	Includes significant errors in grammar, usage, and/or mechanics that render its meaning unclear
1	Fails to demonstrate any grasp of the argument at issue	Provides no support for its main points	Is extremely disorganized or excessively short	Is very unclear due to pervasive incorrect word choice or sentence structure	Includes pervasive errors in grammar, usage, and/or mechanics that render it indecipherable
0	Addresses a topic other than the one assigned, is written in a language other than English, is nothing more than the words in the topic and/or task instructions, is nothing more than random characters, is not legible.				

Scoring the Argument Essay

Using the Argument Essay rubric, check the box in each column that best describes your work. If each of the boxes you have checked is above the shaded area, add those five scores together and calculate their average.

Calculating Your Overall Score

To determine your overall Analytical Writing score, add the scores for both essays (Issue and Argument) together and divide by 2. The overall score is given in half-point increments, so you should round up to the nearest half point when calculating this score. As an example, if you earn a score of 5 on the Issue Essay and a score of 4.5 on the Argument Essay, your overall Analytical Writing score will be 4.75, rounded up to 5.

Section 2—Verbal Reasoning

1. **D, E**	6. **D, E**	11. **A, E**	16. **C**
2. **B, E**	7. **D**	12. **C, D**	17. **A, C**
3. **A, C**	8. **E**	13. **B, F**	18. **E**
4. **B, D**	9. **E**	14. **B, D**	19. **B**
5. **C, E**	10. **C**	15. **A, E, G**	20. **D**

Section 3—Quantitative Ability

1. **D**	6. **C**	11. **2/9**	16. **49**
2. **D**	7. **B**	12. **D**	17. **D**
3. **D**	8. **C**	13. **94**	18. **E**
4. **B**	9. **B**	14. **A, B, C, D**	19. **B**
5. **A**	10. **C**	15. **E**	20. **3/5**

Section 4—Verbal Reasoning

1. **C, D**	6. **C, D**	11. **B, E**	16. **A**
2. **A, D**	7. **D**	12. **B, D**	17. **D**
3. **B, F**	8. **C**	13. **A, D**	18. **D**
4. **A, C**	9. **B**	14. **B, F**	19. **B**
5. **A, E**	10. **A**	15. **D**	20. **A**

Section 5—Quantitative Ability

1. **A**	6. **B**	11. **D**	16. **C**
2. **C**	7. **A**	12. **A**	17. **66**
3. **B**	8. **D**	13. **B, C, D**	18. **A, C, D, E, F**
4. **A**	9. **A**	14. **800,000**	19. **B**
5. **C**	10. **52**	15. **B**	20. **D**

ANSWER EXPLANATIONS

Section 1—Analytical Writing

PROMPT #1

"Public secondary school students should be required to pass a standardized national exit exam in order to receive a high school diploma."

Compose an essay that presents your opinion on the policy presented, explicating your rationale for this opinion. As you build and provide evidence for your argument, you must take into account the likely effects of applying the policy and describe the impact these potential effects have on your argument.

SCORE 6 ISSUE ESSAY

Since the publication of the report, "A Nation at Risk," in the early 1980s, policy makers and pundits have decried the poor quality of American education. They argue that our public schools, once the envy of the world, have lost their way. Business leaders complain that many high school graduates lack basic skills, creating a shortage of qualified workers. Critics also lament the significant achievement gap between students in wealthy suburban communities and their peers in many of the nation's largest urban school systems. This frustration has led many to support the implementation of a standardized national high school exit exam in order to set high standards for all students. Unfortunately, there is no simple answer to the challenges facing the American system of public education, and the consequences of implementing a standardized national high school exit exam are likely to be both counterproductive and discriminatory.

A standardized national high school exit exam is more likely to harm the quality of American education than it is to improve it. Standardized tests are ideal for measuring subject matter knowledge, but they are inadequate instruments for measuring skills like writing and problem solving. If a standardized national high school exit exam is implemented, schools will be evaluated and ranked based on the scores their students achieve. This ranking will create pressure on administrators and teachers to improve student test scores, and "teaching to the test" will be an inevitable consequence. Tragically, because these tests privilege recall of facts over demonstration of skills, school districts will alter their curricula in order to maximize their students' performance on the national test. Class time that was once dedicated to writing and hands-on problem solving will be given over to rote memorization and drill, creating students who are less skilled and prepared than their predecessors.

Not only will a national standardized high school exit exam fail to improve the quality of education in the United States, but it will also exacerbate the inequality for which some propose it as a remedy. Standardized testing cannot shrink the achievement gap between wealthy suburban students and their less fortunate urban counterparts. Without improved resources to address the systemic causes of the achievement gap, students in failing districts will continue to struggle. Only now, with a standardized national test, all students will be held to the same standards, regardless of the advantages or disadvantages they face. The upshot of this is that high school graduation will become a more distant goal for the very students who struggle the most. The dropout rate in large urban districts will rise, and the unfortunate products of these schools will find themselves less employable. As businesses abandon these communities due to a shortage of qualified workers, unemployment will increase. As local economies decline, so too will property values, which are the basis of the taxes that support public education in most areas of the country. Finally, with even fewer resources available, the students in these struggling school districts will fall ever further behind their more fortunate peers.

Adopting a standardized national high school exit exam is a simplistic response to a complicated problem. If we want to improve the quality of education for all students in the United States, we need to recognize that one size does not fit all. We need to develop instruments and methods that better evaluate student skills, and we need to provide resources to address the wealth and opportunity gap that drives the achievement gap. We cannot improve the quality of education if we focus on measuring outputs without doing anything to change inputs.

APPLYING THE RUBRIC	
Argument	6
Support	6
Structure	5
Fluency	6
Conventions	6
Total	29

The average is 5.8, rounded up to a likely score of 6.

ARGUMENT   The essay presents a clear and perceptive argument that a standardized national high school exit exam will be harmful. The essay is especially good at meeting the requirement to examine the consequences of implementing this policy, doing so by describing the chain of events that could be expected to follow its implementation.

SUPPORT   The likely consequences of implementing the policy are well supported by strong reasoning. One excellent example of this is the description of how decreases in the number of high school graduates will harm the economy, affecting tax revenues, ultimately resulting in reduced resources for schools and even poorer educational results.

STRUCTURE   The essay is well focused and organized, with logical transitions between ideas.

FLUENCY   The essay displays sophisticated and powerful vocabulary. Its sentence structure is varied throughout.

CONVENTIONS   Outstanding. The essay includes no noticeable errors in grammar, usage, or mechanics.

SCORE 5 ISSUE ESSAY

High school graduation is a rite of passage, a ritual through which young people show that they have completed one stage of their development and are ready for their next. But what does it actually represent about the education of those young people? What does it certify that they are skilled enough to do, that they are learned enough to understand? In theory, a high school diploma indicates that certain basic skills have been attained. In reality, however, the only thing we know for sure about a person who graduated from high school is that they that completed four years of high school. Even a student who has met state requirements for graduation may have met very different requirements from a student with the same amount of schooling from another state.

Assessment of student success varies dramatically from state to state, district to district, school to school, and even teacher to teacher. Some schools do not even have a common standard for what a passing grade is. Teacher A might consider 55% a D. Teacher B might consider 55% an F. One student with a 55% passes the class, even if just barely. Another does not. Standardization is necessary in that school. But it's easier to manage at a school level than on a national level. We are not willing to put the kind of time and money into standardization that it would take for schools to even educate their faculty about common grading rubrics (even schools that have such rubrics often have no "grade norming" in which teachers undergo professional development training to ensure that they are applying the rubric in similar ways). If we are not willing to fund more professional development for teachers to do something on as small of a scale as their own school, what on earth would demonstrate that we are willing to fund the development of a national standardized test?

While a national standardized test might seem like an obvious solution to ensure that students across the country demonstrate the same knowledge, the actual implementation of such testing would further shift the focus of education toward quantifiable outcomes. The consequence of this is turning students into information regurgitators rather than scholars. The purpose of public education is not just to prepare students for the workforce, but also to prepare them to become responsible citizens.

Completion of high school as a rite of passage is so culturally ingrained that students, and their families, expect that any student who put in their time should be prepared for the world. If a student puts four years into high school and still cannot pass a standardized test, has the student failed or has the system failed? I'm not suggesting we just ignore any possibility of standards in favor of allowing students to bide their time until graduation. I am, however, suggesting that smaller educational communities struggle enough with figuring out how to help students learn; adding to the burdens of overburdened, underfunded schools would mean even fewer graduations for those schools. This would affect already-disadvantaged communities more than it would affect privileged communities. The de facto national exams that exist—the SAT and ACT—are already more accessible to students from better resourced schools, both logistically and in terms of test content. Implementing a standardized national high school exit exam would duplicate this unfairness.

Without standardization, assessment is something of a wildcard. With it, schools become beuracracies in which teachers must focus on delivering measurable results rather than helping young people learn.

APPLYING THE RUBRIC	
Argument	5
Support	6
Structure	5
Fluency	5
Conventions	5
Total	26

The average is 5.2, rounded down to a likely score of 5.

ARGUMENT   The essay presents a clear and thoughtful argument that the implementation of the proposed policy will negatively change the focus of teaching and present an unfair burden to some schools.

SUPPORT   The essay includes concrete examples of how implementing a standardized national high school exit exam will change what schools teach and present a special burden to some schools.

STRUCTURE   The essay is generally well focused and organized, though the discussion of the lack of will to fund the teacher training needed to implement standardization at a national level is less clearly a description of the writer's views on the policy than it is an indictment of the likelihood of its being adopted. Transitions between ideas are logical.

FLUENCY   The ideas in the essay are clear, and its vocabulary use is appropriate and effective. Sentence structure is varied.

CONVENTIONS   The essay demonstrates solid command of the grammar, usage, and mechanics of standard written English, despite the presence of a few minor errors that do not obscure meaning.

SCORE 4 ISSUE ESSAY

It is no secret in America that we have an education crisis. Our students no longer rank at the top of the charts in terms of meeting standardized educational goals. Other countries have surpassed us and now boast better education systems than the one here in the United States. While there are many solutions to this problem, including an increase in funding and a national standard of higher compensation for teachers, this essay will focus on one possible solution. By requiring public secondary school students to pass a standardized national exit exam in order to receive a high school diploma, schools can set an achievable standard that can help return America to the top of the educational charts.

Though they are controversial, there is great need to create a national standard that will strengthen our national education system. Limiting the curriculum a teacher can present may be a good thing. Too often teachers complain about the heavy amount of preparation time that is needed for them to do their jobs. Moving to a strict and standardized testing system could help alleviate this stress. Though the tests do teach a narrow set of skills, they do not have to focus on rote memorization. Many exams also require a critical thinking or analytical section that is not about memorization of facts. A standardized testing still allows students to take elective courses which supplement their test preparation. While these exams can create anxiety, it can also open the door to a conversation about how to manage the this stress and prepare them for the real world. This creates a learning experience that would not otherwise happen. Setting achievable goals is an important part of passage from being a high school student into adult life.

It is clear that the debate about standardized tests will continue. They can be used to determine a standard of education that must be achieved in order to continue with education or enter the workplace. The set of skills taught can be wide and varied, and do not have to exclude other forms of creative education. Finally, since standardized tests are often the metric of entrance into higher education, this type of testing creates an opportunity for learning good test taking skills early on in one's educational career, which is a skill that cannot be underestimated.

APPLYING THE RUBRIC	
Argument	4
Support	4
Structure	4
Fluency	4
Conventions	4
Total	20

The average is 4.

ARGUMENT The essay presents a clear argument that adequately responds to the task instructions. In answering common fears about standardized testing, it describes ways in which these concerns could be worked around. The argument would be stronger, however, if it examined the likelihood of these scenarios.

SUPPORT The essay includes adequate reasoning and some specific descriptions of how a number of the feared consequences of a standardized national exit exam could be avoided.

STRUCTURE The essay is reasonably well focused and organized, though the introduction is a bit misleading. It focuses more on the need for improved education than it does on the ultimate subject of the essay, the possibility of avoiding some of the negative consequences of standardized testing.

FLUENCY The ideas in the essay are clear, and its vocabulary use is generally appropriate.

CONVENTIONS The essay demonstrates adequate command of the grammar, usage, and mechanics of standard written English. There are a few minor errors, but not enough to obscure meaning.

PROMPT #2

The following appeared in a letter to the editor in the journal *Health Matters*.

"Statistics gathered over the past three decades show that the death rate is higher among those who do not have jobs than among those with regular employment. Unemployment, just like heart disease and cancer, is a significant health issue. While many health care advocates promote increased government funding for medical research and public health care, it would be folly to increase government spending if doing so were to affect the nation's economy adversely and ultimately cause a rise in unemployment. A healthy economy means healthy citizens. Reining in government spending is, therefore, the best medicine."

Compose an essay that identifies the questions that must be answered before deciding whether the conclusion and the argument supporting it make sense. In writing your essay you should describe the impact that the answers to these questions would have on your assessment of the conclusion.

SCORE 6 ARGUMENT ESSAY

According to a letter to the editor of *Health Matters*, three decades of research shows that people without jobs have a higher death rate than those who work. Thus, argues the writer, any public policy that increases spending on healthcare and medical research is misguided if that spending would destabilize the economy and thereby increase unemployment. The writer concludes, therefore, that decreased government spending will create a healthier population. This conclusion seems, on its face, both simplistic and unlikely. To test it, there are two questions that must be answered.

The first and most fundamental question raised by the letter's conclusion is whether unemployment does, in fact, cause death. Correlation is not causation. In other words, the fact that two conditions exist in proximity to one another does not mean one is the cause of the other. Higher mortality among people without jobs does not necessarily mean that unemployment causes higher mortality. For one thing, the writer does not specify whether people without regular employment are the same as "unemployed" people. Elderly people do not have regular employment because they are retired, and they have a high mortality rate because they are elderly. Their lack of employment does not cause their high mortality rate. The same is true of people who suffer from serious illnesses like cancer and heart disease. They lack regular employment because they are sick, and they suffer from high mortality for the same reason. The correlation between lack of regular employment and high mortality does not prove that the former causes the latter.

The second question that must be answered in order to evaluate the claim that reducing government spending saves lives is whether that spending would be great enough to cause harm to the economy. The writer makes this broad claim about government spending in the context of spending on healthcare and medical research, thus the question is properly whether this spending in particular would harm the economy. There are several reasons to think that it would not. First, government spending on healthcare keeps people in good health so that they can work. Without that spending more people will be too ill to work, and they, as a result, depend on government programs for their support. In this way, government spending on healthcare may strengthen the economy and, in the long run, reduce or stabilize government spending overall.

An additional way in which government spending on healthcare and medical research may strengthen the economy is by providing jobs. When the government funds healthcare and research, it doesn't just pour money into a hole to nowhere. Those monies enter the economy as wages for doctors, nurses, and researchers. They pay construction workers who build hospitals, custodians, and cafeteria workers. This in turn increases overall employment, raising revenue from income taxes and decreasing spending on social welfare programs. There are logical reasons to conclude that government spending on healthcare and medical research would strengthen the economy, while the claim that it would harm the economy is an unwarranted assertion.

"Reining in government spending" sounds like an admirable goal. Curtailing financial crisis through fiscal responsibility is, by definition, a good idea. But the claim that increased government spending on healthcare and medical research will have the paradoxical effect of increasing the death rate is supported by neither evidence nor reasoning.

APPLYING THE RUBRIC

Argument	6
Support	6
Structure	6
Fluency	5
Conventions	6
Total	29

The average is 5.8, rounded up to a likely score of 6.

ARGUMENT   The essay successfully identifies two questions that must be answered in order to evaluate the argument presented. The essay explicitly and thoroughly answers these questions, providing well-reasoned explanations that support the essay's thesis on the relationship between government health spending and mortality rates.

SUPPORT   The essay provides detailed and persuasive support for its main points, in one case describing how the argument's author has likely confused correlation for causation, and in the other case outlining theories for how government health spending might logically strengthen, rather than weaken, the economy.

STRUCTURE   The essay is well organized, expressing its position clearly and in a logical progression. Transitions between the main ideas in the essay are clear, and the concluding paragraph summarizes the essay's argument well.

FLUENCY   The essay expresses ideas effectively, with appropriate word choice and varied sentence structure.

CONVENTIONS   The essay displays impressive command of the conventions of standard written English, with no noticeable errors in grammar, usage, or mechanics.

SCORE 5 ISSUE ESSAY

In this letter to the editor of *Health Matters*, there are many questions that stand to be answered and little to no proof to hold up its conclusion. There are three main assumptions underlying its conclusion that the government should not spend more money on healthcare: 1. unemployment causes death in citizens, 2. government spending is a problem that outweighs the benefits of government-funded medical research, and 3. government spending creates unemployment. No evidence exists to substantiate any of the claims made.

First and foremost is the question of whether unemployment causes death. It is important to remember correlation does not mean causation. In other words, just because two things might happen at the same time doesn't mean that one causes the other. In this instance, the author clearly thinks that unemployment causes an earlier death, but doesn't think that they are merely correlated. But there are many other reasons for the correlation between unemployment and death. If an individual is unemployed, chances are their stress levels are higher. Furthermore, there might be a reason they don't have a job. For example, they could be sick and that sickness might be the reason they both don't have a job and they die earlier. In another instance, they could have a substance use disorder that would prevent them from being a productive worker without receiving help first.

The second assumption is that government spending is a problem that outweighs the government funding medical research. But does it? I think not. For example, the US government funds over 90% of the world's research on substance use disorders through NIDA (National Institute on Drug Abuse). Without the government, a lot of major medical breakthroughs wouldn't happen because there is no way at this point in time that the private sector would pitch in enough to fund as many innovations as the government helps create.

The final question is whether government spending on medical research causes unemployment. Once again, no data is provided for this. No economic theory is stated or quantitative data is presented to solidify this claim. Based on history, I would think that government spending actually creates jobs. During World War II, the American economy was booming and the government was spending lots of money on the war effort.

In sum, there are many assumptions made in this letter to the editor, with very limited evidence offered in support. A little data would go a long way toward supporting the author's case. Without it, the argument has no merit.

APPLYING THE RUBRIC

Argument	5
Support	5
Structure	5
Fluency	4
Conventions	5
Total	24

The average is 4.8, rounded up to a likely score of 5.

ARGUMENT The essay successfully pinpoints and responds thoughtfully to three questions that must be answered in order to assess the conclusion that government health spending is counterproductive.

SUPPORT The essay provides thoughtful and reasonably persuasive support for its main points. It is strong in its discussion of alternate causality, but weaker in its use of World War II as proof that government spending strengthens the economy (the scale of spending in these two instances does not seem comparable).

STRUCTURE   The essay is well organized, with suitable (though not always smooth) transitions between ideas.

FLUENCY   The essay generally uses vocabulary effectively to express its ideas, though it reads awkwardly in places.

CONVENTIONS   The essay displays solid command of the conventions of standard written English.

SCORE 4 ARGUMENT ESSAY

There is no way to accept at face value the letter to the editor in *Health Matters*. The author of the letter makes several logical leaps that require further examination. While the analogy of the healthy economy draws up images of prosperity for everyone, the conclusions this author makes are fundamentally flawed.

There are any number of reasons for the correlation between death rate and employment; this author examines none of them. To accept this premise I would need to know if "regular employment" included retired people, older people, veterans or others on permanent disability, and children. Unless the statistical data of death rate was limited to eligible workers of working age, then the statistics presented are skewed in favor of the author's ultimate point. They use this shocking claim to draw in the reader and the analogy of health to appeal to the broadest set of people. Health is not a politicized issue; everyone, conceivably, wants to be healthy. However, this analogy is still just an assertion used to support an argument for reducing government spending.

To create a healthy society and cure diseases like cancer, heart disease, and, per the author, unemployment, government spending will likely have to increase. Another question I would need to answer to evaluate the conclusion is where the author thinks money to combat unemployment is going to come from. Other than a thinly veiled jab at healthcare professionals for seeking increased funding, the author has no identifiable solution. I would also need to know whether healthcare spending was going to "affect the nation's economy adversely" and lead to the spike in unemployment promised by the author. It would seem likely that more funding for "medical research and public health care" would create more jobs rather than less of them.

Ultimately, this author uses their health metaphor to assert that "Reining in government spending is . . . the best medicine." This health metaphor has come full circle; earlier in the letter, the author argues that increased spending for medical research would lead to a rise in unemployment, but has no problem touting his solution as the best medicine.

```
┌─────────────────────────────────────┐
│        APPLYING THE RUBRIC          │
│                                      │
│        Argument        4            │
│        Support         4            │
│        Structure       4            │
│        Fluency         4            │
│        Conventions     4            │
│                     ───────         │
│        Total          20            │
│                                      │
│   The average is 4.                 │
└─────────────────────────────────────┘
```

ARGUMENT   The essay identifies and responds to questions that must be answered in order to evaluate the argument presented. The essay's discussion of the argument's use of health as a metaphor is, however, somewhat tangential to the task at hand.

SUPPORT   The essay provides sufficient support for its main points, though it does a better job of identifying where the argument provided lacks support than it does in offering counterexamples or reasoning.

STRUCTURE   The essay expresses its ideas reasonably clearly, and but could benefit from more graceful transitions. The internal organization of the second and third paragraph, could be stronger.

FLUENCY   The essay generally uses vocabulary appropriately to express its ideas.

CONVENTIONS   The essay generally displays command of the conventions of standard written English, despite the presence of a few minor errors that do not interfere with meaning.

Section 2—Verbal Reasoning

1. **(D)(E)** Note the two key phrases "Given the human tendency to suspect and disbelieve in" and "it is unsurprising that." People who view the unconscious with suspicion or disbelieve in it are as a consequence likely to *deny* or *gainsay* (contradict) its effect on human interactions.

2. **(B)(E)** In contrast to his reputation, the author is not markedly taciturn (uncommunicative; disinclined to talk). In fact, he seems inclined to talk. In other words, he is not at all *averse from* or *opposed to* conversation.

3. **(A)(C)** To call a country "the land of the free" while allowing the institution of slavery to exist struck Mrs. Trollope as evidence of *hypocrisy* or *sanctimoniousness* (the act of making a false display of righteousness or piety).

4. **(B)(D)** The key word here is "passionate." Paul finds himself attracted to a woman who is *ardent* (fervent; keen) and *wholehearted* (fully enthusiastic) about her likes and dislikes.

5. **(C)(E)** Soap operas and situation comedies are derivative of contemporary culture: they take their elements from that culture. Therefore, they serve as *evidence* or *indices* (signs, indications) of what is going on in that culture; they both point to and point up the social attitudes and values they portray.

   Note that the soap operas and comedies here cannot be *determinants* of our society's attitudes and values: they derive from these attitudes and values; they do not determine them.

6. **(D)(E)** Whatever word or phrase you choose here must apply equally well both to slander and to counterfeit money. People who would not make up a slanderous statement *circulate* or *spread* slander by passing it on. So too people who would not coin or make counterfeit money *circulate* or *spread around* counterfeit money by passing it on.

   Note how the extended metaphor here influences the writer's choice of words.

7. **(D)** The author cites Meredith's intelligence (*brilliance*) and his splendor of language (*linguistic grandeur*).

8. **(E)** Rather than refuting the claim, the author clearly acknowledges Meredith's inability to evoke the reader's sympathy.

   Choice A is incorrect. From the start the author points out how Meredith leaves readers cold.

   Choice B is incorrect. The author reiterates Meredith's virtues, citing muscular intelligence and literary merit.

Choice C is incorrect. The author quotes several such imagined criticisms.

Choice D is incorrect. The author indicates that if readers choose to avoid dealing with Meredith they shall be doing a disservice to the cause of criticism.

Only Choice E remains. It is the correct answer.

9. **(E)** Speaking of the "challenge and excitement of the critical problem as such," the author clearly finds the prospect of appraising Meredith critically to be stirring and *invigorating*.

10. **(C)** The author wishes us to be able to recognize the good qualities of Meredith's work while at the same time we continue to find it personally unsympathetic. Thus, she would agree that criticism should enable us to appreciate the virtues of works we dislike.

Choices A, B, and E are unsupported by the passage.

Choice D is incorrect. While the author wishes the reader to be aware of Meredith's excellences, she does not suggest that the reader should ignore those qualities in Meredith that make his work unsympathetic. Rather, she wishes the reader to come to appreciate the very ambivalence of his critical response.

11. **(A)(E)** The off-Broadway and Broadway theatres are contrasted here. The former has *manifested* or shown a talent for improvisation, extemporaneous or spontaneous performance. The latter has manifested no such talent for *spontaneity*.

Note the use of *whereas* to establish the contrast.

12. **(C)(D)** People had complimented her for her *fluency* or eloquence; it was therefore surprising that she proved *inarticulate* or tongue-tied at her inauguration.

Note the use of *although* and *surprisingly* to signal the contrast.

13. **(B)(F)** The filmmakers wish neither to *reject* nor to *vitiate* (impair; weaken) a strong sense of place. Instead, they take pains to *impart* (communicate; convey) a strong sense of the places they film as well as of the characters they film. Thus, their films become portraits of the *spaces* their characters *inhabit*.

14. **(B)(D)** The key phrase here is "they remained the dominant viol size." The text is discussing changes over time in the popularity of different sizes of bass viols. Before 1600, larger consort bass viols were in fashion. After 1600, the larger consort bass viols were *displaced* by the smaller

division viols. The division viols continued to be popular until some time in the 1700s, when they *went out of fashion.*

15. **(A)(E)(G)** Particles have no need to be wound up because the property of spinning (*rotation*) is built into their makeup: it is *intrinsic.* That is the significant *difference* between the spinning of particles and the spinning of tops.

16. **(C)** To the author the concept is both simple and traditional, dating as it does from Newton's time.

17. **(A)(C)** Question A is answerable on the basis of the passage. As the area's density increases, its gravitational field increases in strength. Likewise, Question C is answerable on the basis of the passage. The end result of the process is the formation of a gravitationally bound object, a new-born star. Remember, you must have selected *both* A and C to receive credit for this question.

    Question B is not answerable on the basis of the passage. The passage nowhere states what disturbs the gas.

18. **(E)** The passage compares the Quechua empire to a *mandala* because "it was divided into four parts." Thus, a *mandala* is most likely a "figure composed of four divisions."

19. **(B)** The author refers to the Quechua as existing in "a state of unremitting anxiety, which could not be resolved by action" and which the Quechua could only deal with by looking into himself and struggling with the depths of his own psyche. This suggests that the Quechua world was *highly introspective.*

20. **(D)** Both the unremitting anxiety of Quechua life and the recurring harvest failures that brought starvation to millions illustrate the *harshness and frustration* of Quechua existence.

Section 3—Quantitative Ability

Two asterisks (**) indicate an alternative method of solving.

1. **(D)** Could m and n be equal? Sure, if each is 5. Eliminate Choices A and B. Must they be equal? No, not if $m = 1$ and $n = 25$. Eliminate Choice C, as well. Neither quantity is always greater, and the two quantities are not always equal (D).

2. **(D)** Since $\frac{2}{3} = 66\frac{2}{3}\%$, which is clearly more than 65%, it *appears* that Quantity B is greater. *Be careful!* That would be true if *a* were positive, but no restrictions are placed on *a*. If *a* = 0, the columns are equal; if *a* is negative, Quantity A is greater. Neither quantity is always greater, and the two quantities are not always equal (D).

   **Just let *a* = 0, and then let *a* = 1.

3. **(D)** Could the quantities be equal? Could *c* = 5? Sure, if this is a 3-4-5 right triangle. Must *c* = 5? No; if the triangle is not a right triangle, *c* could be less than or more than 5.

   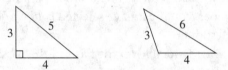

   Neither quantity is *always* greater, and the quantities are not *always* equal (D). (*Note*: Since the figure may not be drawn to scale, do *not* assume that the triangle has a right angle.)

4. **(B)** You don't *have* to solve for *a* and *b*. If *a* – *b* > *a* + *b*, then –*b* > *b*, and so *b* is negative and Quantity B is greater.

   **You *could* solve. Adding the two equations yields $2a = 49 \Rightarrow a = 24.5 \Rightarrow b = -0.5$.

5. **(A)** Since in the given figure *OA* and *OB* are radii, each is equal to 5. With no restrictions on *x*, *AB* could be any positive number less than 10; and the larger *x* is, the larger *AB* is.

   If *x* were 90, *AB* would be $5\sqrt{2}$, but we are told that *x* > 90, so

   $AB > 5\sqrt{2} > 7$.

   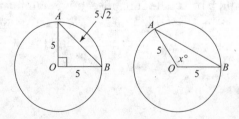

6. **(C)** The distribution consists of 20 numbers: four 1's, five 2's, two 3's, three 4's, and six 5's:

$$1, 1, 1, 1, 2, 2, 2, 2, 2, 3, 3, 4, 4, 4, 5, 5, 5, 5, 5, 5$$

- The median is the average of the two middle numbers, which are both 3, so the median is 3.
- The mode is 5, since there are more 5s than any other number.
- The quantity in Column A is 4, the average of 3 and 5.
- Since the range of a set of data is the difference between the largest and smallest values, the range is $5 - 1 = 4$.
- The quantity in Column B is also 4.
- The quantities are equal.

7. **(B)** Do not waste any time evaluating the two standard deviations. We don't need the values of the two quantities, we only need to know which quantity is greater. The standard deviation is a measure of how far, on average, the pieces of data are from the mean. The closer the data are to the mean, the smaller the standard deviation; the farther the data are from the mean, the greater the standard deviation. In List 1, the mean is 75, and the five data points are 50, 25, 0, 25, and 50, respectively, away from the mean. In List 2, the mean is 150, and the five data points are 100, 50, 0, 50, and 100, respectively, away from the mean. The data in List 2 are further from its mean than the data in List 1 are from its mean, so the standard deviation of List 2 is greater.

8. **(C)** If there are x seats on each bus, then the group is using $\frac{4}{5}(3x) = \frac{12}{5}x$

seats. After $\frac{1}{4}$ of them get off, $\frac{3}{4}$ of them, or $\frac{3}{4}\left(\frac{12}{5}x\right) = \frac{9}{5}x$ remain.

What fraction of the $2x$ seats on the two buses are now being used?

$$\frac{\frac{9}{5}x}{2x} = \frac{\frac{9}{5}}{2} = \frac{9}{10}.$$

**To avoid the algebra choose appropriate numbers. Assume there are 20 seats on each bus. At the beginning, the group is using 48 of the 60 seats on the three buses. When 12 people left, the 36 remaining

people used $\frac{36}{40} = \frac{9}{10}$ of the 40 seats on two buses.

9. **(B)** Since d divisions each have t teams, multiply to get dt teams; and since each team has p players, multiply the number of teams (dt) by p to get the total number of players: dtp.

    ****Pick three easy-to-use numbers for t, d, and p. Assume that there are 2 divisions, each consisting of 4 teams, so, there are $2 \times 4 = 8$ teams. Then assume that each team has 10 players, for a total of $8 \times 10 = 80$ players. Now check the choices. Which one is equal to 80 when $d = 2$, $t = 4$, and $p = 10$? Only dtp.

10. **(C)** Since, in 1990, $2p$ pounds of potatoes cost $\frac{1}{2}d$ dollars, p pounds cost

half as much: $\frac{1}{2}\left(\frac{1}{2}d\right) = \frac{1}{4}d$. This is $\frac{1}{4}$, or 25%, as much as the cost in

1980, which represents a decrease of 75%.

    ****In this type of problem it is *often* easier to plug in numbers. Assume that 1 pound of potatoes cost $100 in 1980. Then in 1990, 2 pounds cost $50, so 1 pound cost $25. This is a decrease of $75 in the cost of 1 pound of potatoes, and

$$\% \text{ decrease} = \frac{\text{actual decrease}}{\text{original amount}} \times 100\% = \frac{75}{100} \times 100\% = 75\%$$

11. $\frac{2}{9}$ There are nine positive integers less than 10: 1, 2, ... , 9. For which of

them is $\frac{9}{x} > x$?

Only 1 and 2: $\frac{9}{1} > 1$ and $\frac{9}{2} > 2$. When $x = 3$, $\frac{9}{x} = x$, and for all the others

$\frac{9}{x} < x$. The probability is $\frac{2}{9}$.

12. **(D)** If Jason were really unlucky, what could go wrong in his attempt to get one marble of each color? Well, his first nine picks *might* yield five blue marbles and four white ones. But then the tenth marble would be red, and now he would have at least one of each color. The answer is 10.

13. **94** If a represents Jordan's average after 5 tests, then he has earned a total of $5a$ points. A grade of 70 on the sixth test will lower his average 4 points to $a - 4$. Therefore,

$$a - 4 = \frac{5a + 70}{6} \Rightarrow 6(a - 4) = 5a + 70 \Rightarrow$$
$$6a - 24 = 5a + 70 \Rightarrow 6a = 5a + 94 \Rightarrow a = 94$$

**Assume Jordan's average is a because he earned a on each of his first 5 tests. Since after getting a 70 on his sixth test his average will be $a - 4$, the deviation on each of the first 5 tests is 4, for a total deviation above the average of 20 points. So, the total deviation below must also be 20. Therefore, 70 is 20 less than the new average of $a - 4$:

$$70 = (a - 4) - 20 \Rightarrow a = 94$$

**Backsolve, starting with Choice C, 86. If his 5-test average was 90, he had 450 points and a 70 on the sixth test would give him a total of 520 points, and an average of $520 \div 6 = 86.666$. So, the 70 lowered his average 3.333 points. That's not enough. Eliminate Choices A, B, and C. Try Choices D or E. Choice E, 94, works.

14. **(A)(B)(C)(D)**

(A) In 1991, more than 50% of the adults whose highest degree was at least a bachelor's degree participated in adult education, whereas those whose highest educational attainment was a high school diploma or GED (high school equivalency diploma) fewer than 25% participated. (A is true.)

(B) From 1991 to 1995, among those adults whose highest educational attainment was grades 9–12, without earning a high school diploma, the rate of participation in adult education increased from about 15% to 23%, an increase of about 50%. None of the other groups had nearly that great an increase. (B is true.)

(C) Since the population of the country grew between 1991 and 1995, and the rate of participation in adult education programs increased in every category, the total number of people participating had to increase. (C is true.)

(D) From 1991 to 1995 the rate of participation in adult education for those who had attained at least a bachelor's degree increased from about 52% to 58%, the least increase of any group on both an absolute and percent basis. (D is true.)

(E) Without knowing how many adults have earned a college degree and how many have attended some college without earning a college degree, it is impossible to make this conclusion. For example, 50% of 100,000,000 is much more than 58% of 50,000,000. (E is false.)

15. **(E)** 50% of 100,000,000 = 50,000,000; 20% of 40,000,000 = 8,000,000. 50,000,000:8,000,000 = 50:8 = 6.25:1, which is closest to Choice E, 6:1.

16. **49** Assume that there were 1,000 adults in the workforce. Then 80 were unemployed and 920 were employed. Since 50% of the employed adults and 40% of the unemployed adults participated in adult education, the number of participants was 50% of 920 + 40% of 80 = 460 + 32 = 492.

So, the rate of participation was $\dfrac{492}{1000} = \dfrac{49.2}{100} = 49.2\%$.

Rounded to the nearest whole percent, the answer is 49.

17. **(D)**

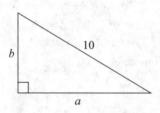

By the Pythagorean theorem,

$$a^2 + b^2 = 10^2 = 100$$

and since the area is 20, $\dfrac{1}{2}ab = 20 \Rightarrow ab = 40$.

Expand:

$$(a + b)^2 = a^2 + 2ab + b^2 = (a^2 + b^2) + 2ab$$

Then

$$(a^2 + b^2) + 2ab = 100 + 2(40) = 180$$

18. **(E)** To find the average of three numbers, divide their sum by 3:

$\dfrac{3^{30} + 3^{60} + 3^{90}}{3}$. Now use the distributive law and divide each term in

the numerator by 3: $\dfrac{3^{30}}{3} + \dfrac{3^{60}}{3} + \dfrac{3^{90}}{3} = 3^{29} + 3^{59} + 3^{89}$.

19. **(B)** Since the radii of the four small semicircles in the figure are 1, 2, 3, and 4, their diameters are 2, 4, 6, and 8. So the diameter of the large

semicircle is $2 + 4 + 6 + 8 = 20$, and its radius is 10. The perimeter of the shaded region is the sum of the circumferences of all five semicircles. Since the circumference of a circle is πd or $2\pi r$, the circumference of a semicircle is πr. So, the perimeter is $\pi + 2\pi + 3\pi + 4\pi + 10\pi = 20\pi$.

20. $\frac{3}{5}$ $a + 25\%(a) = 1.25a$, and $b - 25\%(b) = 0.75b$.

So, $1.25a = .75b$, and $\frac{a}{b} = \frac{.75}{1.25} = \frac{3}{5}$

Section 4—Verbal Reasoning

1. **(C)(D)** The key phrase here is "his extravagance and his free-spending lifestyle." *Ironically* is an implicit contrast signal: it indicates that you are looking for an antonym or near-antonym to *extravagance*. The mayor practices extravagance but preaches thrift, that is, *economy* (financial prudence) or *austerity* (strict economy; restraint).

2. **(A)(D)** Working on commission, the portrait painter seeks proper *recompense* or *remuneration* (payment or reward for services) for undertaking the job.

3. **(B)(F)** Stripped of descriptive phrases, the sentence simply states that jazz would *spawn* or *generate* (give rise to) an industry. Note that the verb *spawn* occurs here with a secondary meaning.

4. **(A)(C)** Several clues suggest that this *brief* essay is an abridgment or synopsis of more extensive critiques ("arguments rehearsed in much more detail elsewhere"). Thus, it can be described as a *condensed* (shortened) or *synoptic* (concise; summary) version.

5. **(A)(E)** If Mrs. Woolf combines both radical and non-radical elements in her fictions, then she presents *an anomalous* (unusual; not fitting into a common or familiar pattern) or *curious* (highly unusual) image. Here *curious* occurs with its secondary meaning (arousing interest or curiosity) rather than with its primary meaning (inquisitive).

6. **(C)(D)** The key phrase here is "move on." If editors have to travel from firm to firm to succeed in their field, then publishing can be classified as an *itinerant* or *mobile* profession, a profession marked by traveling.

7. **(D)** Immediately before quoting Praz, the author states that the general view of Shelley depicts her as "a transparent medium through which

passed the ideas of those around her." The quotation from Praz provides an excellent example of this particular point of view.

To answer this question correctly, you do not need to read the passage in its entirety. Quickly scroll through the passage, scanning for the name Praz; read only the context in which it appears.

8. **(C)** The opening sentence points out that Shelley herself acknowledged the influence of her unplanned immersion in the scientific and literary revolutions of her time. Clearly, the author of the passage concedes this as true of Shelley.

9. **(B)** The concluding paragraph distinguishes Frankenstein from the other overreachers in his desire not to extend his own life but to impart life to another (by creating his monster). Thus, his purpose is *atypical* of the traditional overreacher.

To say that someone *parts from* the traditional figure of the over-reacher is to say that he *differs* from it. Thus, to answer this question quickly, scan the passage looking for *overreacher* and *different* (or their synonyms).

10. **(A)** Clearly religious ideas and concepts do not *obviate* (hinder), *preclude* (rule out), or *deny* the practice of medicine and delivery of health care. Neither do they *reiterate* (repeat) the practice of medicine. However, religious ideas and concepts do *inform* (pervade; permeate, with obvious effect) medical practices.

11. **(B)(E)** The embittered benefactor thinks of them as *ingrates* (ungrateful persons) because they do not thank him sufficiently for his generosity. He does not think of them as *misers* (hoarders of wealth): although they are stingy in expressing thanks, they are extravagant in spending money, that is, being "wasteful of his largesse." He certainly does not think of them as *prigs* (self-righteous fuss-budgets): the specific attribute he resents in them is ingratitude, not self-righteousness, or exaggerated propriety.

12. **(B)(D)** The physicists have had good reason to believe in the principle because it has *survived* rigorous or strict tests. These tests have *established* (proved) that the principle is accurate.

Note how the second clause supports the first, explaining why the physicists have had reason to be confident in the principle.

13. **(A)(D)** The actress had *a knack* or talent for getting people to do things for her and was delighted that her new friends were *assiduous* (diligent) in finding new ways to meet her needs.

Note that it is useful to focus first on the second blank as you answer this question. The key phrase here is "to her delight." The actress would have no particular cause for delight if her new friends proved *dilatory* (tardy; slow) or *stoical* (impassive; unemotional) in finding new ways to meet her needs.

14. **(B)(F)** The presence of inconsistencies (discrepancies; contradictions) in someone's story would *warrant* (justify) some incredulity (disbelief) on anyone's part. Even someone who was not a *skeptic* (person who maintains a doubting attitude) would be justified in doubting such a tale.

15. **(D)** The author takes the reader through Wegener's reasoning step by step, describing what led Wegener to reach his conclusions.

16. **(A)** Since the existence of the correspondences between the various coastal contours was used by Wegener as a basis for formulating his theory of continental drift, it can be inferred that the correspondences provide evidence for the theory.

    Choice B is incorrect. The passage does not indicate that Pangaea's existence has been proved.

    Choice C is incorrect. It is the relative heaviness of sima, not the level or depth of sima, that suggested the possibility of the lighter continents drifting.

    Choice D is incorrect. Mobility rather than immobility would provide evidence for continental drift.

    Choice E is incorrect. The continents are lighter than the underlying sima.

17. **(D)** Choice D is answerable on the basis of the passage. The next-to-the-last sentence of the second paragraph states that the Americas "apparently drifted toward the west."

18. **(D)** Houston believed that the battle had to begin at the graduate level "to mitigate fear" (relieve *apprehension*) of race-mixing and miscegenation that might otherwise have caused the judges to rule against the NAACP-sponsored complaints.

19. **(B)** The separate-but-equal doctrine established by *Plessy* v. *Ferguson* allows the existence of racially segregated schools.

20. **(A)** In assessing the possible effects on judges of race-mixing in the lower grades, Houston was *psychologically canny*, shrewd in seeing potential dangers and in figuring strategies to avoid these dangers.

Section 5—Quantitative Ability

Two asterisks (**) indicate an alternative method of solving.

1. **(A)** Quantity A is the product of 8 negative numbers and so is positive. Quantity B is the product of 9 negative numbers and so is negative. Hence, Quantity A is greater.

2. **(C)**

   Quantity A: Since $(a^9)(a^9) = (a^{18})$, and since $a > 0$, $\sqrt{a^{18}} = a^9$.

   Quantity B: $(a^2)(a^3)(a^4) = a^{2+3+4} = a^9$.

   The quantities are equal.

3. **(B)** Assume that the price of a small pizza is $10; then the price of a large pizza is $10 + 0.30($10) = $10 + $3 = $13.

   On sale at 30% off, a large pizza costs 30% less than $13.

   $$\$13 - 0.30(\$13) = \$13 - \$3.90 = \$9.10$$

   So, Quantity B is $10 and Quantity A is $9.10.

4. **(A)** There is not enough information provided to determine the values of a, b, c, d, e, f, and g, but they are irrelevant. Since the sum of the measures of the seven angles is 360°, their average is 360° ÷ 7 ≈ 51.4°. Quantity A is greater.

5. **(C)** There are 9 ways to choose the first digit of a 5-digit palindrome (any of the digits from 1 to 9); there are 10 ways to choose the second digit and 10 ways to choose the third digit (any of the digits from 0 to 9). Since the fourth digit must be the same as the second digit, there is only 1 way to choose it. Finally, the fifth digit must be the same as the first digit, so again, there is only 1 choice.

   Therefore, the number of 5-digit palindromes is $9 \times 10 \times 10 \times 1 \times 1 = 900$.

   In exactly the same way, the number of 6-digit palindromes is

   $$9 \times 10 \times 10 \times 1 \times 1 \times 1 = 900$$

   The quantities are equal.

   **There is a 1-1 correspondence between the set of 5-digit palindromes and the set of 6-digit palindromes: *abcba* corresponds to *abccba*. So the two sets have the same number of members.

6. **(B)**

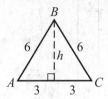

Quantity A: If h is the height of equilateral triangle ABC, then by the Pythagorean theorem $3^2 + h^2 = 6^2 \Rightarrow h^2 = 27 \Rightarrow h = 3\sqrt{3}$. So the area of triangle ABC is $A = \frac{1}{2}bh = \frac{1}{2}(6)(3\sqrt{3}) = 9\sqrt{3} \approx 15.59$.

Alternatively, if you know the special formula for the area of an equilateral triangle, you don't have to find h:

$$A = \frac{6^2\sqrt{3}}{4} = \frac{36\sqrt{3}}{4} = 9\sqrt{3} \approx 15.59$$

Quantity B:

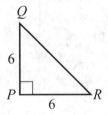

The area of isosceles triangle PQR is $\frac{1}{2}(6)(6) = 18$.

7. **(A)** The simplest solution is to notice that if a 1 is chosen first, of the remaining three slips, two of them have –1 on them and one of them has 1 on it. So there are 2 chances in 3 that the second number will be –1 and the product will be –1. Similarly, if a –1 is chosen first, there are 2 chances in 3 that the second number will be 1 and, again, the product will be –1. Quantity A is $\frac{2}{3}$ and Quantity B is $\frac{1}{3}$.

**Given 4 numbers, a, b, c, and d, there are 6 possible products: ab, ac, ad, bc, bd, and cd. If $a = b = 1$ and $c = d = -1$, then 4 of these products equal –1 and two of them equal 1. So Quantity A is $\frac{4}{6} = \frac{2}{3}$ and Quantity B is $\frac{2}{6} = \frac{1}{3}$.

8. **(D)** Since 8% of 100 is 8, John saved $8, and thus paid $92 for the DVD player. He then had to pay 8% sales tax on the $92: $0.08 \times 92 = 7.36$, so the total cost was $92 + $7.36 = $99.36.

9. **(A)**

A cube has 12 edges. (In the diagram, each shaded square base has 4 edges, and there are 4 edges connecting the two bases.) So, if e represents the length of each edge, we have that $12e = 3 \Rightarrow e = \dfrac{1}{4}$.

Since $V = e^3$, we have $V = \left(\dfrac{1}{4}\right)^3 = \dfrac{1}{64}$ cubic feet.

10. **52** How many pages did Mary read in 30 minutes? Since Mary started on page 10, she read the first 24 pages, except pages 1–9: She read $24 - 9 = 15$ pages. So she read at the rate of 15 pages every 30 minutes, or 1 page every 2 minutes. Similarly, if Mary reads pages 25 through 50, she will read $50 - 24 = 26$ pages. At the rate of 1 page every 2 minutes it will take her 52 minutes to read 26 pages.

11. **(D)**
   - If $(m - 5)(m - 45)$ is positive, either both factors are positive or both factors are negative.
   - If both factors are negative, m must be less than 5, so m could be 1, 2, 3, or 4 (4 values).
   - If both factors are positive, m must be greater than 45, so m could be 46, 47, . . . , 100 (55 values).
   - The answer is $4 + 55 = 59$.

12. **(A)** Since the diameters of the two mosaics are 30 and 20, the radii are 15 and 10, respectively. So the area of the larger mosaic is $\pi(15)^2 = 225\pi$, whereas the area of the smaller mosaic is $\pi(10)^2 = 100\pi$. So the area of the larger mosaic is 2.25 times the area of the smaller mosaic, and hence will require 2.25 times as many tiles.

   **The ratio of the diameter is $\dfrac{30}{20} = \dfrac{3}{2}$. So the ratio of the area is

$$\left(\dfrac{3}{2}\right)^2 = \dfrac{9}{4} = 2.25$$

13. **(B)(C)(D)** Let S = the number of students at Central High School that year.

     If 70% of the students attended the rally, then $0.70S = 1,435$, and so $S = 1,435 \div 0.70 = 2,050$.

     If 85% of the students attended the rally, then $0.85S = 1,435$, and so $S = 1,435 \div 0.85 = 1,688$.

     So, S must satisfy the inequality $1,688 < S < 2,050$.

14. **800,000** From the top graph, we see that in 1975, 54% (35% + 19%) of all college students were male, and the other 46% were female. So there were 5,400,000 males and 4,600,000 females — a difference of 800,000.

15. **(B)** In 1975, of every 100 college students, 46 were female — 32 of whom were less than 25 years old, and 14 of whom were 25 years old and over. So, 14 of every 46 female students were at least 25 years old. Finally, $\frac{14}{46} = .30 = 30\%$.

16. **(C)** From the two graphs, we see that in 1975 54% (35% + 19%) of all college students were male, whereas in 1995 the corresponding figure was 45% (28% + 17%). For simplicity, assume that there were 100 college students in 1975, 54 of whom were male. Then in 1995, there were 140 college students, 63 of whom were male (45% of 140 = 63). So the ratio of the number of male students in 1995 to the number of male students in 1975 is 63:54 = 7:6.

17. **66** Let x represent the number of envelopes Eric can address in 99 minutes and set up a proportion:

$$\frac{40 \text{ envelopes}}{1 \text{ hour}} = \frac{40 \text{ envelopes}}{60 \text{ minutes}} = \frac{2 \text{ envelopes}}{3 \text{ minutes}} = \frac{x \text{ envelopes}}{99 \text{ minutes}} \Rightarrow$$

$$2 \times 99 = 3x \Rightarrow 198 = 3x \Rightarrow x = 66$$

18. **(A)(C)(D)(E)(F)** Start with the least expensive option: 2 regular slices and 2 small sodas.
    • This option costs $5.00. (A is true.)
    • Changing anything would add at least 50 cents to the cost so $5.25 is *not* possible. (B is false.)
    • Increasing two items by 50 cents each—say, buying 2 medium sodas instead of 2 small sodas—brings the cost to $6.00. (C is true.)
    • Now replacing a medium soda with a large soda adds 25 cents, so $6.25 is also possible. (D is true.)

- 2 pepperoni slices and 2 medium sodas cost $7.00. (E is true.)
- Replacing one of those medium sodas with a large soda adds 25 cents, so $7.25 is possible, too. (F is true.)

19. **(B)** Since a normal distribution is symmetric about the mean, and since in a normal distribution 68% of the scores are within one standard deviation of the mean, 34% are within one standard deviation below the mean and 34% are within one standard deviation above the mean. The other 32% are more than one standard deviation from the mean, 16% are more than one standard deviation below the mean, and 16% are more than one standard deviation above the mean.

So 16% score below 400, 34% between 400 and 500, 34% between 500 and 600, and 16% above 600. Set up a proportion:

$$\frac{\text{number of students}}{\text{percent of total}} = \frac{10,200}{34} = \frac{x}{16} \Rightarrow \frac{16 \times 10,200}{34} = x \Rightarrow x = 4,800$$

20. **(D)** $\dfrac{1}{x} + \dfrac{1}{y} = \dfrac{y}{xy} + \dfrac{x}{xy} = \dfrac{x+y}{xy} = \dfrac{10}{20} = \dfrac{1}{2}$

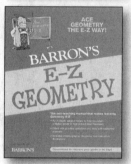
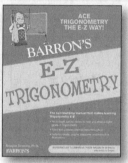
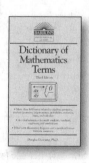
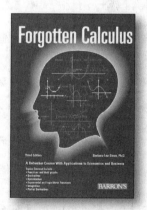

GRAMMAR GRAMMAR & MORE GRAMMAR

For ESL courses . . . for remedial English courses . . . for standard instruction in English grammar and usage on all levels from elementary through college . . . Barron's has what you're looking for!

501 English Verbs, 3rd Ed., w/CD-ROM

Thomas R. Beyer, Jr., Ph.D.

An analysis of English verb construction precedes 501 regular and irregular verbs presented alphabetically, one per page, each set up in table form showing indicative, imperative, and subjunctive moods in all tenses.

ISBN 978-1-4380-7302-6, paper, $18.99, Can$21.99

Grammar in Plain English, 5th Ed.

H. Diamond, M.A. and P. Dutwin, M.A.

Basic rules of grammar and examples clearly presented, with exercises that reflect GED test standards.

ISBN 978-0-7641-4786-9, paper, $14.99, Can$16.99

Painless Grammar, 4th Ed.

Rebecca Elliott, Ph.D.

Focused mainly toward middle-school students, this book takes a light, often humorous approach to teaching grammar and usage.

ISBN 978-1-4380-0774-8, paper, $9.99, Can$11.99

E-Z Grammar, 2nd Ed.

Dan Mulvey

Barron's E-Z Grammar is written primarily for high school seniors and college freshmen and emphasizes the simple logic underlying correct grammar and clear expression. The author covers all parts of speech and correct sentence structure.

ISBN 978-0-7641-4261-1, paper, $14.99, Can$16.99

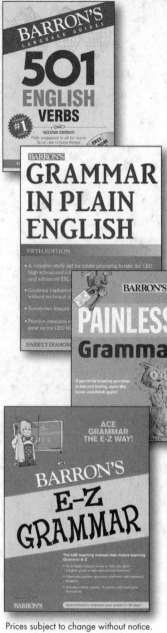

Prices subject to change without notice.

Available at your local bookstore or visit **www.barronseduc.com**

Barron's Educational Series, Inc.
250 Wireless Blvd.
Hauppauge, NY 11788
Order toll-free: 1-800-645-3476
Order by fax: 1-631-434-3217

In Canada:
Georgetown Book Warehouse
4 Armstrong Ave.
Georgetown, Ont. L7G 4R9
Canadian orders: 1-800-247-7160
Fax in Canada: 1-800-887-1594

(#90) R11,